Parting Company

Understanding the Loss
of a Loved One

The Caregiver's Journey

Cynthia Pearson and Margaret L. Stubbs

Seal Press

Cover design by Joseph Kaftan
Cover photo: Photodisc
Author photo: Rocky Raco
Text design by Laura Gronewold

Library of Congress Cataloging-in-Publication Data
Pearson, Cynthia.
    Parting company : understanding the loss of a loved one : the caregiver's journey / Cynthia Pearson and Margaret L. Stubbs.
    Includes bibliographical references.
    1. Death—Psychological aspects Case studies. 2. Terminally ill—Home care—Psychological aspects Case studies. 3. Caregivers—Psychology Case studies. 4. Terminal care—Psychological aspects Case studies.
    I. Stubbs, Margaret L. (Margaret Louisa), 1947–   .
    II. Title.
HQ1073.P43   1999   306.9—dc21   99-23702
ISBN 1-58005-019-0

Printed in the United States of America
First printing, July 1999

10   9   8   7   6   5   4   3   2   1

Distributed to the trade by Publishers Group West
In Canada: Publishers Group West Canada, Toronto, Ontario
In the U.K. and Europe: Airlift Book Company, Middlesex, England
In Australia: Banyan Tree Book Distributors, Kent Town, South Australia

We dedicate this book to all who find themselves
caring for others in their last days.

Acknowledgments

First we offer our thanks and appreciation to the caregivers who gave us their time and their stories. Although the experiences of only fourteen caregivers appear in this book, there were many others who spoke with us, both briefly and at length. There would be no book without them, and the learning that their stories has engendered in us continues over time, as it now will for our readers.

When you work at something for more than seven years, you know you will not recall everyone who deserves a word of thanks, but we hope to include as many of those people as possible in these acknowledgments. In the beginning, there was Jacquie Powers, and we thank her for helping us to frame our original questions. Other much appreciated contributors to the thinking behind this project include Bob Arnold, Belle Foss, Carol Heape, Dianne Kelleher, Linnea McQuiston, Henry Pearson, Martha Sanger, Rich Southard and Helen Vantine. For their helpful editorial feedback, we especially thank Sara M. Rath, Anne Kuhn, Frank Mediate, Evelyn Pearson, Lynne Rokavec, Regina Sestak, Arlene Shubock and Mona Strassburger.

We offer our thanks to feminist scholars in general, especially Lyn

Mikel Brown, for bringing to light so much information about women's experiences and for giving stature to qualitative methods of inquiry. We also wish to acknowledge the Winchester Thurston School (where we first made one another's acquaintance in the fifth grade) and the Wellesley Centers for Research on Women, for fostering original thinking and the will—and skill—to apply it.

For their technical assistance, we thank Megan Cameron, Kaiya Korb, Anita McClellan and Bobbie Thrash. For patience and encouragement beyond the call of duty, we thank our family members: Lincoln and Richard Allen, and Courtney, Sam and Tom Turich.

For providing a forum to present portions of our work to a broader public audience, we thank the editors of *The Maine Scholar*, the Association for Women in Psychology, Kathy Blee, Director of Women's Studies at the University of Pittsburgh, Alan Meisel and Lisa Parker of the Center for Medical Ethics at the University of Pittsburgh School of Law, and the Department of Women's Studies at the University of Maine at Farmington.

And last, but certainly not least, we thank Seal Press for taking on this book, and especially Jennie Goode for her cordial and insightful editorial guidance.

Table of Contents

Parting Company

Introduction

The Wisdom of the Witness

The focus for this work developed one rainy night as we, friends since childhood, prepared for a funeral. Peggy's mother had died three days earlier, after Peggy had cared for her at home during her end-state cancer. Cynthia had managed the care for her paralyzed father for two years before his death and was currently assisting a beloved niece who was dying at home of a brain tumor. That night, we began comparing notes on our experiences of caring for the dying. Our conversation grew increasingly candid and emphatic. We had both been astonished to find that nothing we came across in the existing literature had prepared us for what we had been—and were still—enduring.

When the time came for us to take charge at the deathbeds of our loved ones, we were filled with sadness, anxiety and a great sense of duty. We also felt ignorant. We had never had the responsibility of caring for someone who was dying, and we wanted to know more, much more, about what it would entail and how we could manage it. We both assumed that, just as we had done when we were pregnant, we would be able to find support, information and guidance by reading about the subject. But none of the reading spoke to the reality we were experiencing—the intense emotional, physical, intellectual and spiritual significance of being in attendance during a loved one's death. Indeed, much of what we consulted brought frustration and self-doubt instead of enlightenment and solace.

Most of the books were by professionals who presented remote, generalized ideas about death and dying. But we were experiencing death as pragmatists, not philosophers. When we tried to understand our own circumstances in terms of these generalizations, we seldom found a fit. We wondered then whether there was something wrong with us or our family members. When we looked for more particular cases to address our immediate and practical concerns, we found personal memoirs. These accounts were too specialized and time-consuming for us, however, as we frantically sought to anticipate the actions we might be called upon to take.

We eventually concluded that the main problem was that most of the literature on death and dying was about how we die. Very little was about how we *live* while those in our care are dying. The spotlight was consistently on the person dying. While valuable to us in terms of what we might do to help or understand a loved one better, there was little that helped us to help ourselves. No material spoke directly to the transition we experienced as caretakers of the dying, to our feelings of disorganization or to our fears about how we would fare both during and after our loved one's death.

Fortunately, as we reflected on our respective crises after the fact, we developed an alternative perspective on the mismatch between what we read and what we learned from experience. We came to realize that being with a dying person and witnessing death had simply not been adequately detailed. Eventually, we resolved to write the book we wished we could have read while going through the deaths of our family members. In it, we sought to place what had been missing for us—information from the survivor's perspective about the true phenomenon of being in attendance during dying. We now identify this experience as "death-in-life": the transformative experience of being present at another's death as a caregiver, witness and survivor.

Throughout the research and writing of this book, we maintained the perspective of untrained, unpaid and thoroughly committed caregivers. What was it we had needed to understand, and how could we learn about it? We began by talking about what would have been helpful to us, speaking with hospice professionals and designing interview questions we hoped would evoke the insight and information we had needed when we were dealing with the deaths of our family members. Then we began talking to other survivors and caregivers and recording their answers to our questions.

Parting Company presents many perspectives on the experience of attending to the dying, including those of both lay and professional caregivers. The first-person accounts we have gathered and the observations we have made about them in the commentary at the end of this book place the caregiver at center stage. We wanted to record people's real experiences: what *actually* happens rather than what can or should happen. We hope that these accounts will inform and enlighten those family members and other loved ones who are confronting the death of someone close to them.

These interviews provided us with insights into how death happens within our ongoing lives; how we as caregiving family members come to reckon with a loved one's dying; how we come to accept death when it occurs, or sometimes refuse to accept it; and how we stretch, or cannot stretch, to accommodate death-in-life.

At the outset of our project, we understood our need for the details of dying as witnessed by caregivers. But we did not fully appreciate their wisdom or the importance of their perspective until we were well into our research. The interviews, with caregivers like ourselves, confirmed our experience that the struggle to understand and make meaning of death-in-life is largely absent from public discussions about caring for the dying. The main consequence of this omission is that the caregiver's experience remains hidden; isolation and lack of information remain the norm. An equally important consequence is that the caregiver's reality has been ignored in formulations of public policy intended to help us with the end of life. For too many of us, the result is that such policies do not meet their intended goal.

⟶

When computers were new to the average American, teachers of computer literacy began to use the term "FUD factor." This referred to the fear, uncertainty and doubt that plagued their students as they encountered a completely new and sophisticated technology for the first time. As we collected interviews from a diverse group of people who have experienced the passage of others into death, the notion of a FUD factor became a valuable tool for us. Fear, uncertainty and doubt form the matrix in which we perceive death and dying.

A primary step in our identifying and understanding death-in-life was discovering the concept of "liminality." This term, derived from the Latin word for threshold, *limen,* was coined in 1909 in a seminal anthropological study, *The Rites of Passage.*[1] When human beings go through life transitions, there is often a ceremony involved, typically called a rite of passage. By studying these ceremonies and rituals, social scientists discovered that there are generally three phases: separation, transition and incorporation. The middle, transitional stage often involves the crossing of a threshold, either literally or symbolically. But in all cases, that middle phase is a state in which the individual is "betwixt and between," neither here nor there. The concept of liminality has been taken up by contemporary scholars to describe many states of a transitional nature. For example, a 1990 study of the families of coma victims describes the family members' positions as liminal, because their loved one is alive and yet, in most respects, dead to them and to the world.[2]

We recognized in these descriptions our position as caregivers at the deathbed. When we are living with dying, we too are in a state of liminality as our loved ones' conditions and circumstances continuously change over time. Along with sadness, living with dying is full of fear, uncertainty and doubt, and leads one inexorably to ponder the most human and existential uncertainty of all: What happens when we die? The more we gathered the honest particulars of experience that characterize the turbulence and transcendence of death-in-life, the more we learned. We now think of this liminal experience of participating in the dying of another as a significant marker in the life course—one we hope will be more readily understood as caregivers' perspectives become more prominent in our understanding of death and dying. Understanding the liminality of caregiving for the dying became the underpinning for the three central principles we have derived from our research: Every death is unique, God is in the details, and the past is prologue.

How do we come to grips with a situation as profound as a loved one's dying? Many caregivers search for templates, in religion, for example, or in therapy, or by taking a course on death and dying. We too searched for templates, but eventually realized that with a subject as socially taboo and innately mysterious as death, we are unlikely to discover a how-to formula that will help us manage the ungainly monster that death is. We did not learn what we really needed to know until we began to speak personally and at length with others. Over time, as we reflected on our own experiences and talked to others about theirs, we came to understand that no amount of data can be amassed that will account for every death, nor is any one paradigm adequate to describe this human experience. Our first principle became clear: Death is unique in every case, and however any source might describe the experience, there is no right way to die or to attend the dying, no twelve-step program that can be applied in every situation.

We realized that we could learn more about this transition by embracing its ever-changing form than by trying to pin it down once and for all. Especially after we gathered several interviews, we found that we would benefit from adopting the stance in the well-known parable of the blind men feeling the elephant. In the parable, none of the blind men was able to completely describe the beast, because each had a unique and limited relationship to it. Yet each could describe a portion of the reality, and combined, their descriptions rendered more of the truth. Though we are similarly blind with respect to death, bits and pieces of what others have perceived will illuminate our own experiences. Daunting as death is, other landmark life events—for example, menstruation, making love and childbirth—have all been similarly mysterious, as is any experience before it becomes one's own. We think the best we can do in these situations is to ask others about their experiences and use the information they provide to give us a sense of what *does*—not necessarily what *should*—happen.

As soon as we began conducting interviews, we realized that such firsthand accounts were what we had needed while coping with our loved ones' dying. In a new way, we understood the saying that God is in the details, our second principle. People's own stories conveyed the breadth and depth and mystery of dying that we had experienced during this transition. They shared common themes and concerns, yet each situation was unique. Most importantly, these stories provided what had been missing from "the experts" and other sources.

The third principle we came to understand is that how we cope with death-in-life—indeed, how we survive it—has to do not only with our current situation but also with our history: What is past is prologue for the caregiver. That is, how death has happened to loved ones in the past, how our families did or did not manage serious illness or sudden death, and how we learned what death was like have an enormous effect on what happens to us as we live with dying, and as we go on to survive the death of those close to us. For most of us, there is a store of death experience, usually unarticulated, which informs our current reactions. Our lives are full of unexamined instances of loss. We have found that when people explore these instances, they often recognize parallels between past and present experiences. This recognition often brings participants a wider array of possibilities for action in the current crisis.

Reflection on the past reveals unanswered questions, unaddressed feelings and unquestioned but characteristic patterns of family beliefs and rituals that have been carried out in response to death. These insights can help people to identify troubling areas, especially aspects of the current experience with which they are likely to need help. Just as often, people are able to identify strengths they or other family members brought to bear in times of death and mourning. Discovering that courage and ways of coping lie within their own past experience—and realizing that a store of strengths is already available to them—can be immensely comforting.

When fear, uncertainty and doubt derail us, we sometimes feel especially reactive, thoughtless, out of control. Our past experiences, including confusions as well as strengths, accompany us through our crises. Unless we pause to identify them—easier said than done at the height of a crisis—we may be at their mercy, rather than able to use these insights or skills to our best advantage. Recognition of and reflection on our past experiences with death and loss can help to put us back on track as we try, once again, to ride out an essentially mysterious journey.

You will find in these chapters a wide range of accounts. The majority are voices of lay caregivers whose experiences range from providing full-time care at home to confronting a sudden and unexpected death. Our contributors are of varying ages and discuss the loss of spouses, parents and friends. Also, because caregivers must interact constantly with professionals, we have included an array of voices from health care, pastoral and funeral vocations. These accounts offer two valuable benefits—the perspective of those experienced in dealing with dying, and useful insight into how each views those who are dying and their caregivers. We urge you to take whatever you need from this collection in whatever order works for you.

The accounts are framed by this introduction, which puts caregiving in historical perspective to help us understand our own experiences, and a closing commentary, in which we survey this collection and point out the themes and truths that we have noted over our years of working with these stories. These perspectives are by no means exhaustive, however. Indeed, as you read each chapter, we invite you to notice what makes the most sense to you, what stands out as meaningful or helpful or, by way of contrast, what seems most at odds with your own experiences or with the picture in your mind's eye of what death and dying entail. We encourage you to add your own notes and comments, and a page is provided for this purpose at the end of each chapter.

These stories form a very complex tapestry with many motifs and colors. Because we were surprised to discover new meaning in each interview as we revisited it, we suggest that you, too, may find new insight if you revisit these stories a second or even a third time. In an appendix we provide the two sets of interview questions used, one for lay caregivers and one for professionals. We include these not only to offer background, but to open up the discussion in general. Time and again, upon completing an interview, an interviewee would say to us, "It has been very helpful to talk about this with you. Thank you." A clinician later pointed out to us that such interviews are now being called "narrative therapy." We are not clinicians but want others to know that it may be helpful to invite someone who is grieving or struggling through caring for someone seriously ill to tell their story. We hope these questions may serve as a point of departure.

A few of our interviewees requested that we use their real names: Paulina McCullough, Richard T. Murray, Jane Spahr and Rhonda A. Wiles-Rosell. Otherwise, our subjects' names are pseudonyms, and we have changed details of their stories to protect their privacy. To each of the more than forty people who agreed to speak with us at length, we offer our thanks for their participation, for their honesty and, most of all, for their examples. To readers who are health care professionals and policymakers, we hope this material will help you to understand the caregiver's reality and recognize its importance to end-of-life issues. But most of all, to readers who are providing care to dying loved ones, we hope this helps.

The Roots of Our Experience

We may take for granted how we deal with sickness and death in our culture, but current customs have evolved over time. Indeed, that we found ourselves both determined to care for our dying loved ones and utterly unprepared to do so is rooted in history. Women's traditional role as caregiver, the emergence of modern, male-dominated medicine in Western culture and most recently, shifts in where we care for our dying have all been factors. We now turn to these broader issues.

Women's integral roles in both curing and caring in our culture has typically not been common knowledge. However, women's studies scholars are well aware that "women have always been healers . . . [and that in the past] it was woman, as it is today in tribal cultures, whose task it was to tend the sick, manage labors, and ease loved ones through their last repose."[3] In their now classic 1973 pamphlet, *Witches, Midwives and Nurses: A History of Women Healers*, Barbara Ehrenreich and Deirdre English "recapture the history of women as health workers."[4]

They explain that women have historically been

the unlicensed doctors and anatomists of western history. They were abortionists, nurses and counsellors. They were pharmacists, cultivating healing herbs and exchanging the secrets of their uses. They were midwives, travelling from home to home and village to village. For centuries women were doctors without degrees, barred from books and lectures, learning from each other, and passing on experience from neighbor to neighbor and mother to daughter. They were called "wise women" by the people, and witches or charlatans by the authorities.[5]

Over time, women were systematically shut out of medical practice. In the Middle Ages the wisdom of women healers was denounced as magic, and many were burned as witches. Their focus on experience— observing what does and does not work and applying that knowledge— was a special threat to religious doctrine, which Ehrenreich and English characterize as "a profound distrust of the senses."[6] They continue,

The witch was a triple threat to the Church: she was a woman, and not ashamed of it. She appeared to be part of an organized underground of peasant women. And she was a healer whose practice was based on empirical study. In the face of the repressive fatalism of Christianity, she held out the hope of change in this world.[7]

What the Church did not manage to quash, the emergence of male-only universities did. By the 1800s, formally trained doctors—whose "heroic" methods included bleeding and massive doses of purgatives— began to differentiate themselves from lay practitioners. Despite the fact that "lay practitioners were undoubtedly safer and more effective [because] they were less likely to do a patient harm," by mid-century in the United States, the "regular" doctors were successfully applying the political clout available to them as white, male, middle class and able to vote.[8] By the 1900s, although folk and immigrant healers continued to serve the poor and the disenfranchised, the work of lay practitioners was largely illegal. "In state after state, new tough licensing laws sealed the doctor's monopoly on medical practice."[9] In the United States, unlike other industrialized countries, even midwifery was outlawed.[10] Women who wanted to become legal healers were directed to nursing, and once there, were instructed to strictly follow doctors' orders.[11] Bedside care was relegated to nurses so that doctors could diagnose, prescribe and move on.[12] Ehrenreich and English note,

> *Curing became the exclusive province of the doctor; caring was relegated to the nurse. All credit for the patient's recovery went to the doctor . . . the nurse's activities, on the other hand, were barely distinguishable from those of a servant. She had no power . . . and no claim to the credit.*[13]

We have been heartened recently to see expanded coverage of end-of-life issues in response to the Supreme Court's consideration of physician-assisted suicide. But the news reports and available books on this issue continue to suggest that doctors are the most worthy spokespeople on the issues of death and dying. Dr. Timothy E. Quill's A *Midwife Through the Dying Process*,[14] for example, includes some caregivers' accounts but with the objective of concluding that physicians should have an expanded role in easing terminal patients into death.

That Quill, a male doctor, chose to use the word "midwife" in his book title seems a perfect example of co-opting the caregiver's work. This is disappointing because the real "midwives"—lay caregivers—are not being heard as clearly as they might be. Nor are feminist scholars, who have been keen critics of medical practice and have an historical perspective on women's systematic exclusion from all but the scut work of health care. Hospice nurses have provided the best documentaries about what the dying person experiences (see *Final Gifts: Understanding the Special Awareness, Needs and Communications of the Dying* by Maggie Callanan and Patricia Kelley for an example).[15] But no one to date has offered a feminist analysis of death and dying—an analysis that acknowledges the costs, both financial and personal, for caregivers and voices these as issues for health care policymakers to consider.

Perhaps one reason that attention has not been given to the

caregiver's reality is that it has been taken for granted as women's work, which is expected to be given for free by women. In our culture, caregiving has traditionally been expected from women for so long that we don't readily consider the impact of gender-role expectations on the system or quality of care for the dying. Indeed, we ourselves served as unpaid—and largely unquestioning—female caregivers. It was not until we thought about what we did in the context of what our interviewees were telling us that we began to entertain the notion that gender-role expectations had influenced our decisions to care for our dying relatives, or that our own gender-role expectations contributed to an internal sense of duty, motivating us to accept exhaustion and at times overwhelming despair. Least obvious to us in the midst of caring for our dying loved ones was that the health care systems with which we were working depended on the unpaid labor of our love.

Although many men find themselves needing to care for a dying loved one at home, the typical twenty-four-hour-a-day caregiver is female. Women currently constitute the majority of caregivers in all categories. They are 77 percent of adult children caring for parents and 64 percent of spousal caregivers.[16] Furthermore, there are gender differences in how spousal caregivers manage that twenty-four-hour-a-day care: Men, for example, are more likely to hire additional female help to care for their ailing wives, while women tend to their husbands themselves.[17]

These trends are likely to continue, given that policies are increasingly reimposing the burden of long-term care on family members in response to the reigning view that the United States cannot afford the projected high costs of institutional care for its burgeoning numbers of elderly.[18] Current hospice practice also supports this trend, providing minimal inpatient care and a preponderance of outpatient, at-home hospice services.

It is interesting to view the hospice movement against the backdrop of the history of women and caregiving. The idea of providing special, comfort-based palliative care for the dying gained ground after the first model, St. Christopher's Hospice in England, opened in 1967 under the direction of a woman, Dr. Cicely Saunders.[19] Hospices were developed for those patients for whom there was no hope of a cure, and thus no heroic treatments left to prescribe. In the 1980s, hospice services in the

United States became reimbursable under Medicare, and today there are more than one thousand hospices in the country.[20] But most hospice patients do not receive care in an inpatient facility like St. Christopher's. In fact, "Most care is provided by . . . groups that do not have freestanding facilities. Typically, hospices provide a range of medical, nursing and psychosocial services to patients and their families, with the aim of supplementing care received from other health care institutions."[21]

A patient who is not being cared for in a facility is being cared for at home, twenty-four hours a day, seven days a week. Having someone die at home was the normal course of events in the distant past, but in this century most deaths in the United States have taken place in hospitals.[22] It is only recently that hospice, and the home death that it makes possible, has become an option. Those who take that option face a surprising dilemma: Unless we have medical training, we have no idea what to expect. Several generations have come of age in the United States without meaningful exposure to the care of the dying. No wonder we felt ignorant.

Although we welcomed hospice services in our own situations and we value the humane approach of palliative care for the dying, we are concerned that even within this perspective the role of the home caregiver is minimized. Indeed, in a letter to the *New York Times*, Jack D. Gordon, president of the Hospice Foundation of America, defined hospice as "care in the home by a team of professionals—doctors, nurses, social workers, clergy, aides."[23] He did not mention a crucial factor that consumers should understand about hospice, namely that the twenty-four-hour-a-day caretaking falls not to any of the aforementioned professionals, but to the patient's loved ones.

It is our opinion that among its benefits, hospice provides an expedient alternative for health care insurers and providers. "Home care" has become a popular, money-saving principle throughout the health care system precisely because it leaves the lion's share of the work to unpaid caregivers. For many this may prove to be an overwhelming burden, and one they will not learn about ahead of time from official quarters, because the caregiver's ordeal is typically underarticulated.

Because cost-benefit analysis has become the basis for health care decisionmaking in this country, it deserves a closer look—especially by caregivers. Based on social exchange theory, this "rational choice perspective" is an economic model which assumes that human beings only make choices that promise to be more advantageous than disadvantageous.[24] But as we experienced the dying of our loved ones and then talked with others who had done the same, we discovered that caregivers typically "stretch themselves way beyond any sane limits," as one health care aide we interviewed observed.[25] The term "rational" is hardly adequate to describe one's decision to care for a dying loved one—family history, necessity, love or obligation often supercede a clear analysis of what is advantageous or not.

The "costs" to caregivers have been identified by some analysts. A study by public health researcher Emily Abel of those who care for the frail elderly reveals some particulars of the financial, social, physical, emotional and psychological costs of providing "informal care."[26] For example, wage earners suffer an array of financial consequences, from losing their competitive edge, to taking time off without pay, to having to quit their jobs. If caregivers manage to hold on to their jobs, Abel notes, they completely sacrifice their leisure time.[27] Confined to the home to care for a loved one whose condition only worsens, caregivers also find themselves isolated from others. There is no preparation for experiencing dying in one's day-to-day life, no counterpart to the childbirth classes or the bonding with other families that characterize the transition into parenthood, for example. Abel cites data suggesting that caregivers experience three times as many symptoms of stress as noncaregivers.[28]

In contrast to the reality of home care that our interviewees describe, what is available for the general public to consider is an overly positive picture of home care in general, and especially care for the dying. In fact, the more we have thought about the messages in the media and in promotions from the health care industry, the more we have realized that we are saturated with a "pro" home health care public relations campaign. This reminds us of the public relations campaign after World War II, which was a concerted effort to convince women who had been in paid employment during the war years to return to unpaid duty at home: an environment that was ever so much more pleasant, thanks to all the labor-saving devices produced for them there.

Consider a recent television news report about an innovation in home health care. It featured a special recording device that is connected to a client's home telephone. A health care practitioner can telephone the client with this device, ask about general health, and even (depending on the client's ability) ask the client to measure and record pulse, temperature and blood pressure information on the spot. Health practitioners can also use this equipment to remind clients to take their medications. There is even a way for clients to record when and how much medication they take, by pressing the appropriate buttons.

On the surface, this is an uplifting report, emphasizing cost savings within the health care system—to the extent that its use could substitute for a home visit or for on-site care—and extolling the benefits of a client's comfort in the home. But to us, it only adds to the perception that home health care is easy. With more technology to assist in home care and with the support of visiting health practitioners and hospice workers, caring for the dying at home looks reasonable and manageable. To see such renderings of the task helps us undertake it, and we are already willing. Most of us think that taking care of our own, especially when they are dying, is the right thing to do, something we should do. A terminal illness means that this is our last chance to provide what love and care we can. As one psychologist we interviewed explained about caring for his dying companion, "I have no right in this. The man is dying. You only get to die once. You should get to do it decently."[29] The situation brings an acute sense of urgency to the fore.

The conviction that in-home care is the right thing to do is further fueled by the thought of our dying loved ones facing their last days in impersonal hospitals, hooked up to machinery, perhaps ignored, and in great pain, as recent studies suggest is the case for many.[30] And so we welcome news of any advance that will help us keep our loved ones at home, where we believe they will be more comfortable. The first-person accounts offered in *Parting Company* reveal these and other aspects of caring for the dying. In sum, these accounts present a much more complicated scenario of home care than the glossy overlay that is typically presented to the public. These stories carry a warning that an overly optimistic portrayal of home health care leaves lay caregivers unprepared for the difficult task they have undertaken.

Our culture's collective experience with death has changed systematically over time. In *The Hour of Our Death*, Philippe Ariès points out that "the hidden death in the hospital, which began very discreetly in the 1930s and '40s . . . became widespread after 1950."[31] But in recent years, modern medical technology has prolonged many terminal cases, health insurance benefits have been curtailed and the hospice movement has grown. More and more, inexperienced family members and loved ones are becoming primary caregivers, yet most of us grew up in a society where death was a stranger, and few of us lived in households where decline and dying were accommodated. Consequently, most of us are now without a past sense of tradition or a shared understanding of death; we lack a basic literacy of dying, even as it intrudes into our lives.

To seek more understanding is to encounter a strong taboo, which, Ariès explains, has been reinforced by the very practices that placed the dying in hospitals and care facilities for more than two generations. Once a familiar part of life, death has been "hushed up," with the result that "our senses can no longer tolerate the sights and smells that in the early nineteenth century were a part of daily life, along with suffering and illness."[32] Modern Western society regards death as a personal failure, a special affront to technological progress and its implied promise of control, with the modern doctor-technician feeling that failure perhaps most acutely. Against the backdrop of this taboo, it is not surprising to find limited general acknowledgment of and information about the realities of dying. Less obvious is the fact that we don't really want to imagine how difficult this reality can be. Having to deal with death is formidable enough; it doesn't take much more to make people back away even further. Because of this, discussing the difficulties associated with caring for the dying is hard to broach. It scares people.

Professional health care practitioners and even hospice workers are not likely to inform us fully about the difficult aspects of home care for the dying. Sometimes this is because they are trying to support us in our desire to do it. They want to honor our wishes to make our loved ones more comfortable at home, and so they focus on the positive aspects of what home care might hold for us and our family members. It would seem cruel to focus on how hard it might be to care for a dying person when bolstering our resources would seem to be the thing to do. Even so, it is important to realize that health care professionals are also driven, and in some cases mandated, to advocate the financially cost-effective course of action.

The pressures to provide this care are personal, social, economic, gendered and powerful. The lay caregiver is unlikely to appreciate any of this, especially in the midst of a crisis. Consequently, over time she is all the more likely to find herself in over her head. When the reality of caregiving overwhelms her, no one, least of all the dying loved one, is well served. The system breaks down as the back of the worker on whom the system relies is broken. This happens because all too often there is no Plan B; the questions "What if it proves too much?" and "How will I know if it's too much?" are not fully framed at the outset of making the very important decision about what one should do when a loved one is dying. Although it may be utterly appropriate to take on this awesome task, too often we respond without thinking; we respond according to our unarticulated but powerful beliefs about caregiving, which are reinforced by a system that relies on us to respond in just these ways.

So what is the prospective caregiver to do when confronted with the option to take a loved one home to die? You may be told that it's good for the patient, but you also need to understand that it is good for the institutions involved, including Medicare and private insurers as well as hospitals and hospices. Their interests are represented by corporate and government policymakers, lobbyists and foundations; yours are not. You will have the twenty-four-hour responsibility but limited power to exercise your judgment on behalf of your loved one.

Furthermore, although hospice presents itself as providing complete support—and that is its intent—it may not. When that happens, you discover the worst aspect of all: that a patient who is certain to die falls outside the checks and balances of normal medical accountability. If the nurse fails to show up for an appointed visit or the doctor neglects to order the stronger medicine, the outcome will not change. And so you must be proactive. When the costs of caregiving have taken their toll on you, that is often when you must become a ferocious consumer. In the last hours, when you are the most exhausted and saddened, expect to fight—for adequate pain medication, for the respite care that was promised or for staff to hear you out.

It is clear from our own experiences and from those of others that when you escort a loved one to the threshold between life and death, *you also* embark on an unfathomable journey. The individual stories of death-in-life collected here reveal the true depth of this experience, including for some of us the hidden costs of home care. These costs would probably have eluded us without the benefit of stories from other caregivers. Against the backdrop of others' accounts, we began to understand more fully what the reality of end-of-life care entails. Each interview is embedded with nuggets of experience and understanding that cannot be summarized and indexed. As caregivers tell their own stories, the rich details and particulars speak in their own honest ways. We have concluded that with a subject as taboo and intimate as dying, word of mouth is the best educator.

We offer this work not to discourage people from undertaking home care for the dying, but to help them more realistically make decisions for themselves and their loved ones. Nor is it our intent to castigate the tireless efforts of front-line hospice and palliative health care practitioners. Rather, we wish to identify the areas that need improvement. Broader access to what caregivers know will enable a fuller discussion than is currently taking place about the circumstances of death-in-life. This will help our society to design a system of enhanced care not only for the dying, but for the living who care for them as well. On one hand, these stories may seem depressing, especially to someone who has never confronted this experience. On the other hand, and to us, they are profoundly inspiring, revealing human resilience and our capacity to be courageous and loving. As a result of this work, we are personally more fully prepared, not only because we understand more about the reality of caregiving but also because we have gained invaluable new insights and advice from each narrator.

Trying to Do It All

Claire Levine

Claire, a social worker, was thirty when her husband, Robert, died in their home of malignant melanoma. Four years earlier, she had noticed that Robert had a mole that looked unusual. Cancer was diagnosed and, after treatment, went into remission. Claire and Robert then married, and he completed two medical residencies, in internal medicine and dermatology.

It had been a little over a year since his death when we spoke with Claire. She's a friendly, slender woman who proves to be both dynamic and delicate. She began the interview by showing us a photograph: She and Robert are standing together at a wedding, shortly before they will announce their own engagement. It is still a secret, and you can see that in the picture. Claire, encircled in his arm, is grinning broadly. Robert, tall and handsome, wears a sweet expression of contentment. Claire explains that the sweetness was characteristic. Its visibility in this picture is the reason she brought it to the interview.

They had been married for two years and Claire was looking forward to starting their family when Robert's remission ended. As Claire told their story, we were struck by the relentless clarity of their situation. As a physician, Robert knew, and worried about, his prospects. As a social worker, Claire understood the needs of a couple in crisis. But despite their knowledgeability, they were no less overwhelmed by what happened to them.

They were young and personally unacquainted with death. Neither had ever lost anyone dear to them. Robert's parents were survivors of the Holocaust and had lost their families before Robert was born. This may have been a factor in Robert's saying that he always thought he would die young, a belief that seemed to increase his anxieties, according to Claire. She grew accustomed to minimizing Robert's worries over his health, so much so that on the night of her thirtieth birthday when he noticed two tender spots under his skin, she was sure he was exaggerating. That was in August; Robert died five months later, on January 31. He was thirty-one.

Asked when she knew that Robert was dying, Claire paused. This was a hard question to answer, she said, and thought about it for a long moment. Then she began with a slip of the tongue.

"Okay, I know when I knew I was dying—I mean, *he* was dying. I say *I* was dying because I think I felt a part of me—that *I* was dying. I think it was when he was in the hospital in October." At the time, Claire was working full time and sleeping at the hospital, trying to "do it all. I thought, 'I can work and he'll be at home and we'll get on with life.' I think I was denying it." One day when the oncology nurse called her at work, Claire was not getting the answers she needed. "The nurse was being very evasive, and then I said, 'How long does he have?' No one was coming right out and saying anything to me because Robert didn't want anybody to say he was dying or that he wouldn't make it. He just wanted everybody to fight with him and beat this thing. And yet here I am, I needed to know what life had in store for me. Because if he was leaving, I'd be left—you know, reality.

"The nurse said, 'If he keeps getting these infections, he won't last till spring.' And then it really hit me: holy cow! Then I was really mad that she told me that. 'How could you tell me that!' I said. But—I had asked her.

"But then I still had hope. There are other miracle cases, and he could still be the one miracle. In reality, intellectually, I knew things were not good, but emotionally I thought, 'We're going to beat it. It's not going to take control of us.'"

Claire and Robert continued their fight to the end. During the last weeks, Claire was "feeling so exhausted and so angry. I couldn't get any sleep. My mother and his mother stayed with us for a month, and my father traveled down on weekends. I remember thinking, 'I can't stand this.' It was great that everyone was there to help us, but we didn't have any privacy either. About a week before he died, I felt like, 'I can't do this anymore, I gotta get outta here. I want to run away and never come back. This is just a horrible nightmare.'

"I remember getting impatient with Robert. He needed a lot of physical care, and I was the one who did it. The hospice nurses did a little, but they weren't there twenty-four hours a day. I was. I did everything. Bathing, feeding—he was only on liquids, which meant hooking up the NG [nasogastric] feeding tube and cleaning it out. And I felt angry and tired and wished I had more help with his physical care. Also, that was the time he started becoming incontinent. He could still use the bathroom but sometimes he just couldn't make it by himself. One time he was sitting in the chair he always sat in—we had this cream-colored furniture—and he just pooped on the chair. And his mother called me. I wished that someone else could have taken him to the bathroom. I was so tired.

"I can't believe that I actually did all that I did. Sometimes when I think of those things now, I get panicky and nauseated. But when I was going through it, I just did it. I didn't think about it, even at the end, when things got really complicated and gross. Cancer is not a pretty disease."

The week before Robert died, one of his brothers arrived for a last visit, to say goodbye. A conversation among the three of them marked the time in Claire's mind when Robert began to acknowledge that he was dying. Claire opened the journal she kept that week and read: *January 22—Robert and I spoke of his feeling of being tricked into death. If he's dying he doesn't know it, but he doesn't know if he wants to know, because then he'll just give up. He wants to live and continue to fight. It's so frustrating. He feels that the doctors have given up on him. He's so happy that I understand how he feels. He feels he will live as if he has four months, have his family visit, but then have a formal goodbye and try to live each day that way.*

Then he has all his options covered. He's frustrated because he feels he can't have a plan to die. It's happening too fast. He can't get a handle on it. This is out of control.

January 26—Robert thought all day about his disease and possibly coming to an acceptance of what is happening to him. He feels confused because he doesn't know how he got so sick so fast. When he looked at himself in the mirror, he was shocked at his physical appearance, because inside he felt like the same person. He's trying to come to terms with the quick progression of his disease. He says that he won't fight God anymore, but if God is trying to get him to feel more comfortable, he will.

Claire explained that it was during these days, as she was writing these entries, that she also acknowledged that Robert was dying: January 28—I feel so sad today. I want my husband back. There are glimmers of the old Robert, but so much of the time he's so sick and so distant. I want my old house back, my old job back, my old life back. It was so great, so warm, loving and wonderful. Now I pray for moments when Robert will share a thought with me just so we can be close again. I just can't think of losing that. My life will never ever be the same. Mom said my innocence is gone. She's right. Sometimes I feel so bitter about what's happened. My head is spinning so much of the time. My days are filled with caring for Robert, calling about health benefits, answering the phone, running errands, trying to protect Robert.

These busy things really protected me today from my own pain. The mothers and Robert were napping. It was so quiet. Just me in a quiet house. I wondered, "Oh my God, is this how quiet my future is?" Panic, fear, feeling ill set in. I want it like it used to be. I'm so frightened. I spoke to my therapist today. "Just try to make it through this grieving time, try not to plan too much for the future," she said. I just cried through most of the session.

When I came home, Robert awoke from napping. He told me about vivid dreams, which I'm trying to make sense of. Robert sometimes thinks they're real. I don't know whether it's from the morphine, but today he dreamt that we were in an investigation. I was making a "femor." I said, "What's a femor?" and he said, "It's an omelet with surrounding cheese. It was protecting the cheese." When he woke up, it all melted. The other part of the dream was that we were in a Purim play. [Purim is a festive Jewish holiday during which children perform the Purim play, re-enacting how Queen Esther saved the Jews *from a murderous rampage.] It was such an effort for him, but he stuck it out. I could find out information through this play, somehow, to save him. Somehow he was helping me to find out what the information is. In the dreams he has all of the knowledge of his disease. When he wakes up, it's lost.*

On January 30th, the day before Robert died, Claire wrote: *I'm getting really scared now. Robert's sleeping more and more and getting more and more confused. It's so frightening to see him this way. I can't believe I can watch Robert this way and not fall apart. . . . Robert seems so distant at times. It's so painful. Tonight he felt like the nurses were trying to plot against him. Where did he get this idea? This is not like my husband. It's so weird. The morphine needle was bleeding. The feeding tube wasn't working as well.*

January 31—Robert died today at 4:11 P.M.

Claire looked up, she had written no more. She said thoughtfully, "Something was really different that day." She described how she woke first that morning. Robert slept in a hospital bed in their room, and when she looked over at him, "there was a grayish tint to him. Something about him looked different. I got really scared. I tapped him, then started shaking him, and was thinking, 'He's in a coma.'" Claire had once asked the doctor how Robert would die, and had been told, "He'll just go into a coma." She shook him some more.

"It took him a really long time to wake up. His breathing was really labored. It took a long time, and then when he woke up he looked at me and didn't say anything. I walked around the other side of his bed, and he looked at me and said, 'Would you please go get my wife?'

"I said, 'Honey, it's me Claire. I'm your wife.' It took him a really long time to realize this was me.

"And then he said, 'Were we on vacation?' I said no, and he said, 'We just went on a vacation and it was really great.'

"'Really?' Then I said, 'No, you've been here, you've just been sleeping.'

"'Well, don't let me go back to sleep, because if you do I will die.'

"'You're crazy, don't talk like that.' And then I got really scared."

The hospice nurse came that day and Claire asked her, "Robert says he's going to die today, what do you think?" The nurse said, "Well he could, or it could be a few days."

"I knew it but I didn't want to know it. It's not like you say, 'I know he's going to die,' and that's it. You go back and forth. And you keep hoping. I think I knew because I canceled my plans to go out that day.

"He never went into a coma. The nurse cleaned him and gave him a massage. He was relaxed, he wasn't agitated. They say that seventy-two hours to a half hour before somebody dies, they get real calm. Then he talked to his other brother on the phone and he said something like, 'Goodbye, I'm going to die today.' I was thinking, 'How does he know this?'"

Claire and Robert watched their favorite TV show together that afternoon, and then Claire went to take a nap in the other bedroom. "At four o'clock my mother-in-law came to me and said, 'He wants to talk to you.' I went in to him and lay down on my bed. I took his hand and was stroking him. He said to me, with a smile on his face, 'Tell me three special things about me.'

"I said, 'Oh, you're wonderful,' and he said, 'No, no, that's not good enough.'

"So I said, 'You're a very loving person, you're a fighter and you're wonderful.'

"Then he said, 'And promise me you'll take care of the fund.' We had started a melanoma fund at the cancer institute where he was treated. And he said, 'Everything for the fund is taken care of, it'll be okay?' and I said, 'It'll be okay. Don't worry, I have everything under control.' And then his head rolled back, and he went into a seizure, and that was it."

Claire's voice became more emphatic as she continued. "We had been *talking,* like you and I are talking, like normal people, and then his head started to roll back and then," she gasped, reliving it, "I got so scared, I started screaming his name. 'Robert, Robert, Robert!' And the mothers came, and the nurse came running in. I was screaming, 'Is it really happening, is it really happening?' And the nurse said, 'Yes, it's really happening.' I was hysterical. This was *not* calm, like how they'd said he would die. He'd started a seizure. They sent me out of the room, and I didn't want to come back till it was over. But I did come back. It seemed like hours, but it was a matter of seconds.

"It was very peaceful after. He turned very, very yellow immediately, because his whole liver was filled with the disease, not working. I just held him for awhile. Then another hospice nurse came. The feeling was, 'I just don't want to let him go. I'm not ready to let him go.' The funeral people came. Robert was being transported to New Mexico, he was being buried in New Mexico where his parents live. So, I guess I had anger because they said, 'It's time,' and *I* wanted to make that decision.

"I think they thought I could just stay there forever with him, and I guess they thought it would be healthier for me to let go, that it was time for me to let go. I had done everything I could and there was no point to me hanging on. But I do regret that. They should have let me decide when to release him. But, I don't know, I was in such a state that maybe no matter how long of a time I would have had, it would have been too soon or too rushed."

It was the hospice nurse who was trying to hurry the process along, and "she did it in a very sensitive way. She said, 'Claire, it's time.' Maybe I was there a long time. My memory is very clouded and vague. I think I was there about forty minutes. That's a good amount of time, but I just wasn't ready, and whenever it was, I wouldn't have been ready. It was like, oh, he's sleeping. I kissed him, I held him, I laid my head on his chest. He wasn't breathing, his chest wasn't moving up and down. But it was like, 'Oh, he's just sleeping.' That's how I felt. I guess whenever they would have taken him, I wouldn't have been ready. I just wasn't ready, I wasn't ready to let him go. *He* made the decision to go. I was just talking to him and then he just decides to die. I still have a lot of anger about that. Like, 'Robert, give me some warning,' you know? But Robert was a very private and quiet individual and didn't want to cause problems for anybody. He felt very, very guilty about being sick and being a burden. He didn't want to be a burden, and he just did things in a very mellow, understated way. That's the way he lived his life and that's the way he died.

"I think to compensate for the rushed feeling I had with letting him go, I keep going back to that actual time of death, replaying it in my mind. To help me let go."

⌒

Claire felt cautious about describing some of her experiences after Robert died, because others had characterized some of them as hallucinations. With our reassurances that she would not be considered "crazy," Claire proceeded.

"It feels so good to share this," she began. "When I was in New Mexico the morning of the funeral, my sister and her husband and I took a walk around the block. And this butterfly kept following us. And I just knew that was Robert. I never saw a butterfly like that. It was black with yellow pinstripes, like a shirt." She smiled. "He wore those oxford pinstripe shirts. He was pretty conservative. As I looked I was thinking, 'That's an interesting butterfly—oh hi, Robert! You're walking with us! It's nice of you to join us.'

"In Judaism there's something called *shivah*, it's like an extended wake. You don't view the casket and the body, but people come to the home for seven days. You have a lot to eat, and in a weird way it's like a party. In a way, I hated that. I was so exhausted, and I didn't want to deal with these people I hardly knew. I just didn't want to make small talk. That whole week when I felt, 'I can't deal with these people,' I would go outside and sit, and read, and this butterfly would just keep flying around. The same butterfly, that whole week. I'd say, 'Robert!' I'd say, 'Thank you,' or I would question, 'Why did you do this to me? Here you are a beautiful butterfly, and here I am in pain and suffering.' But when I had these questions, it would just fly away. It wouldn't answer.

"Another experience was about a week and a half after the funeral, shortly after I came back home to our apartment. My mother was staying with me for a week. It was the first or second night home. It was four o'clock in the morning and I was sleeping, and I was woken by Robert whispering, saying, 'Talk to me,' just like that, 'Talk to me.' I felt his breath on my ear. This was not comforting to me. I freaked out. I was so frightened, so scared. I was screaming for my mother because it was very, very scary for me. My mother said, 'You were just having a bad dream, you're just hallucinating. Robert's not here, how could he be here?'

"That really caused a lot of problems for me. Nighttime became a really scary time. I had trouble sleeping because I did not want to experience this again. I remember—I'm not sure when we had this conversation, whether it was before or after the melanoma recurred—Robert and I had this conversation in which I had said, 'Don't come back as a ghost. I don't want to see you.' But I don't think I ever said, 'I don't want to *hear* you.'" Claire laughed at this distinction, adding, "I just meant, 'Don't scare me. I don't want to be spooked like that.'"

Claire found some relief when she went to her hometown to spend some time with her family. "My mom had met this wonderful cancer therapist that she had been seeing when Robert was ill, so I went to see her. I told her about this experience. I told her, 'I can't sleep, and I think I'm going crazy.'

"She said, 'Well, just tell him.'

"I said, 'What? Just *tell* him?'

"'Tell him that you don't want him to talk to you,' she told me.

"I said, 'Oh. I never thought of that. Okay.'

"She was very calm, didn't think I was nuts. It had never occurred to me that I could tell him not to do this. That evening I had a conversation with him. But I felt really guilty, because I didn't want him to be hurt. I still wanted him to contact me, but not in that way. The therapist told me, 'Don't worry. He's in a place where nothing could ever hurt him. He'll understand, believe me.' She was great. I kept in touch with her for a long time.

"Then I went through a stage where I was really, really worried about him. Was he okay? Who's going to take care of him? Is he lonely? I was obsessive about this. And then I had this dream. I was at my parents' house." She described the incident in her journal:

March 14—Robert came to me while I slept. I was driving some sort of chair in a room with barriers on a long black road. Then all of a sudden, two beautiful white birds flew overhead. I was not afraid, but almost wanted to kiss them. Then I found myself in the most incredible outdoor scenery I have ever seen or felt. I can't even describe it. I remember gasping and going, "Oh! Oh! Oh!" I couldn't believe how beautiful this place was. I wanted to cry. I was standing on top of a gorge or a mountain ledge, looking out. I saw beautiful evergreen trees covered with mist. Everything was peaceful and gorgeous. This was no dream; this was Robert. Thank you, Honey. I just wanted to stay in that place. Our souls were connected for that second. Everything was so vivid.

I woke up feeling, "What just happened?" trying to go back to that place. I knew this was no ordinary dream, but that Robert had spoken to me. He is in a beautiful place. I had to tell someone, but Mom thought I was nuts.

"The next day, I told my mom again about this experience, and she started to cry because she wanted to experience this and she hadn't. She felt really sad that she wasn't able to experience things like this.

"This was the first time that I realized there's something beyond. Even writing it doesn't describe the feeling I had. I'll tell you, it's better than this place we have, this earth. After this experience, I've had no fear of death. I fear pain and the process of dying, but no fear of the afterlife. The scene was just amazing. I didn't see him, I didn't hear him, but it was him—the whole scene was him. I'm so happy I experienced that. People say it was just a dream, but I call it an experience because it wasn't just a dream.

"Shortly after this, I went to visit my sister and stayed with her for a month. At this point I wanted to know what Robert was doing. I went to a Tarot card reader, and it was really interesting. A lot of the things he said have evolved. But that night, I saw Robert. I was in bed, at four o'clock this time. I looked over and saw him lying next to me. He looked healthy. He looked *really good*.

"My initial reaction was, 'Omigod!' and I wanted to scream for my sister. Then I felt, 'Wait a minute, he's not going to hurt me. This is *Robert*. Furthermore, he hasn't been in my bed for months. I'm going to see what this is all about. I want to get through this and see what's going to happen.' He was sleeping, and then he looked over at me and smiled. And then—you know how in cartoons, when the cartoon character dies, and then the body . . . " Claire gestured that the body floats up and away. "That's what happened. His body just rose up. And that was that."

While Robert was dying, Claire thought a lot about the afterlife. She thinks her interest may have been a factor in why these incidents have happened to her. "I just needed to know. I was very open to knowing. I think I was already open to a dimension other than this life. Maybe that's why."

The fear these experiences engendered is sometimes still troubling to Claire. "Even a year later, nighttime is still not a very comfortable

time for me. I'll look around, try to see if I see his ghost. I scare myself!"
No other family members or friends reported any experiences of this nature. "I felt so alone, I really did."

Claire described how Robert's death had been in character. "Being a physician, the kind of person he was, he had to have a plan. Robert had to plan everything. This is what was so emotionally painful for him with his illness. That he couldn't have a plan to die was so frustrating for him. He would try. He would write down what he was going to do. 'First I'll take a shower, then I'll get my feeding tube cleaned. Then I'll take a nap.' Real detailed like that. It was so specific, and that was his way. He needed to have a plan." But at the time, "I couldn't talk about dying with Robert. I would talk about it with my family, but without feeling. I'd talk about getting my finances in order, seeing about a job, what I'm going to do about my social life, without ever realizing the kind of emotion I would have.

"The summer after he died, I would really feel the sadness and feelings of panic. When I would talk about his illness or think about his physical deterioration, I would get a very sick feeling physically. Panic attacks, nausea. I continued to work with my therapist. Through arranging Robert's fund at the cancer institute where he was treated, I was offered a job, probably because I seemed so much in control. But now, six months later, working day in and day out around cancer makes me physically ill. It takes all my energy, all my cognitive work to say, 'This is not the same time as it was a year ago. These people aren't Robert. You're in control, you're okay.' It's just been recently that I'm less anxious when I talk about it. I can feel the sadness but still maintain control.

"While I was going through it, I was very in control, going through it like a trouper. Then there was a period of time that I was feeling very out of control, that I couldn't deal with this. But gradually I'm feeling back in control. It's a part of my life, I have to live with it and I have to find a place for it. It has definitely been a yearlong process, and there are different phases that one definitely goes through. I was very busy when I first came back after the funeral, seeing people, doing interviews on the radio with his doctor; I did a benefit for his fund. I was all over the place. I got a full-time job at the cancer institute. I was running, and then it just sort of hit. I felt like, 'I'm losing it. I can't deal with this. I don't want to have this history. I don't want to be a widow. I don't want to talk about it.' Now I'm trying to weave this tragedy into my life.

"What I really struggle with is coming to terms with Robert's physical deterioration. I've never ever experienced someone so physically ill, his body being out of control. Every part of his body did not work. And then he got that death look. Going from being a beautiful man to a look of death—I don't think I'll ever come to terms with that."

But "the experiences have been very helpful, the scene experience and the butterfly experience. They have reassured me that he was in a very beautiful place and that he was okay. It hasn't reassured me that it was okay for him to die, the way he did, but at least he's okay. I don't worry about him the way I used to."

Religion has helped too. Claire has felt supported by the religious community and has "become much more observant since his death." Her family has been another source of support. "Throughout the illness, as angry as I would get sometimes for lack of privacy, I couldn't have done it without my family and Robert's family—parents, my sister, his brothers. That was the core thing that helped me get through, before and after. That's what helped me move on."

Looking back, Claire wished that she and Robert "could have been more sharing about death, and about afterlife, about what would happen to me, and what he felt would happen to him. Only once, for two seconds in passing, with great difficulty, I said, 'If things don't work out the way we want'—I couldn't even say, 'If you die, well, you know, what's going to happen to me?' I couldn't be specific about it. He just said, very matter-of-factly, 'Well, you'll feel really bad for a while, you'll be really sad, your family will help you and then you'll move on. You'll meet somebody, you'll get married and you'll have a family.' I was covering my ears the whole time. I didn't want to hear it. I'd asked him, but I didn't want to hear. I thought he was going to say, 'Oh, no, I'm going to be here forever.' But he didn't. So I wish that we could have been more open, more explicit."

Claire also regretted that Robert's father, an elderly man with many health problems, was not able to be part of the process. "I wish that they could have shared. I don't know how Robert felt about that. I wish that they somehow could have connected at some level.

"I definitely believe now that when you die, you go to some beautiful place. I can't imagine there's a hell or purgatory after what I've experienced. I do believe in a soul, and it goes to this beautiful place. I don't know how, or when, or with whom, but I believe it goes somewhere. I don't know how you get to this dimension. People describe going through this tunnel. I don't know about that. With the experiences I had, I felt that I was connected in some way. I was consciously aware that this was death—or the afterlife. That's the only basis I have to describe what it was like. I also feel it can be a lot of things. Robert could be in the trees, or a waterfall, or a butterfly. He could also be a bird. It's not defined by space and time. You can just go anywhere. I *do* feel there's a sense of being very free—very, very physically free and very, very spiritually free. Robert was suffering so much in his body. He didn't want to die, he didn't want to let go, but I think that once he did let go, there was an incredible sense of freedom for him. Who wants to be in a body that's deteriorating and full of pain?

"On that last day, when he was sleeping and I couldn't wake him up, I believe somebody came to him. I don't know who. He actually mentioned somebody's name. He said, 'Write down this name—*Hargrove.*'" Claire learned later that "Hargrove" was the name of a character in a P. G. Wodehouse novel that Robert had read. She continued, smiling at the memory, "So I wrote down that name, *Hargrove.*" She laughed and shrugged but then grew more serious. "I do believe there was a guide who came to him and told him, 'It's time.'" This was how Robert knew that he was dying that day, she believes. He woke up thinking he'd been on vacation, "someplace really nice. It seemed to me that he had been with somebody in someplace beautiful. This Hargrove, whoever he is."

After all that she had been through, Claire had a lot of advice for those who find themselves in similar situations. "Be patient with all the feelings that you experience. They're all valid and they're all real. In the grieving process, after you see somebody die, you're left with so many questions, so many emotions. You really do go through different phases and you don't know it at the time. A year later, I can reflect and see that. First I was exhausted, then I was in shock, then I was running, then I was *really* feeling. If you can, get somebody who can be a support system for you—a therapist or a friend or a family member. Be really open with feelings. Find somebody you can really share with, not somebody who's going to deny your feelings and say, 'That's not real,' or 'That's not true.' It's really important to have that kind of support."

Claire also felt that it was important to say goodbye, even though she was not able to do it directly. "The way I said goodbye is that I wrote in my journal about all the things that Robert meant to me, and the things that we'd shared. Shortly before he died, I read that to him. Having the opportunity to say goodbye is important for the person who's left. I was thanking him for being a wonderful husband and for the times that we shared, but not actually saying goodbye. In my mind I knew, this was my symbolic way. And that turned into the eulogy that I asked my brother-in-law to read.

"I said goodbye, but Robert didn't. He didn't say goodbye the way I wanted him to say goodbye, but at least I did. At least I thanked him, and I told him I loved him, and that he was a wonderful husband."

Claire further advised, "Expect the unexpected. Things change, especially with an illness like cancer, a terminal illness. You just get through. Take one day at a time. It's such a cliché but it's true. Just get through it, and then, after it's over, take care of yourself. Pamper yourself. You can try and do that while you're going through it, but oftentimes it's too hard. Afterward, become a baby again. Get your parents to take care of you, or get somebody to pamper you. My sister literally fed me, and literally dragged me to the shower. I regressed so much. I think you have to do that to get back to being a whole person. You feel so vulnerable, and so *unwhole*. I remember feeling, 'What's wrong with me? I must be this horrible person since this person died on me, I couldn't save this person.' I'm a social worker, so I should have helped Robert have all these positive thoughts. He should have survived, because I could have helped him with his positive imagery. That kind of guilt."

The keenness of her situation was striking. This couple's considerable expertise had been no defense in the face of their ordeal. All they could do, in Claire's words, was to "get through it." Even so, guilt was part of the aftermath. There has been "no guilt about the care I gave him, because I did everything. I was there twenty-four hours a day for months." But she still feels guilt about what it means to survive. It took months before Claire began to feel better at night and the fears began to abate.

"There was a time, in the early fall, when I think Robert moved on. I met a gentleman who I have since fallen in love with. It's not without guilt, or without conflict. It probably would have been better if I'd met him after the first year, but he's also really helped me through this first year. I've been going through a lot of anniversary dates since we met."

Claire spoke about the anniversary of Robert's death. It was freezing that afternoon, and she was surprised to hear birdsong. She looked out her bedroom window to see two birds together in a tree. As she turned from the window, Claire glanced at her clock. It was 4:11 P.M., the exact time of Robert's death.

Notes

It's Time to Start Helping Him Die

Nurse Elena Martinez

When she began caring for Mr. Lovejoy, Elena Martinez was a private-duty nurse in her early forties, newly divorced and on the verge of career burnout. She had grown up in her father's country, Costa Rica; her mother is a native of Virginia. Having worked in obstetrics, intensive care and an inpatient hospice unit, Elena had hoped that private duty would mean less stress. She was dismayed to find that private patients were often demanding and difficult, but the elderly Mr. Lovejoy was a wonderful exception. Elena grew fond of him and experienced considerable conflict between her professional and personal impulses during his decline. At the end, she felt privileged to have been at his bedside when he died. We asked Elena to describe her relationship with Mr. Lovejoy. She shook her head, smiling, and began.

"This was someone I never would have come into contact with if I hadn't been in this profession. Mr. Lovejoy was a high-level executive, a multi-millionaire. I would have had no reason to ever know this guy if it hadn't been for the fact that he was sick and dying and needed somebody to take care of him."

Elena had begun caring for him eighteen months earlier. "He was

36

ninety, going on ninety-one. He had emphysema, real bad." He fought and endured his illness and the discomfort of its treatment until his activity became so limited that he could no longer do the things that mattered to him. Then he seemed to stop trying. Even so, "it was more than six months before he actually died.

"Initially, I was just taking care of him, like I would any patient. And then there came a time when I realized I was starting to feel things for him in my heart. But I was afraid to go with those feelings, wondering, 'Am I crossing over the boundary of professionalism?' So I had to take my time with that. I had to wait for affirmations, for signals from him."

Mr. Lovejoy's family sent Elena a photograph after he died. It was taken of the two of them together during one of his later hospitalizations. "He looks really happy and so do I. There was something about his eyes, something about his smile that felt like there was much more shining through this human body than initially met my eyes. That's the only way I can describe it."

Elena described how, after she began dating someone special, Mr. Lovejoy knew about it before she told him. "It got so he would say things that I wasn't sharing with him, and he knew what was happening with me." This was important to Elena, for it demonstrated that this was not a one-sided situation. She no longer worried that she might be projecting personal needs onto her patient. "Mr. Lovejoy made comments about how he could tell that I was in love because of the way I was around him, and how neat love really is because not only does it makes you feel good with that person, but it makes you feel all these great things for other people."

A few days before Mr. Lovejoy died, when he was still able to get up, Elena was sitting with him, talking, when she suddenly "felt something come into the room and just go"—she smacked one hand with the other— "right into his body. And as soon as I felt that, I knew that it was death. I remember just looking at him and seeing his face change and thinking, 'Oh, so you're here.' That day I knew that he was going to die soon."

After work that day, Elena had an appointment with her therapist.

During the session, she spoke about her impressions about Mr. Lovejoy. "So we worked on that, and I grieved the death of Mr. Lovejoy before he died. I cried and cried and cried. And when I went back to work the next day, I was energized and ready to do what I had to do as a helper.

"Within the next forty-eight hours, I went in and Mr. Lovejoy was really agitated. I remember talking to him for about an hour, trying to calm him down. He was very hard of hearing, so I was really yelling. Nothing was working, and he was really short of breath. Then I decided to massage him because he liked to have his hands and feet massaged. So I started on his hands, and then I moved down to his feet and he started to really relax.

"When I was rubbing his feet, I found myself wanting to say, 'It's all right, you can let go,' so I did, very softly and hesitantly. He shouldn't have been able to hear me, because I was far away from his ears and I was speaking very softly. But I felt that he *was* hearing me, and I kept telling him to relax, and that it was all right to let go, and that I was with him. Things like that—that he had struggled real hard and he had fought, and he was a good father and a good grandfather and all these things. I told him that it would be all right, that it was all right to go.

"This man went from being completely frantic and short of breath and unable to do anything, to being calm. His breathing was regular and he was quiet—and he seemed to be listening. And so I figured I'd just go with it. It wasn't like I was thinking what to say, I just started saying things. He didn't object, he just stayed really quiet. I sensed that he was going very deep.

"That was around eight o'clock in the morning. I thought for sure he would die that day, he had changed so much. It was the next day that he did die, but he stayed in that same state for twenty-four hours. I called from home that night to see how he was doing and was surprised that he was still alive. I went in the next morning and he was still lying there completely quiet, hadn't gotten agitated or anything in that twenty-four hours.

"I thought, 'Now what do I do?' I had a feeling that if I bathed him, it would be the end, that he wouldn't be able to live through that, but I knew that he liked his bath. So I went about my business bathing him and just took a long time, putting lotion all over him because I knew he liked that. He was really tenuous during that bath. His breathing was so shallow and his lungs were getting full, and I was afraid that when I turned him he would die, but he lived through the bath. But then I just sat down next to him and I was holding his hand. He took a deep breath and then he didn't breathe for about thirty seconds. I thought, 'Oh,' and I just sat there and looked at him and waited. He took another breath, and he did this for about five minutes—take a breath and not breathe again. During this time he started to change. He started getting waxy looking, and going from looking like a human being to . . . what you see when you see a dead body, which is just this . . . shell. That's when he started to change over into that state.

"Then he started to breathe normally again for a few minutes, but very, very shallowly. And then he just stopped. He definitely looked dead to me, but I waited and checked his pulse and listened for his heart and looked at his pupils and all that other stuff before I called the family. Because the last thing you want to do is tell family members that their loved one has passed away and then have them come in and find out he's still alive. Sometimes it's hard to tell. So I just waited."

Although Mr. Lovejoy's suffering was finally over, "it still just feels really crummy when a patient dies. In many ways, I had been wanting for him to die for a long time before he actually died, and there were times I felt guilty about that. Society is so structured toward helping somebody to live, that when you start to pick up that somebody's going to die and you say, 'Okay, it's time to start helping him die,' everybody around you is still into helping him live, and there are times you feel guilty. You think, 'Who am I, *what* am I, to think that I want this man to go ahead and die? What's wrong with me?' There are those thoughts, and I'd been going through that struggle with him for a long time. I wanted to get about the business of helping him, but I seemed to be the only one who was ready to do that."

Elena recalled similar circumstances with a cancer patient, Karen. Four years earlier, Karen had been at the hospice unit where Elena worked.

Although she was not expected to live for more than a week or two when admitted, Karen surprised everyone and stayed alert and alive for months. During that time, Elena came to admire and respect her, and Karen became an inspiring influence in Elena's life.

"That was the first time I was close to a patient to that extent. . . . Karen was just so special. She also had those eyes, like Mr. Lovejoy's, something about their eyes. I guess what it is is somebody's spirit just shining through, just *shining* through. You see so much beyond these two little circles, there's a whole world of something behind all that. She was only forty-two or forty-three years old when she died. She was such a beautiful person. As much as I hated to see her suffer and knew that she needed to die—and I often wondered how she could stand it—still, when I knew that she was going to be gone, I knew I was going to miss her *so much*.

"I remember going in to her one day shortly before she died. I couldn't stand it anymore because she was rotting. Her body was rotting, and she was in incredible pain all the time, and I couldn't stand to see her like that. I remember one day sitting at her bedside and I started to cry. I just told her, 'Karen, I can't stand to see you suffering. And I don't want you to misunderstand me,' because here I was telling her essentially, 'I want to see you die because I can't stand to see you live this way, I can't stand to see you suffering.' And she just listened and then said, 'But I'm not suffering.'

"I couldn't understand that. She said, 'I'm in pain, but I'm not suffering.' And I could not for the life of me figure out what she was talking about at that point, but it really hit me. Something about that exchange made me understand that what was going on with this woman was way beyond what you could see. Here was a woman who could not get out of bed and was in excruciating pain almost all of the time, yet she got such pleasure out of life. I remember watching Olympic ice skating with her, and I was uncomfortable. I thought, 'How can she stand to watch this, those beautiful girls and their legs while her leg is rotting off of her body and she's in pain?' But she loved it! She just took such pleasure in life and wasn't resentful or angry or anything. It amazed me."

The day Karen died, "I was in my backyard and I was really thinking about her. Remember, Karen was one of these patients expected to die months earlier. We couldn't understand how she could keep going, same as with Mr. Lovejoy. She had a strong will and a strong spirit too. So, finally, because she was on my mind, I called the hospice. They said, 'She's really bad.' And I *immediately* got in my car and went over. It didn't take ten minutes, but when I got there, she was gone.

"When I walked in the room, I just collapsed on her body and cried. I don't know why it was so emotional for me. Maybe if I'd had the opportunity to grieve for her before she died, like I did for Mr. Lovejoy, I wouldn't have felt so overwhelmed.

"When I first came into the room, she still looked like herself, she hadn't changed over too much. Then she became a shell within minutes. There's a process when the body stops ticking. There are still a lot of changes that take place. In fact, with some people you can almost see when their spirit leaves their body. Just like I saw when death came into Mr. Lovejoy, you can see when the spirit is gone, you can see that happening.

"In Karen's case, suddenly I looked at her and went, 'Oh, this isn't Karen anymore.' You're just looking at this mask, a costume. And you go, 'Wait a minute, Karen, where are you?' There's nothing there anymore that you recognize. That's what really makes you *know* that what makes us is not our bodies. You *think* it is—you see someone's body and you go, 'Oh, their cheeks are so pink and their eyes are shining and what a cute nose!' But that's not what does it—it's that spirit that they have in them that comes through."

Karen had become a spiritual beacon for Elena. "We had talked a lot about prayer, because she had a very strong belief in God and she prayed every day. I can't remember if she actually encouraged me to pray or not, but by her example she did." Elena began to pray regularly, and even after Karen's death, she felt Karen providing spiritual support through an arduous year of personal and marital crisis.

Elena had worked at both ends of the life course in her nursing career. Originally, she studied midwifery, but because of the licensure difficulties in her state, she became an obstetrical nurse. "When I was working with women in labor, I put myself in the here and now and didn't worry about anything else. There's a certain state that I know I'm in when I'm in it, and I don't quite know how to describe it except that it feels like there's . . . radar or something. Like I'm picking up on signals everywhere. When I'm in that state, it's different than when I'm just functioning in my head. And definitely with women in labor, I was able to tell a lot intuitively about what was going on with them, what would help them, what wouldn't help them."

Elena felt that often her most valuable service was "just helping a woman calm down and relax to the point where she could have the baby. When women were overcome with fear, or fear of the pain, I could just somehow calm them down, with my voice, or with my hands, and let them know that everything was fine. It was similar to what I said to Mr. Lovejoy, and sometimes I didn't quite know where all this was coming from. How do I know that this is fine, how do I know that this is going to help this woman? I think there's something about the quality of my voice when I'm talking like that, and maybe where it's coming from, that makes the difference. It's not really coming from any intellectual space."

It seemed with both birthing and dying, Elena's job was to help patients move beyond their agitation so that they can get on with what is happening to them. Elena described how "with women in labor, I've used massage a lot. That's *very* effective. Back massage was effective, leg massage was *really* effective. The thighs, especially. Something about getting a woman's legs to relax really helps her to deliver. With pain, you tighten up those muscles. Partly because I am a woman and I've had a baby, I was able to say, 'I know that you feel this way, but let me tell you that you don't have to be afraid of that. *This* is what's going to happen. You're not going to split open.' And it was good that I could do that with these women because they wouldn't tell you what they were thinking. I'd tell them, 'I know this is what it feels like, right?' And they'd say, '*Arrgh*.' And I'd say, 'Guess what? Your body's going to be fine and your baby's going to be fine.'"

Elena would like to see more candor on the subject of death as well, but "for some reason, society as a whole doesn't want to acknowledge death. I think the very first step is just acknowledging death and saying it's *painful* when somebody dies. It's painful for everybody. Even if in a way you're relieved, even if in a way you're glad for them and you don't want them to suffer, you're still losing somebody, and that's very real. It doesn't matter how old you are, or even what it is that died if it has meaning for you—whether it's a pet or a person. Whatever the emotional meaning, it needs to be acknowledged and respected, and that person has to be comforted."

For example, Elena recently had to tell her young daughter about the death of her great-grandmother. She thought it important to try to put into words what she believed her child was feeling, and then to hear out what the child was thinking. "The grieving process does not last forever, but if you don't let it happen, it's not going to go away. I think kids especially need for an adult to acknowledge the death and the pain of it and what a loss it really is, and let them feel it.

"For adults, or anyone around somebody who's dying, when you feel the death thing, which comes way before the death occurs, most of us want to negate it. Then we say, 'I'm being so pessimistic! Of course he's not going to die!' But it's not necessarily being pessimistic—it's *sensing* the upcoming death. Acknowledge that you're feeling these things. Know that you're getting these signals. Death is coming, and it's time to start getting ready, to say the things that you need to say to this person. And that's scary because you're acknowledging it, and how do you say to somebody, 'God, I know you're dying.' It sounds so crass.

"It's really important to acknowledge the process of death when we start to feel it—and I think we all feel it, it's just what we do with those signs and signals. We usually don't share them with each other and acknowledge them in a positive way. But it should be like when a woman starts to go into labor, and says 'Ooo, something's happening,' and everybody starts to anticipate the birth. It's the same kind of process. Understand that it's *okay* to acknowledge death and go about the business of helping somebody you care about to go through this passage that we all have to go through. Understand that that's our role, to do these things. And that's not bad. What's bad is fighting it, pretending like it's not there and never doing what we need to do for the person who's dying and for ourselves.

"It happens a lot that people are so busy fighting death that by the time the person dies, they haven't said what they needed to say. They haven't done for the person what he or she might have liked, which is why the hospice concept is so nice. You're acknowledging that a person is dying and you're trying to work through the grieving process before the person actually dies, and say your goodbyes and cry your tears, and let the person know how much you love them before they go. I think people need to know that, that they've been of some value and meaning in life. Instead of having a stiff upper lip and saying, 'Oh, you're going to be fine,' and, 'Oh yes, we're fine.' That's like saying, 'Even though you're dying and we're never going to see you again, we're fine.' Well, I wouldn't feel so good about that, if someone came to my bedside and told me that they were just fine and I was about to die. I'd like to feel that maybe they were going to *miss* me! Wouldn't you?" Elena laughed and shook her head, and grew serious again. "Many times people hang on to life, waiting for something to happen so that they can go. Until their business is finished, they can't depart. There are a lot of stories about people being on the verge of death forever, and then some family member comes in and says something, or another family member dies, and then they die. It's just as important for the living people as for the dying person; it's a two-way street. I know for my part that it was important for me to say what I had to say to Karen about her suffering, and to tell Mr. Lovejoy that I loved him. That was a very hard thing to do."

Elena had finally spoken up to Mr. Lovejoy "just a few days before he died. I'd been wanting to tell him how much I cared about him, and I'd held back because of the professional thing. But also because I was afraid he'd misunderstand me. He was a very wealthy man and I thought, 'If I tell him I love him, is he going to think I'm after his money? Like I'm trying to wheedle my way into his will?" But with encouragement from her therapist and her boyfriend, Elena was finally able to speak her mind. "I tried not to make it too mushy. I figured it would be easier for him—for both of us—if I tried to make it kind of light. I just said, 'Mr. Lovejoy, I think you know this already, but I just want to make sure you do know how much I love you.' He didn't make a big deal out of it, but he heard me. It felt good. I was glad that I did that."

"I don't really know what happens when we die, except that I definitely am beginning to believe more in reincarnation. I have a sense, during a death, that a spirit exists that actually leaves the body. . . . So I'm beginning to believe that in some way, spirits continue to live. Now, I don't know whether we're actually old spirits that come back in different bodies, or whether spirits come in and out of the bodies we have now, but I definitely believe that when you die, it's just this physical shell that's dying. It has nothing to do with who you are. You're definitely still alive and well at some level." Elena likened her impressions to the movie *Cocoon*, where otherworldly characters "zipped out of their skins." So it is with the embodied spirit, she said. There is more to us "than this costume we wear."

Elena remembered another hospice patient, "an Asian woman who had some form of cancer in her abdomen. It was really gross—it had ruptured through and so she had fecal matter pouring out of her abdomen. No matter what you did, you couldn't make it smell good in her room.

"Sometimes we would talk, and she was an interesting woman. Somehow we got to talking about this cancer, and her kids, and her grandchildren. She told me that she had been very miserable for many years. She had tried to tell her husband and her children, and it was as though nobody could hear her. Her family was very segmented, divided. She said she'd been the happiest since she got this cancer, because the family was united. Her perspective on this whole thing was that this was a blessing. She had had so much pain for so many years and felt so distanced from her family. And if what had to happen was for her to get cancer and die for her to have the closeness and the love and the quality of family that she wanted, this was what she had to have. It was okay with her.

"That really struck me. It was similar to Karen telling me that she was having pain but she wasn't suffering. Somehow that's been a real lesson for me. I'm not sure I completely understand it yet, but more and more I understand that there is a difference between experiencing pain and suffering. Somehow we choose to suffer. We don't always have a choice about whether we have pain or not, but it's definitely our choice whether we suffer or not. There's a difference between living with pain and living in that suffering state."

Elena talked for a long time about hospice care and how it differs from hospital care. Although hospices are not exclusively for people with cancer, most patients are cancer cases. Cancer means "long-term, drawn-out death, and we don't have the cures for cancer that we have for other diseases. There's only so much we can do yet with cancer." She continued: "A hospital setting is more for taking care of somebody in a crisis, getting them through it and then back on their feet again. Hospice patients are sick enough that they need physical care and medication, but there's nothing you can do for them that's going to make them well."

But what about a patient who is dying less predictably? A hospice-managed death is quite different from one like Mr. Lovejoy's, where there are sporadic declines and hospitalizations and what's happening is not well defined. Family members often do not get the support that a hospice can provide. However, families still have to make decisions.

The conversation turned to the case of the seventy-nine-year-old father of a friend of Elena's, and his last days in the hospital. Paralyzed from a stroke and suffering from organic brain syndrome, he had pneumonia and septicemia (blood poisoning). He could no longer talk or swallow, and it was clear to all four of his daughters that he was dying. Even so, they had to coax the hospital to discuss the measures they did not want to have taken. In a hospice-managed case, the approach would have been, "Let's help this family prepare for this death." But during this patient's last hours, a staff doctor stopped in and ordered a blood transfusion. One of the daughters chased him down the hall and asked him to cancel the order. He obliged, but if she had not caught him, both patient and family would have gone through more hours, and perhaps days, of suffering.

Later, the family would try to reconstruct how this happened. When they had made it clear to the staff that they knew their father was dying and wanted to limit how much would be done to keep him alive, they had been given a form headed, "Palliative Support Care Guidelines." Twelve measures were listed with spaces to check "yes" or "no." They had quickly checked "yes" to measure one: "Comfort measures only (analgesics, anti-emetics, sedatives)." Other entries, such as intensive care and tube feeding, were easy no's. But when they came to arrhythmia control, IV support, antibiotics and transfusion, a nurse cautioned them that each of these could also provide considerable comfort. No one wanted to withhold something that would ease their father's way, so they had checked "yes" to each. They surmised that the staff doctor that day was simply going by the guidelines that were in the chart when he wrote his order. Yet it was obvious that the man was dying when that transfusion was ordered. He passed away that night.

"Dying is *the* sin in the hospital. It's the bad word," Elena said. "So it's really important to find out what someone's wishes are before they get into that kind of situation." Helping people make choices should be part of the process, she said, as should helping them to stick up for those choices if necessary. "Someone has to be an advocate" for the patient.

"It's a really touchy subject. There were times when I've wanted to say something to the family. But you have to be really careful. Nobody wants to be the bad guy. It took me weeks before I could say to Mr. Lovejoy's wife, 'I hate making him do these things. He tells me he doesn't want to do them and the doctor says he needs to. I just want to be nice to him. I don't want to give him a hard time.' Trying to say to his wife, basically, 'He's not going to get better by doing all these things. It's going to prolong his time here with us, but I know he's not ever going to be well.' But the doctors are saying, 'Let's do this and let's do that.' You're putting yourself in a funny position. Maybe that's what families need more of, another professional coming out and saying, 'Listen, I know the doctors are telling you that if he has these breathing treatments five times a day, he's going to get a lot better and stronger. But my opinion is, that's not going to happen and all we're doing here is prolonging his time. He's not going to improve.' I think of it as being a patient advocate."

She added that many times family members cannot absorb that kind of information, because they are not ready to hear it. The problem is circular, however, because family members are dependent on the interpretations provided by medical personnel. Often, the medical personnel do not mention the nasty part of the results of what they're doing. Their position is that this is going to keep him alive. They also often fail to mention the potentially even greater pain that will be incurred if this person lives to suffer another day or week. Those considerations are typically not addressed.

Elena felt that the real problem was denial and avoidance of the subject of dying. "Until more of this stuff is talked about out in the open, things aren't going to change. People have to start talking about it and saying, 'There's more to this than what the doctors are telling us.'" It can be very strange for family members to arrive at a point where their instincts change from, "What more can we do for our loved one?" to "What *less* can we do?" Even a professional like Elena can come to feel, "I wish this person's suffering would be over."

Citing a recent news story, Elena posed the question, "Why do you think some of these nurses give lethal doses to patients in hospitals? I understand it completely. I don't think it's right, but when I worked in intensive care, I got to the point where I couldn't stand it anymore. I could not stand causing pain and suffering to people just to keep them alive on these respirators month after month. They're human beings! If you for one second put yourself in their place, you know damn well you don't want to be there. And you have people who are saying, 'Please don't,' or, 'Disconnect me.' Or they're signaling to you, 'Please take me off this ventilator.' They're asking you to. And you have to pretend they're not asking you, or just tell them 'I can't do that,' and go about suctioning them and turning them and doing all these things that the doctor's telling you to do to keep them alive. That kind of stuff is just awful, and it goes on all the time for the sake of keeping people alive. For what? I think that's just torture."

And yet, what about those cases where, after months of minimal hope, a patient comes back? Isn't that always the gamble? Elena allowed that she had never had to deal with this on a personal level, "Thank God, not with my parents or my children. But at this point in my life I believe there are more important things than keeping somebody alive.

Now, if my child were lying in a bed on a ventilator, would I be able to say, 'It's time to get that ventilator off and let her go,' understanding that her life is worse for her than death could ever be? I don't know. But certainly from my experiences so far, from people dying or being very very sick, I feel that way. We don't know what death really is, but I'm beginning to feel more and more that it's a release. You get out of that body that's sick and horrible and hurting, and then the body is laid to rest and the spirit is freed. What's so awful about that? I think the worst part is for the people who stay behind and have to say goodbye and don't want to let go."

Notes

Shock Is What You Feel More Than Anything

Nell Mihalich

Nell sat in a rocker at the Mihalich family beach house where her husband, Frank, had spent his summers as a child. It was the weekend of his birthday, and she had come to join Frank's parents and siblings to commit his ashes at the seashore. When he had died the previous November, Frank and Nell were three months shy of their twenty-fifth wedding anniversary. Their nest had emptied: Their twenty-three-year-old daughter lived out of town, and their son, nineteen, was away at college.

Nell spoke in a low, steady voice. Having worked as a dancer and a flight attendant before marriage, she projected a composure that has helped her to succeed as a businesswoman in marketing. As she began to describe how it was when Frank died, this self-possession both served and contrasted with the content of her experience.

Six months earlier, Nell had come home from work one afternoon to find her telephone answering machine indicating more calls than usual. This small signal was quickly succeeded by more prominent omens that something was terribly wrong. In fact, her fifty-two-year-old husband had already died of a heart attack while playing basketball after work. But it would be a long time before anyone would tell her so.

51

"The shock is what you feel more than anything," she began. "Particularly in my case, without having any idea. I came home from work, pressed the button on the answering machine and was told to call all these people. The next thing I know, the police are in my driveway and I thought, 'This is not good.'"

As Nell recounted the events of that day, she characterized them as "a comedy of errors." The messages on the machine instructed her to call her husband's employer, a Fortune 500 company, and a hospital. She called the hospital immediately, but "they hung up on me. I called back again and they said, 'The doctor wants to talk to you,' and put me on hold. As that happened, the police drove up, so I hung up on them."

The police told Nell to go to the hospital immediately, "and everybody else kept saying that, the hospital and the company." After speaking to the police, she called the hospital back, but "they still wouldn't tell me anything." Nell then called her sister's home and spoke with her brother-in-law, Mark. "He normally wasn't even home at that hour; it was a fluke. Mark picked me up and phoned my parents. He kept telling me all the way over to the hospital, 'Oh, it's nothing. You know Frank, there's nothing going on.' But I knew, I knew that Frank was either dying or dead, because they don't send police to your house when there's nothing going on.

"But I kept thinking, 'Don't be negative, think positive, maybe it's just not going to happen.' Once we got to the hospital, this guard in the emergency room grabbed me and said, 'This is the wife!' He kept pointing at me and shouting this through the crowded emergency room. I'll never forget, I felt like crawling under the floor."

Nell was then introduced to "two of the guys who had been playing ball with Frank when he collapsed, and they had a very difficult time talking to me. They really couldn't say anything, they looked away. You know, you think, if *they* can't, if they couldn't even look me in the eye . . . " The staff then "stuck me in a room and my parents arrived and we sat in this little cubby of a room knowing that something . . . and the nurse came in and said, 'The doctor's doing all he can.' Finally after about twenty minutes, the doctor comes in and says—I think this is a *horrible* thing to say when somebody dies—he said, 'Mr. Mihalich has expired.' It sounded like a credit card, you know? And of course we all let out with a yell and a scream and everything and then started getting into what happened."

What happened next to Nell was "an even worse shock." When the family was finally allowed to see Frank, they walked back through the emergency room to find that he had been "mutilated. It was absolutely horrifying. I didn't realize what they had done until they were gutsy enough to send a hospital bill to my house." Nell learned later that Frank had died literally in midstride on the basketball court, running to retrieve a ball before it went out of bounds. "When he hit the floor, he was dead." According to his friends, it took about ten minutes for the emergency medical service to arrive, but "they couldn't bring him back." By the time he was brought to the hospital, Frank had been dead for half an hour. Nell was incredulous at what was done next: "They did a tracheotomy on him. The doctor told me that when Frank came in, there was no heart beat, no breathing rate, no pulse. So what do they do? They do a tracheotomy on him. Well, if somebody's dead and then you slit their throat like that . . . the blood pocketed and it just all blew up his face and neck, and the whole thing was purple black—the whole side of his face, all the way down. They didn't cover it up. We saw this and we all just screamed. And of course the color is absolutely horrifying; it's very gray, and then you see this purple black, and it doesn't look *anything* like anybody you remember."

Nell related how she touched Frank's hand then, and struggled to explain a subtle impression in the midst of her horror. His hand felt to her as if "there weren't any bones, yet it wasn't completely flaccid. There just wasn't a feeling of rigidity, and that's the clue that this isn't the person; they've *gone*, they've left, there was a shell left." But such reflective perceptions seemed to be crowded out by the impact of seeing her husband so badly disfigured. Indignant, Nell returned to the subject. "It was absolutely criminal. That was so shocking; it took me a long time to get rid of that picture, to get it out of my mind."

Nell believes those procedures were done "because the hospital wanted to make a few bucks. They did everything—the things that were on the bill, suction, all these things that they did on somebody who was dead were unforgivable." Although it doesn't seem possible to add insult to injury in such traumatic circumstances, Nell felt the hospital did. "Everything they did was an absolute horror," Nell said, including approaching her about organ donation as she and her family were turning back to the small waiting room. "That's when I finally said, 'I'm getting out of here. Get me out of here.' We all left, and went to my brother's."

That night was a long one for Nell, "going through things I had never been through before that night. Spending about four hours shaking, and sleeping about two, just shaking, just the horrible shock of the whole thing." She thought back to that summer, when there had been another medical emergency. Frank had suffered mysterious swelling around his eyes and forehead. Later the swelling would prove to be the result of an allergic reaction to a spider bite, but Nell had taken him to the hospital for a CAT scan, "because they thought he had a brain tumor. And at that time I consciously—maybe it's because I'm a planner, not that I wanted anything to happen to him—I started going through what I would do. Because he really looked awful. I thought back to that, and I knew what I had to do. In my case, because we were estranged from Frank's parents, uppermost in my mind was to let them know that everybody would be included. I knew that Frank would not want to have a funeral. However, I felt that because of his family, it was important."

Frank was the eldest of six children of a prosperous doctor and a former nurse. When he was thirty-six, during a visit from his parents, Frank suffered a heart attack. Shaken and concerned, his parents helped out as Frank recovered and gradually returned to a normal life. But eight years later, during a visit to the family beach house, Frank quarreled with his mother over the discipline of Frank's son. The argument escalated and Frank left in a rage, vowing never to see his mother again. He never did, and he kept his distance from the rest of his family as well. In the ensuing years, he made it clear to Nell that if anything were to happen to him, he did not want his family to be informed.

Under these circumstances, Nell's decision to have a funeral and to include his estranged family seemed an extraordinary undertaking. She was able to carry it out by drawing on a goal-setting course she had taken through her work. She used the visualization techniques she had learned there to help herself cope. Although planning the funeral would still be very taxing for Nell, she had prepared. The night that she was unable to sleep, she "started visualizing how all this was going to happen." Later, she was able to go to the funeral home and make all the necessary decisions without serious difficulty.

But throughout the ordeal, there was still a sense of shock. In fact, Nell said, "I think the shock never leaves. There are many, many times that I think back to that funeral. I think that that whole process is really for the survivors. Because you start to think this person isn't dead and then you picture them in the coffin, and you *know*. It helps you enormously."

She also recalled the ways in which the funeral was not helpful. "Other people come to the funeral. I just felt suffocated those three days. There are so many people coming down on top of you, you're feeling overwhelming suffocation. I thought, 'I've just got to get myself away from all this.'" In the days following the funeral, Nell got away by going back to her parents' home for a few days. In a sense, she also went back in time. Comforted by the familiar setting, she discovered, "I was going back to when I grew up and trying to realize that I had to establish my own identity again, when I *did* have an identity without being married. Because that's something you have to do. Your identity changes very quickly."

The shock would go on and on. Nell describes it as pervasive and inescapable, but adds, "I was able to realize I had to keep myself mentally and physically active. I walked a lot, around the block, especially when I felt my feelings were going to overwhelm me. I'd get up and walk around. I walked and walked and walked. And that was helpful."

As she offered more details of her experience, Nell remarked on the importance of her role as wife. It began when she walked into the hospital and "the guard made such a big deal out of my arrival," and then being ushered "into that private waiting room. It didn't take a whole lot to figure out that something was very wrong, and that it wasn't necessarily *me* who had to be there, but *a wife* who could sign off on all these things. I began to feel it wasn't myself as an individual" who mattered, but "because I was 'the wife,' the responsible party. I had to make all the arrangements." As angry as Nell felt about the mistreatment Frank's body received in the hospital—"You know something, I never signed off on those procedures! Outrageous!"—she also felt the limitations of her power: "Was I going to be strong enough to fight?" She realized there would be great difficulties in mounting a formal complaint. It would entail going up against large institutions: the hospital board, her husband's corporation, insurance companies. It was more than she felt she could handle.

Instead of fighting, Nell "decided to do something positive and joined the hospice group, because they don't allow that to happen." Although a hospice typically serves those suffering terminal illnesses and their families, Nell felt the hospice approach suited her situation too. She was drawn to "the philosophy of the patient's right to choose, of giving somebody a choice, and knowing that somebody you love in the last few moments of their life would be allowed to express *how* they want to do this. If *anybody* had given Frank the choice, had he been able to say . . . but there was no chance for him, or anybody who *knew* how he felt, to say anything. They just mutilated him."

Soon after the funeral, an old friend who had lost a child told Nell about hospice. "She kept saying, 'In hospice, our philosophy is much better. We do not allow an ambulance to come near one of our patients. When a certified death has occurred, we wait half an hour. Then we call them. They already know ahead that it's over, and they take them out and that's it. They don't mutilate them.'"

It seemed that Nell had discovered a way she could defend Frank, even if it was after the fact. "Hospice gave me that feeling, like I had done something positive so that maybe that wouldn't happen to somebody else. . . . It offends me deeply that society is so uncaring about somebody dying, about death in general. I like the idea of hospice. These people are so wonderful."

Not long after Frank died, Nell had an experience that surprised her. Her sister, Celia, had been asked by a neighbor, "Has Nell had a vision of

Frank yet, at night?" The neighbor's parents had recently died within weeks of each other, and she felt each parent had visited her. Celia had answered, "Not *my* sister. She wouldn't do that." Nevertheless, "a couple days later, I was sleeping one night and I saw Frank very plainly. He said to me, 'Why are you running around so much? Why are you being so active and so involved?' I said, 'Because you're dead and I've lost my best friend.' And that was it. Whoa! It *does* happen. And it wasn't like a dream, it was just . . . you see this person standing in front of you, and they talk normally. It's more like a vision. I didn't think it would happen to me, but Celia's neighbor was exactly right. Having had that assurance made me feel like it was okay. It wasn't like I was losing it or something."

Nell decided that this was "one of these things that happens in the normal course of a death, especially losing a spouse. . . . And I *know* he'd say that to me, 'Why are you running around doing all these things?' He never liked that, he always wanted me home with him." It was as if Frank were asking, "Why aren't you staying with me?" Nell's reaction was to ask herself, "Why am I alive?"

This is a common reaction among the newly widowed, Nell learned. "You even think, 'God, why should I keep living?'" But after the dream, "that's when I started realizing that I had to start to get on with my life, that I was alone, and what did *I* want?" Nell repeated her internal reflections: "Well, I am alive, and I've got to do *something* with my life. I'm not the one who died, I've got to go on. What do I want my life to be, how do I want it to be? What are my priorities, and so on and so forth. You have to find some way to venture forward with your life."

Nell rocked in her chair and added that her brief conversation with Frank "was very calming. Reassuring. Like I said, it wasn't a dream. It felt like a visitation or a vision. I found it to be very comforting and I think it was important. It leads you on or gives you the feeling like this is what's going to get you through. I didn't feel panicked or upset. I just felt pleased, somehow."

Nell reflected on whether Frank had died the way he lived. "Frank was very lucky he died that way. He was playing his sports and he just fell right over. He didn't have to go through the agony of really hurting. God was really kind to him." She added, "There was a lot of violence in him, and he didn't die violently. A lot of pent up emotional anger. If he died the way he lived, he would have had a long, agonizing, frustrating, something-that-made-him-angry illness."

Nell explained that years earlier, in the months after Frank's first heart attack, he had been a classic "cardiac invalid," afraid of any activity. But after returning to work, and especially after he began coaching Little League, "he got back into society. He loved sports so much. Sports brought him back into it." But "Frank was a very stressed person, and the high stress level he put himself through" continued after his first heart attack. Nell added, "His *life* reflected him more than his death did, his lifestyle and the disease he had, but . . . he would have chosen that death. Anybody would." We suggested that Frank *had* died the way he lived— playing sports, competing, being aggressive. Nell laughed and nodded at this. "Yes! Aggressive and assertive, right!"

It has helped Nell to establish a relationship with Frank's parents again. Even though she was uncertain how they would put eight years of alienation behind them, Nell needed to try. "As a parent, I know that I would feel similar pain to that of a spouse if my child died. And from the time I found out that Frank was dead, I thought, 'How awful for his parents.' That's when I felt I wasn't going to say, 'Sayonara folks, your son is out of my life.' Because you do feel that empathy for somebody else who's sharing the same grief that you have. It helps me that I know they feel like I feel."

Nell added that the more she talks about Frank's death, "the pain's there but it's not this agonizing or ripping-at-you pain that, in the beginning, is just overwhelming." She spoke of the difficulty of wanting to remember but having to relive that shock. "As time passes you're able to see what's happened right in front of you," she explained, and that seems to make it, "easier to talk about."

Reflecting on what has helped her come to terms with this death, Nell again credited her ability to plan. "I tried to visualize before certain things happened how I hoped they would happen, instead of just letting them happen." For example, the day after Frank died, Nell spoke with the family attorney, who mentioned that the holidays and the winter were hard times for the newly widowed. "So right away my little planning mind goes, 'Okay, holidays and winter. So, you have to do something about this.' Right away it was Thanksgiving. What got me through Thanksgiving was being disciplined." She went to her family's large dinner, as she always did. "A couple of times I would need to talk, to get up and move around, to do something. After dinner, I could picture Frank playing pool like he always did, and I took my nieces and nephews down and I played pool, and all night long I just kept moving, moving, moving."

She added, "I appreciate my nieces and nephews so much more. I had a difficult time dealing with my own children at first. It was tough because they were too close to the pain I was feeling." Seeing her children's grief over the loss of their father increased her own suffering for a time, but Nell found it comforting to spend time with other family members: her sister and brother, their spouses, her parents. And "friends. I had more plans to be with my friends, and *different* friends. *That* helped, as did being physically active."

Nell got through Christmas "in much the same way" as she had Thanksgiving. After the holidays ended, she was looking toward the date of their twenty-fifth wedding anniversary in February. "I knew that would be very difficult, so I started planning." The weekend before the anniversary date, she took a short trip with a girlfriend. "That helped. The actual anniversary was on a weekday, so I got through work and I knew when I got home I was going to have some kind of a celebration. A bottle of wine. At first I was just going to tape my thoughts about his death, but then I took out the wedding album and some other pictures. I went through the pictures and tape-recorded how I felt looking at the pictures. I said on the tape recording, 'I bet you think this about this, Darling,' and I got through an hour and a half of it, and it was like a conversation with somebody else, but it was just me. I think saying it out loud helped."

Other things that helped Nell were "the fact that I work, and going through things. Going through clothes, books. A lot of times I'd try to distract myself—sometimes my niece would come over to help me, sometimes I'd turn on the radio." Nell advised in general, "Think of ways this is going to be difficult. Help yourself. Do something that will make it easier for you." Some things have worked out well, she said, but then added, "I think there are some things you can't solve." Despite her ability to carry on through planning and action, it was clear that Nell could only try to make the best of a bad situation.

"I don't know if you were going to even ask this question, but nobody tells you this when you're a widow. All of a sudden at age forty-seven, after having a sexual relationship with one man for twenty-five years, there isn't any intimacy. *That's* difficult." Nell's only frame of reference for widowhood had been "somebody like my grandmother, whose sexual relationship with my grandfather had ended, and the intimacy as well."

Nell elaborated on her social circumstances. "In this day and age, you don't just establish a sexual relationship with *anybody*." Nell has found that meeting people is difficult. She is not often invited out, and when she does join her and Frank's old circle of friends, things are very different. The men in the group have become reserved and the wives seem more formal too. "They watch you. It's a totally different feeling. That's why a lot of widows don't remain friends" with those they socialized with as a couple. "I can see the women fine, when I'm alone with the women, fine, but when you put the women and men together, and *you* don't have anybody so that it equals out, after a while, they don't invite you to couple things. You get used to being with people who are single or divorced." Nell thinks that part of the problem is that younger widows are often perceived as a threat by married women. So, even though Nell may be feeling, "I wouldn't want this guy on a bet," the wives "see it differently. It's a totally different perspective for them and for you."

Nell described the New Year's Eve tradition among their old circle of friends. "We all stood next to our husbands, and that way you always knew that the first person who kissed you at midnight would be your husband. This year, they all stood next to their husbands, and I stood by myself. I thought, 'Oh, this is neat, this is really neat, Nell. Why did you do this?' That's a very difficult time, because it's usually associated with affection, but I got through it. You just realize that you'll probably be spending a lot of time with women, not couples anymore.

"It's a totally different perspective. You just get used to it. The sexual relationship is something you're not going to have, and you're not going to be with other couples. They're not going to invite you, unless you're the extra person. It's difficult for the couples, but it's more difficult for the person who comes alone." Nell described a column she had read on retirement, written by a couple who described their social planning with widowed friends. They will call a widow as a couple and say, "We're going out to dinner on Tuesday night and we'd love you to come." The widows express real appreciation for being asked to join both of them, instead of only the woman. "But when they're older like that, in their seventies, they're confident and willing, and it won't compromise their relationship" to ask another woman to join them.

She recalled another holiday reminder of her status as a widow. "At Christmastime, I went to a party with the people who worked with Frank. In corporate structure the wife learns how to circulate alone, but I always knew I could go back to him and say, 'God I'm so bored. When are we leaving?' You know, my real feelings. Or when you've socialized with so many people and then you're back to your husband and you're together. This time there wasn't any of that. There wasn't anybody. That's a totally different feeling too."

Remarking on this changed status, Nell noted again the importance of the few days she spent at her parents' home after the funeral. "I had the feeling then that I had to have my own identity. And walking the same streets I walked as a child in grade school, I thought, 'In your own way, you were on your own then. You can find an identity again, but it will be so much better.'" Now she would have maturity on her side. "Those three days really gave me a chance to go back and ask, 'How did I walk these streets as a young kid? What was I doing before I attached myself to somebody else, got married?'" In her experience, Nell added ruefully, a woman is valued as somebody else's property. "The women do not count, I don't care what anybody says. In this country, being a woman in the work force, I know that. We make less, we're not allowed to express ourselves like the men are. But I had to go back and find the person that I was, to go back and say, 'Okay, now I know my identity and I can go forward.' That helped me an awful lot, the first three or four days." Especially, she added, because there was a sense of letdown after the funeral.

"I thought, 'I've got to do something.' I wrote my parents a note and told them, 'I'm eternally grateful to you for allowing me to camp on your doorstep.'"

It seemed that Nell's course on planning and goal-setting had helped her to stay clear in the midst of trauma. "After taking this course, I felt more confident about who I was, how I handled my life and how I can constructively channel the need to be the best I can be." Nell continued, "I always felt good about my relationship with Frank. He allowed me to be the person I wanted to be, and I allowed him the same freedom. Oftentimes, I feel that widows feel guilty" about what they may have failed to do for their husbands, "and that's what drives them into the depths of depression. But I didn't feel that way. I didn't ever want to live my life with regrets. Things happened to us and we could have had a lot of regrets." She described how their savings had been lost in a now famously corrupt investment scheme. "But Frank came out of it, we both came out of it, saying, 'Look, this isn't the end of our lives. We're still alive, we can still go on.' That made us stronger together . . . Maybe it's because we lived our lives like that."

When we die, said Nell, "I really think there is something kind of peaceful or enlightening that happens to you when the soul leaves the body. There's some tranquility involved in it. Even though I go to church, I don't know if I believe in a hereafter life with a heaven and you get to do what you want and all that. I think maybe you just finally find a peaceful place, where it isn't the same reality. Maybe you circle the earth as a star or something. But your soul leaves and it leaves behind a lot of troubles. Very peaceful and very content. And I don't think it's a person anymore. I think your energy just goes and dissipates and you're just very peaceful."

Notes

If I Get Him to the Hospital
and He's Still Alive, I Win

Paramedic Michael Andrews

Michael Andrews is a thirty-nine-year-old former steelworker who has worked for five years as an emergency medical technician and paramedic. His pre-school-age son and daughter played at his feet as he spoke; he also has a twelve-year-old daughter from a former marriage. Since recently going on worker's compensation for a back injury, a common hazard for paramedics, Mike has assumed the responsibilities of a full-time parent. When he's working, he goes out on an average of two calls a day.

When asked how many deaths he had attended, Mike replied, "Do you mean patients who stayed dead?" He thought for a moment. "I guess that in all I've been present for twenty deaths. Of those, I'd say twelve didn't stay dead and eight did." It is Mike's job to see that patients don't stay dead.

Those who died were of a broad age range, "from pre-born to after they should have been called, the DNRs." By pre-born, he meant miscarriages and stillbirths; DNR, an order for the terminally ill, means "do not resuscitate." "DNR is a legal thing," he explained. By law, medics must use CPR and other available lifesaving technology unless a DNR form is presented. The form must be physically with the patient or else the medic, the command physician at the hospital and everyone else up the chain is liable for a lawsuit.

Mike said that the most satisfying aspect of his work was "the paycheck." After a pause he added, "And my days off." He grew talkative when we asked what is stressful about his work.

"A lot of paramedics get 'the God complex.' You get so used to following different medical guidelines, and you get so used to taking successful calls to the hospital—that means dropping them off while they're still breathing. That's a successful call. If I get him to the hospital and he's still alive, I win."

This sounded like a game, and Mike refined the analogy: "It's a competition. And psychologically, people don't realize that they're competing against something they can't see. They're competing against an unknown situation. And when you do this enough times successfully, when one patient finally does die—and it does happen, and when you first see them, they might be conscious and they might be talking to you—and there's nothing you can do to stop the process of death, when they do go downhill, or when the call 'goes sour,' as some of us say, then the stress builds quite a bit. You might sit back for days, weeks, thinking, going over in your mind, over and over again, 'What did I do on the call? How could I have made it better?' What's even worse, 'Does anybody else see anything about me that maybe I did wrong? Did I do something wrong? Could I have done something different?' All those questions go through a medic's mind. Outwardly, he may not exhibit any stressful signs, but internally he's churning."

Then there is the stress of responding to an emergency call and "trying to find a location where you're supposed to go—it's like being a delivery driver. The only difference is, instead of delivering a pizza within thirty minutes, you have to pick up a patient and have him at the hospital before he dies. So there's a little bit of stress associated with driving past a house that has no numbers on it, and then, when you finally get there and somebody says, 'What took you so long?'—even though you made it there faster than Domino's Pizza could and without killing anybody, which is still another accomplishment—that's stressful.

"The other stressful part of the job is when you have someone who does pass away and you know there was nothing you could do about it, but you still blame yourself. So I may not seem as though I'm being very serious, I might joke around or say a few off-color things, but that's another form of stress relief. What you have to do is tell yourself, 'Don't take the job too seriously.' If you take it too seriously, you'll take it home with you and you end up having a nervous breakdown."

Mike elaborated on the stress of failure and blaming oneself. Although other medical personnel suffer doubts on the job, none may experience the kind of urgency that the paramedic does. "That's us. We're in an emergency state. Paramedics get paid a lower wage than nurses and other medical professionals do, because they usually burn out in less than ten years. And so they wait for the next young crop of psychologically healthy people to come along; they train them to be paramedics, while they take the burnouts and ship them out to pasture. There aren't that many old paramedics.

"After a while, you either learn how to deal with the stress, or you get out. And some people who do learn how to deal with it realize that they don't want to do this for the rest of their lives. They get into management or get their nursing degree." In some ways, Mike said, that is easier because in the hospital, you "just listen to what the doctor says. If it's a screw up, it's the doctor. That's not to say that nurses don't undergo their own kind of stress. They have to see people pass away who they get to know on a daily basis. They might see a patient for a week before they die, give them their milk, stuff like that. So there's stress all through the medical profession. But I don't get a chance to see their stress, and they don't get a chance to see mine—when I'm sweating my rear end off pumping on somebody's chest and I happen to be in an alleyway somewhere, or in a tight spot in a bathroom, and I have to carry the person down three flights of steps, still doing CPR, carrying all my equipment, and load them in the ambulance along with my partner, still maintaining CPR, and get them to the hospital and hopefully, I can get their heart started on the way there. All that has to be done within twenty-five minutes. And that's protocol. That's what you're supposed to do. And if you took longer than twenty-five minutes, they call you on the carpet and ask you why, what took you so long? I used to be a person who couldn't handle stress at all. I'd get upset when someone scratched my car—before I became a medic.

"A lot of times after I have a particularly bad call, or a run-in with someone who's really ignorant, I just sit back and think about the situation and how I can correct it the next time. Because there's nothing you can do about it now that it's past. Why worry about it? You spend more time worrying about a problem than you do actually facing the music for it. Like when you get a letter to appear before a court because you didn't pay a parking ticket. Most people will worry for weeks before they go to the hearing, when the actual process is only going to last maybe half an hour. So, I access those memories and then I think, 'I'll worry about that when the time comes.'

"I've had to develop a lot of different techniques for handling this stress, you know, take a deep breath, exhale. Hypnosis helps quite a bit. There are other times you get stressed out and you have to catch yourself. You say, 'I'm getting stressed again. I'll cool it.' And then you do. There are some people who can't handle stress, and they'll take it out on their co-workers. Especially in the medical field. And the way they do that is they become critical of each other. It's not just in the paramedic field, but all through the medical profession. You'll see people who are backbiters. If they're more pissed off at somebody else than they are about the thing that's causing them stress, they can forget about it. And that's how they deal with stress. They don't realize they're doing that."

Mike had first learned self-hypnosis to help himself quit smoking and found it worked well. That led him to study hypnosis in-depth and to join the local hypnotism society. He now carries a business card that reads, "Hypnosis for Self Help: Weight Control, Quit Smoking: Group Rates." Mike has found this background useful in his work. He described a long and dramatic call to a construction site where there had been a cave-in. He and his partner were the first medics on the scene. When they found the one victim who was still alive, Mike's first thought was, "This guy's gonna die." With both legs broken and crushed ribs, the patient required a life flight helicopter, but none was available. They were going to have to transport him in the ambulance.

Mike called the hospital for permission to administer morphine but was denied; narcotics would suppress the vital signs that were already dangerously weak. Indeed, the patient seemed likely to lose consciousness imminently, taking him even closer to death. Mike had to improvise, so he asked the victim, "Have you ever been in the Army?" The man said no. Mike then told him, "This is a technique we use on the battlefield. First, I want you to keep yelling the way you are now. Don't stop."

That accomplished two things: It kept the patient oxygenated and it gave him something to focus his consciousness on. As the screams became regular, "it was almost like chanting," and Mike was able to give the patient suggestions. "I told him he'd understand where his discomfort was and be able to tell me about it because this was all really happening on television." Provided with this tool to disassociate himself from his injuries, the victim "could hear and watch but be in control. He could separate from the situation, understand and be more rational." Mike added, "That's how we found out he had a broken arm. We knew his legs were broken, but it wasn't till I touched his arm that he told me it hurt. And he could do that because it was all happening on TV. Misdirecting attention a little bit leads to amnesia," Mike explained, so he also told the victim that afterward, he wouldn't remember the pain.

In the emergency room as doctors inserted a chest tube in the victim, Mike watched and felt sure the hypnotic effects were still working. The patient was not wincing in pain and he even said, "That feels good," as the pressure around his lungs was relieved. Noticing that something positive is happening is a very good sign in someone so severely injured. The patient survived, and when he made it out of the intensive care unit to the step-down unit, Mike called him and asked how he was doing. The man thanked Mike and said, "You know, I don't remember anything about the pain, just like you said." Mike asked if he remembered watching television. "Now that you mention it, I do recall watching TV."

There are limits to how much hypnosis can accomplish in a trauma situation. Mike explained that if he tried to suggest to someone who was badly injured that he was not in pain, it would not work. People will not believe a suggestion that is too incongruous. But telling victims about a battlefield technique does work, because people can accept that idea. Mike emphasized that it is important to meet victims at their level, as when he told the injured man to "keep doing what you're doing." He has helped others to disassociate by asking them if they've ever been drunk. "Everyone has, so it's a good analogy." Being drunk is being disassociated, according to Mike, so asking someone to recall that can help them. Occasionally, it works very well. "I had one guy who, after I gave him the suggestion that he was watching TV, told me he was watching *I Love Lucy.*"

Mike speculated that more than half of his patients are "life threatened," meaning that "without intervention, they'll die. Most others are B.S. calls, like a cut finger, a stubbed toe. There's a few psychological emergencies, where people just go off the deep end; they want somebody to talk to and they'll call you. Now, they're not life threatening, but they're serious."

"The only time I feel funny about treating somebody is when they don't appear to have any thought of me as a human being. In other words, if I get to a patient who happens to have the flu and he's coughing, and he starts treating me like I'm some kind of a servant who's there at his beck and call, and actually coughs in my direction and has no consideration for my health or the health of my family, then I don't want to treat that guy. But I treat him anyhow because that's my job. He doesn't care if I get sick. He sees me for twenty minutes, and then he's done with me. Those kind of people, they bother me. The other kind of people—people who you know are going to die but do want help—I have no problem with helping them. In fact I *want* to help them, I want to make it easier for them. Even if it's just an extra five or ten minutes that they have to get right with one of their relatives, if they have another five or ten minutes of consciousness so that they can talk to somebody before they die, that's good enough for me."

Mike does not concern himself with terminal patients who might be better off not being treated. "When I get called in, I'm there to be the cutting edge between life and death. I'm supposed to get there in time so that they can live." It's his job to save patients at all costs, and to give their family members "a chance to be with that relative a little longer. If they wanted them to die in the first place, they can pull the plug, not me.

"As one slimeball attorney once put it to me, 'You don't save lives, you prolong the inevitable.' And I thought, 'He's right, I do prolong the inevitable.' But," Mike added sardonically, "in his case, I might not."

Mike thinks this work has changed him. "I don't think anybody can do this kind of job without becoming warped. And by warped, I mean morbid. You see things that the rest of the population doesn't. For years, I worked in a steel mill. I never watched anybody die. You see relatives every once in a while who pass away, but I never got a chance to see trauma calls, like automobile accidents and building collapses. People who have AIDS, people who have gunshot wounds. Things that you see on TV, but in this job you see them up close, and then you get to see their families, their kids.

"When I was in a trauma center doing some clinical time, this guy had gotten caught between two railroad cars. They had crushed his hips, crushed his pelvis. It was a week later when I saw him. He was all bloated, what's called septicemia, blood poisoning. His body just went poison on him. He looked like he was going to die. To me he was just another patient, but as I turned around to leave the room, I saw a picture of him on the wall, with his daughter and his dog, and his daughter had written a nice note. And then the human reality came into play, because then I could identify with him and also with *my* daughter, and I felt for the daughter. When I looked back at him, what a change! For the rest of the evening, I was just devastated. Sometimes it catches you off guard.

"To other people you seem morbid, but to yourself you seem normal. Other people see you as being morbid, or callous or cold, because they can't comprehend walking up to an automobile accident and seeing somebody crushed, and their relative sitting beside them screaming and hollering, and you have to block out the person who the coroner's going to see, and deal with the person who's screaming."

Mike spoke about one experience that was particularly significant to him. He began by setting the scene: "It's a nice day, sun's shining, birds are singing, a great day for baling hay. I'm sitting at the ambulance base, and I hear someone outside honking their horn. I was going outside to wash the ambulance at the time, and these two ladies pull up and they have their father with them, a man in his eighties. He was grayish and having some labored breathing. I said, 'What can I do for you?' And his daughter said, 'He's having a heart attack and he needs to get to the hospital, but he doesn't want to go. So we stopped here first.'

"I said, 'Well, what's his name?'

"'James, James Taylor.'

"I said, 'How's it going, James? Can you sing me a tune?' I wanted to get some rapport going with the guy.

"'I wish I had his money,' he said. "I don't need to go to the hospital. I've got this heartburn, this chest pain. I'll be okay, I just need a little rest.'

"'James, you ain't goin' nowhere man, you're coming with us to the hospital.'

"'Nah, I can do it by myself. I can get up.'

"I said, 'No, don't get up.'

"And he said, 'Maybe I better go to the hospital.'"

Mike continued: "The guy's in his eighties, hates hospitals, he's an elderly that never decided to use his Medicare, probably never had health insurance when he was younger. He strikes me as the kind of man who'd have to have his legs chopped off before he'd go to the hospital. So we put him on a cot and rolled him over to the ambulance, which was only four or five feet away, but I wasn't going to get him to walk four or five feet, he's not going to move a muscle. I get him in the back of the ambulance, put the monitor on him, I see what's called a dysrhythmia, which means that he's having a big one. Normally, what a medic would do is stay right there on the spot and start the IV and do all the other stuff right there. But I told my driver to get in the truck and *roll*—do lights, do sirens, let's *go*. 'Cause I had this funny feeling that this guy was going to go sour on me, and I really didn't want him to do it in my truck.

"I start the IV, I've got him on oxygen, I call medical command because I'm ready to give him a nitro tab, and the doctor says give him one nitro and if he needs another, give him a second one. I said okay, so I gave him one nitro, and as we're turning the corner to go to the hospital, I need to give him another one because his chest pain hasn't subsided. I say, 'James, you're going to be okay, bud. Are you sure you weren't around any organophosphates, or fertilizer, or any kind of insecticide?' Because he was complaining about tingling in his lips. It's a side sign. He said, 'No,' and I says, 'I just want to be sure, I want to rule out everything.' As we are backing the ambulance up to the emergency room, I disconnect the monitor, and as soon as I turn it off, James's eyes rolled up and his eyelids started to flutter. I said, 'James, James, wake up buddy.' He didn't wake up. I said, 'Oh, shit.'

"Those are the two words you're going to hear forever. You hear them on ambulance calls, you hear the pilot say it on the recording just before his plane crashes. I started doing CPR right away. I couldn't countershock right there. I'd just shut my monitor off, so rather than start it up again, it was much easier to just pull him out, drag him into the emergency room and scream, 'Help!' And that's what we did. He was out like a light. No pulse, no respirations. Rolled him in there. I stuck the monitor leads on him, popped him one time with the electrodes, shot him up a couple of times with epinephrine, and the whole time we still worked the CPR on him.

"The way I usually have to work a call, it's just you and your partner. But now, I've got the emergency room staff helping. So we shocked him, we filled him up with epinephrine, then we shocked him one more time and all of a sudden he came to. We saw the heart monitor going and the heart rate started real good and real fast. Then we had to give him lidocaine so he didn't go right back into defib again. He went right into what's called a sinus rhythm, which means that the heart started functioning pretty close to normal. We had a tube down his throat and we had two IVs started, had him hooked up to all these wires and stuff. When he woke up, he nearly bolted off the table. There were two people on each side, and one person on each leg, and we were having trouble holding him down. I yelled, 'James, James, calm down! We need to keep the tube in place.' I was glad that he was alive, because that meant we won. But at the same time, I was totally drained of energy. It's like being a wrestler. Everybody who's ever done wrestling in high school knows that after you do that two- or three-minute match, your hands are shaking, you're exhausted, you're drained. That's exactly the way I felt, just like

I'd done a wrestling match.

"His daughters were down the hall. One daughter was riding in the front seat of the ambulance when he arrested. She asked, 'How is he?' She didn't want to ask, 'Is he dead?' I said, 'Okay,' and gave the thumbs up sign. You should have seen the relief that came over her face. She and her sister were crying. When you do something like that, for me that's an emotional reward. I get that feeling too. I cry and laugh along with the families when that happens. I felt good about that. Later on, after James was discharged from the hospital, I called him and said, 'James, I understand you have a farm. Would it be okay if I got some cornstalks for Halloween decorations?'

"He said, 'C'mon, you can have all you want, you can have all the corn you want. . . . I've got deer on the property if you hunt.' So I brought my son and my wife out there to get the cornstalks and James was standing in the front yard and he said, 'Here, I want you to have this.' He has stuck a rolled up twenty dollar bill in my pocket. I said, 'I don't want your money.' I gave it back to him, and then he started chasing me around the yard trying to stick the money back in my pocket. I said, 'James, I don't want your money. Cornstalks are fine. Deer huntin's fine.' He said, 'I want you to have it. At least take your wife out for dinner.' My wife was standing there saying, 'Take the money, take the money,' because James was getting sweaty and all gray again. So, I took my wife out to dinner and the bill came to twenty-five and something, so that was okay with me; it was like getting a discount."

Mike wondered if James remembered anything about the time that he was clinically dead, those now famous markers of the near-death experience, and so asked, "'James, by any chance did you see a light at the end of the tunnel or anything like that?' And he said, 'Nope, nope, didn't see any light at the end of the tunnel, but I do remember you wheeling me into the emergency room. I could see that. I was there on the cot as you were going in and then I was floating above looking down. It was like being both places at once. But I didn't see any light.' And I said, 'Did you hear any harp music or anything like that, see any relatives?' 'No, nothing like that.' He just remembered that he was with the whole process the whole time. He didn't really think that he lost consciousness.

Then he asked me if his heart had really stopped and I said, 'It really did.'"

Mike speculated, "A lot of times, people confabulate. They lose track at point A, and then when they wake up, they're already at point C. So to fill in the gap, their mind will make up B, to give them some continuum of what happened. It happens in automobile accidents all the time." However, although James seemed to have a double perspective of being both in and out of his body, he didn't confabulate according to Mike. James's story was in sync with what actually happened. Had James remembered anything else? "He remembered waking up and being held down, and that was about it."

Mike continued: "When you see someone pass away, it's almost as if a certain glow about them disappears. Like a person has a particular glow, you can tell when they're talking, awake, active. It's not light; it's like a light, but you can't see it. It's like the heat waves over a road. And when they pass away, they just go blank. When you're looking at the person, it almost seems as though the batteries died in a flashlight." There are signs to determine where a person is in the dying process. "Eye movement. That's the marker for me. Skin color is a marker. Muscle tension in the face. When people are losing consciousness and the heart has stopped, blood circulation has stopped, the eyes invariably go up into the head, the eyelids flutter, there's a pallor, a change of color in the face, the mouth opens, the head goes back. I've seen it enough to know."

"A lot of it is horrible." Mike paused, and then continued thoughtfully. "Aside from thinking, 'That might be me some day'—and it probably will be, because you're just prolonging the inevitable, as the slimeball attorney says—I think what happens is when the batteries go dead in your recorder, the information on the tape goes somewhere. That's not to say that I believe in reincarnation, but I think that someone, somewhere, may pick up on memory glimpses of what you had in your life. I don't know how, I don't know why it happens."

He described his hypnotism teacher, a man in his eighties. His wife of fifty years was dying of cancer when Mike brought them a videotape of a woman who was regressed under hypnosis to a lifetime in 1827. "She gave very vivid accounts of that lifetime," and some of the historical details were later checked and proved to be accurate. "After they saw the tape, it gave them some renewed energy and faith, but at the same time I'm sure it gave them a little bit of sorrow too. Because, would he, in his next life, ever find her again?" Since his wife's death, Mike's teacher "has been able to deal with it very well." Mike believed that seeing this video- tape "reaffirmed their faith and their hope, because they're religious people, that there is a life hereafter. It may not be what we have come to think of as a life hereafter, but there is something else other than a great abyss. That's what I think."

Notes

Not at All Prepared for How It Really Was

Lee Adler

Tall and attractive, Lee Adler, a graphics designer and publications consultant, had just marked the first anniversary of her mother's death when we spoke with her. Although married for twenty-five years to a photographer, Lee has remained childless by choice. As the first-born of five sisters with an alcoholic mother, she explained, she had already experienced too much of child care by the time she married.

Several years before her mother died, Lee sought therapy to help her deal with the frustration and grief caused by her mother's increasing binges, and worked hard to maintain her own equilibrium.

Her parents were married and Lee was born as her father was training to fly B-29s during World War II. When the war ended, he returned home and became a successful businessman—and an oppressive family man. "My father was a despot over a houseful of women, and he treated my mother as if she were as lowly a subject as any of her daughters,' Lee began. "As the oldest, and a semi-despot in my own right, I sometimes felt that even I outranked her."

~

"My mother's refuge, and her weapon against relentless and sometimes heartless tyranny, was alcohol. Her escalating dependence on booze was the only thing my father failed to control. For twenty-four years, the first half of their marriage, the conflict spiraled. Finally, the only movement possible was apart. But divorce was untenable for these two—they were welded together in strife. He retreated to Florida, the one place my mother refused to go. For the next ten years, he barely participated in family life or his job, taking full advantage of his executive status to go to Florida for a week or a month, whenever possible. At sixty, he retired and simply moved there, deigning to visit 'home' and spouse for a few days every two months."

Lee's sisters grew up and moved into their own lives, "as far away as possible" from their troubled parents. It was by chance that Lee and her husband found themselves returning to her home town. But that is how, at age thirty-two, Lee began her role as "lonesome participant and witness to my mother's gradual disintegration, fueled by alcohol and the awful grief of abandonment."

Lee's relationship with her mother over the next fourteen years was a mixture of caring and avoidance. "My mother did try her damnedest to be self-sufficient and didn't ask much . . . except emotionally. The biggest stresses on me were the phone calls. They were difficult, emotionally charged conversations. If she was drunk, they would be horrible rows." On special occasions, Lee would bring her mother "lots of cards and multiple presents, and take her out, or do some really special thing like planting hundreds of impatiens in front of her house for her birthday. Everyone else would send stuff from afar, but the many missing people were always a big void. Once I called my sister in Iowa to beg her to come for Mother's Day and she hung up on me."

Lee would visit, but "Mother was often semi-lucid, depressed, with no interest in anything. So we just kind of watched television together. If she was not depressed and had been drinking, she'd be ranting and raving and unreasonable. I'd end up leaving angry, but also afraid to leave for fear she would do something," Lee recalled. "She'd want us to come for dinner, and though I always feared this, I'd say yes. Sometimes she would make all my favorite things and it would be wonderful. Sometimes

I'd walk in at six and she'd just be sitting there staring at the table and nothing done, nothing available to cook.

"My most common activity was house caretaking, discovering things that were undone and doing them. She usually would not ask me to come specially, but when I did come and start looking around, I'd realize everything was falling apart." So Lee would find herself "throwing out the sour milk, discovering mildewed clothes in the washer, trying to save the dying houseplants, cleaning up the dog's old accidents." Lee had bought her mother a Scottie dog for companionship, but eventually the dog became another source of concern. "When things got much worse, I worried about the dog's welfare. She seemed to get fed regularly, but I was a nervous wreck because she was not taken out enough, and her health wasn't watched carefully. I knew the dog was probably experiencing emotional crises and things like Mother's blackouts. I was motivated to check on my mother because I needed to care for the dog."

It was not unusual for Lee's mother to pass out and fail to answer the phone, and one time she had fallen and had to be hospitalized. So whenever Lee couldn't reach her mother, she would make the fifteen-mile drive, torn between resentment and fear. "But as many times as I had imagined going to Mother's and finding her dead, I was not at all prepared for how it really was." Nothing, she said, had prepared her to encounter "the goneness."

It was January and the holiday visitors, including Lee's father, had come and gone from the family home where her mother still lived. Lee's mother reported having some kind of virus, but Lee was never sure what to make of her mother's symptoms, which were usually alcohol related. When she spoke to her on Saturday, however, Lee felt her mother really did have some kind of flu and made a mental note to call back that night. She never did.

The next day, Lee awoke very concerned about being remiss, made "about twenty phone calls during the day and still wasn't motivated to go there—I don't know why." She kept thinking of likely reasons why there was no answer. Her mother might be resting, or in the bathroom, or out with the dog. But "at nine minutes to three, I came down the stairs, put my coat on and said to my husband, 'She hasn't answered yet, I'm going down there.' He said, 'Do you want me to go with you?' But I told him I had to do it myself. When I said those words to him, I was sure of what I expected."

On the way, Lee became "distracted" and took a wrong turn, yet this was a trip Lee had made innumerable times. She kept thinking the trip was taking longer than it should, "but I felt almost lethargic, like 'It doesn't matter, it doesn't matter.' I was real aware of not feeling urgent," she recalled. "In retrospect, when I got there, things were strange. It was a cold, winter day and the front door was ajar. I thought for a moment, 'Oh, she's up!' or, 'She wants to make sure I can get in.' I could hear the TV, it was very loud." Lee started walking down the hall; it seemed to stretch out in front of her. She was calling, "Mother," in cadence with her steps, and "it took a really long time" to enter the TV room.

"The first thing I saw at the door was the TV screen, and I could tell nothing was on the channel. I was real afraid when I saw that. As I came around the corner, on the couch, my mother was lying there. The position she was lying in was exactly like a Chinese medicine figure." These are reclining nude figures made of ivory, used by modest Chinese women to point out to the doctor where they are ailing. "She didn't have a stitch on. That's what made me think of the Chinese doll. I said, 'Mother,' and I thought it was possible she could be sleeping." But within seconds, that possibility evaporated. "And then I thought to myself, 'No. She must be dead or she wouldn't be lying around naked like that.' And I didn't even touch her or go over to her." Still four paces away, she felt "absolute certainty and resolute calm."

Lee went to another room, picked up the phone and dialed 911. She explained that this was not an emergency, that her mother was already dead. But the response was urgent: "We'll be there right away." Then, "As soon as I hung up the phone I thought, 'Oh no, I made a mistake, she's not dead.' And I walked back down the hall and looked at her and shook her wrist, and when it wouldn't give . . . " Lee recoiled.

Before the paramedics arrived, she picked up an afghan from the floor and covered her mother's body "but not her face." Lee realized then that her mother had been covered by the afghan originally, but that the dog, who was jumping up and down frantically, had caused it to slide off. Lee went outside with the dog and waited. The paramedics arrived within minutes. "Two strapping young men went rushing back there, and I thought, 'Why did you bring oxygen?'" With their equipment, their arrival was noisy. Lee followed them but stayed in the hall. "The minute they got back there, I could hear them whispering instead of doing anything. They knew from experience. When she stepped into the room, looking beyond and between the two medics toward her mother, "they closed together like a wall, and I couldn't see her anymore." Lee looked around them and saw that they had covered her mother's face. "It annoyed me, and I was going to go over and pull it down, but then I thought, 'Oh, that's what they do.'"

Lee learned that her mother had been dead for twelve hours and noted that it had indeed been "already over" when she woke up that morning. After the paramedics arrived, so did a police officer, a neighbor and then the undertaker. The journal entry Lee wrote later that night describes the aftermath, revealing how painful the family's situation really was.

The cop is gone. The hearse is gone. . . . Phone calls: Florida, Massachusetts, California, Iowa, New York. Jeez, they all went as far as they could go without falling off the continent and still stay clear of each other. . . . And I don't feel like softening the shock for the father that taught me to be tough.

"I have bad news."

"What kind of bad news?" The telephone shout of the hard of hearing.

"Mom died."

"She did what?" he shouts.

"She died," I yell back.

"Whaddya mean died?"

"You know . . . dead."

"Oh God. I'll get the next plane."

"No, tomorrow is fine."

"Call the girls."

"I am."

It's dark outside by the time I turn my attention to the house. The front door still stands open, and I decide I'm more comfortable with it that way. I just need to straighten things up for everyone's arrival tomorrow. I finally go into the bedroom . . . the king-size bed, unrumpled. A neat triangle of sheet folded back against the expanse of blanket, like she had just flipped it back to get out of bed. It covers a pile of letters and cards from Christmas. She was rereading all the good wishes from decades of friends. Oh. Little plush-lined slippers. Brand-new, a Christmas present. Poised at the side of the bed, waiting for her little feet. Now that's eerie. I'll put those away before someone sees.

I pick them up and slide open the closet to the age-old slipper-putting place and there is something in their spot. Right there at the front of the closet, where for thirty years only slippers rested, two half-gallon bottles stand defiantly empty of bourbon. I grab them up and put the slippers in their place.

"Oh, shit. Mother, are you gloating at me or what?"

Then, "Sour mash bourbon." Sour mash? Why did you always say to waiters in restaurants, "I'll have a bourbon old fashioned, but don't use that sour mash, I hate that." Did you do this in one swoop, all of this?

Sour mash bourbon. Sour mash indeed.

Clearly, reconciling herself to her mother's life and death was not going to be easy for Lee. But there was an overriding "inner experience" that ushered her through her shock and grief, and Lee labored to explain it: "In the instant that I looked at my mother, I felt like I diffused. I was very fuzzy in the moments immediately after. I remember what I was doing, but it's almost like . . . I felt like my head was spread out. It was expansive and enormously calming. It lasted weeks. But in that moment when I first really looked at her face, there was a very, very strong, definite, calming knowledge. Not intellectual knowledge—it was the knowledge that this was where I was supposed to be, and part of that knowledge was a statement that formed in my brain to my mother: 'Well, Mom, we got where we were going together, didn't we? This is where I stay. You're on your own. Bon voyage.' In reflection afterward, I thought that part of me recognized that I was to be there for that. And that's how I took it."

Lee explained that she has since read about shock and adrenaline and the physiological response she was experiencing in those moments. "That's the rational explanation for the feelings that I had." But other "nonrational" experiences were also part of this event, especially those having to do with the house. Lee described the origins and impact of these experiences, revealing the powerful effect of a lifetime of uncertainty about her mother's behavior. Her family had moved into the home where her mother died when her third sister was newborn. The TV room, where Lee found her mother's body, was then the nursery. On Easter of that year, the second sister, then five, reported seeing the Easter bunny in the nursery the night before, standing over the baby's crib and looking at her. Lee's mother, a Catholic, told her daughters that the figure was probably the baby's guardian angel, checking on her. But Lee and her first sister were older and mischievous, and for years afterward tormented the younger children and each other with the probability that the spirit of the house's former owner was haunting them. He had in fact died in that same nursery and TV room.

This detail of Lee's past came back to haunt her in the aftermath of her mother's death. Having taken total responsibility for packing up and selling the family home, Lee found it hard to be alone there, especially in that room. "My mother raised us on a steady diet of fairy tales and ghost stories, and I felt she was fully capable of being able to reach me." This made Lee feel vulnerable and resentful. "You know this will upset me. Leave me alone," she'd mentally tell her mother. "Get lost."

This fear, and the emotional turmoil caused by her mother's alcoholism, made Lee's adjustment to her mother's death even more difficult. In addition, she could not help but acknowledge the feeling that her mother had known this would happen some day, and there had been hints that it would happen soon. "I believe my mother wanted out for a long, long time, and knew the only way she was capable of doing it was to drink enough to finally do it. Events from up to six months before, all the way to finding her front door ajar, make me know that my mother planned to go." During her mother's last week, "she wouldn't let me come down all week long, and when I talked to her the day before, I said, 'You can't go on like this. If you're not feeling better tomorrow, I'm coming down and taking you to the emergency room.' And she said, 'Well, you come tomorrow. By tomorrow everything's going to be just fine.' And even as she said that, on another level, I knew what she meant; I gave her plenty of time."

There were other portents. After a holiday gathering less than two weeks before the death, Lee's husband had taken leave of his mother-in-law with a heartfelt "I love you." It would be the last time they saw each other. "It was almost like an announcement in front of everybody. I'd never seen him do or say anything like that. And Mother said, 'I love you, too.' I thought it was so odd at the time. After she died, I felt that what had gone on there was a definite 'goodbying.'"

Sorting out what was knowable and unknowable has been an ongoing concern for Lee. She has discovered that "mystical can be in the guise of emotional and vice versa—especially vice versa." This prompted her to relate another meaningful coincidence:

During the funeral week, Lee had found in her mother's room "a funny little music box that had yellow birds on it and played 'Yellow Bird,' a Jamaican song." One sister told her, "Didn't you know 'Yellow Bird' was Mom's theme song?" Lee had not.

"A while later, I had to pack that thing up and do something with it. I wound it up and just looked at it for a minute before I packed it away. And when the music started to play, I was infused with, not that feeling of big and wise but, oh, great love for my mother, which is not my normal condition of thought for my mother. And I actually fell down onto the floor and cried for a long time. It was something about that song, that whole thing, that had not occurred when I had packed her scarves and gloves, or her jewelry, or her books, or even a letter she had been in the process of writing that night to a friend. None of that touched me, but something in that music really did, and I thought that that was when I let her in. And then I chased her out again." Lee packed the music box so carefully that there was no chance she could accidentally hear it again. She had struggled hard to defend herself from the pain her mother caused while she was alive. It was hardly surprising that Lee was unable to relax her emotional vigilance for months after her mother died.

In the fall, Lee went to Florida to spend Thanksgiving with her father. "So I'm sitting, talking to my father, and I look and there's this yellow bird sitting on his shoulder. I said, 'What is *that?*' It's a real live canary. It lives in my father's apartment, no cage. He dumps seed out in an ashtray on the kitchen counter and it comes. I asked, 'Where did this come from, Dad?' He said, 'Jeez, I dunno where the hell it came from. It's been here since summertime. We were in here one day, and someone said, "Look at that, this bird's trying to get into your apartment," so we opened the glass door and it walked in and it's been here ever since. I'd hate to live without it now. I love this thing!'"

To Lee, this was simply incredible. Her father hated pets and had refused to let his children have one. She asked rhetorically, "How many Floridians do you suppose have a canary walk up and just move in? I mean, my father especially! It sits on his shoulder. In the morning my father gets in the shower and sings, and this bird wakes up and comes in on the shower door and sings with him. It tickles my father because people come and go and this bird just swoops back and forth. People don't even know it's there until it does something. There are four ceiling fans along the length of the room, and it flies up and down, through the paddles, while they're on."

The correspondence between her mother's favorite song and the yellow bird who had moved in with her father, the widower World War II flyer, was significant to Lee. It appeared to relieve her of the awful burden of having to care for her mother all by herself, even after death. Now Mother was reunited with Father, and free as a bird. This "happy ending" seemed to mark the beginning of Lee's internal recovery, not only from the shock and grief caused by her mother's death but from years of witnessing her unhappiness and suffering. Asked to describe her current beliefs about death, Lee answered thoughtfully, "It's like a shadow play." She explained how the projections of invisible puppets on a screen are for her a metaphor of the invisible sources of physical life. "And," she continued, "my death can be part of the drama. I try to see it like fiction or a dream. The characters don't exist after death, but the consciousness that invented them does."

Notes

Instead of Being Able to Spend Time with My Mother, I Was Busy Managing Her Case

Susan Briggs Russell and Family

Forty-four-year-old Susan Briggs Russell leads a very active life. Her rural New England home seems like a Noah's Ark of house pets—cats, dogs, turtles, fish, birds, hamsters—which she maintains with her husband, Harris, and their son, Brad. In this household Susan holds the full-time job, teaching child development at the local college. Harris is a musician who works when work is available; otherwise he is occupied as a househusband. Both are clearly devoted to Brad, an easygoing and agreeable third-grader.

After pointing out the room just off the living room, where her mother stayed during her last days, Susan settled in and began to describe how little she had known about what would be required of her in her role as caregiver. She had never cared for a dying loved one before and in fact had never been in attendance at a death. When her father had died, Susan was at her home in New England, far from the Midwestern city where she had grown up and where her parents had remained. Indeed, although Susan had decided to take care of Bernice when her kidney cancer reached its end-state, she was not sure how to judge when it would be time to step in.

~⁀

87

"I think my mother actually started dying in June, before we got to their summer camp. She and my brother lived during the winter months in Cincinnati, where I grew up, but they spent summers at our camp on Lake Erie. It was there that my mother had fallen out of bed and had to be hospitalized and transfused. It was the most serious physical failing that she had encountered and doubly scary because James, my brother, who had been able to provide a good deal of her care—he kept her company, got the groceries, helped her with meals—didn't even know she had fallen out of bed.

"James was my only sibling. He was a lawyer when he suffered the onset of mental illness in his late twenties. Although his psychotic symptoms were generally well controlled by medication, he was unable to hold a job and so he lived with our parents. In addition, my brother had developed a drinking problem. He was less functional toward evening, and he often slept too soundly to rouse easily. When my mother fell that night, she had apparently lain on the floor for quite a while. It was only the following day, after calling me, that they decided to go to the emergency room and she was admitted. I think that for her, this was a brush with 'the beginning of the end.'

"This experience set the stage for my mother allowing Harris and me to be a part of her care and gradually take over. We hadn't talked much about it. At first, when it was clear that the prognosis was bad, I had offered to take her home with me. I knew James wouldn't be able to be with her when she died, to have her be at home. I really wanted to try to do it. My dad had died postoperatively in the hospital after surgery to repair an aneurysm. Even though Mother and James had visited him, he was alone and disoriented during that hospital stay. I wasn't even in town. So I really wanted to be there for my mom.

"This death was different; we could anticipate it. I knew it meant bringing her to New England, and I was aware of how problematic that was going to be—what would happen to James? Would he come too? If he didn't, would he be okay by himself? I didn't know. I just offered and we never really talked about it again; we didn't know how it was going to happen, or when. The plan we did articulate was that we would spend that summer with her. When we got there in June, we didn't really know how much more time she had left.

"The first clue I had about what might happen, about how I would know how sick she was, was from a hospice nurse who came for a home visit at the camp. I asked her what I could expect, how would I know, what did she think was going to happen. The nurse laid out a scenario for me of how the deterioration would probably happen in my mother's case. She said my mother would probably have respiratory problems and that gradually she would need more and more help moving around. She was having heart palpitations, so one of the first things we did was to make a space for her downstairs, so that she wouldn't have to climb the stairs. Even though she was walking at that point, the nurse said that she would probably need to use a walker to get to the bathroom. And she did. That helped her pull herself up from the toilet. And then she wanted a portable potty right near her bed, so that she didn't have to get to the bathroom. And then, just like the nurse said, she wanted to use the bedpan. And gradually, the circle of her activity would become bed-oriented, and eventually she would be in bed. And that scenario really helped me; it helped me prepare, helped me see what I might have to do."

Because the rest of the family slept upstairs, Susan got a baby monitor so that she could hear her mother call for her in the night. However, "I started losing sleep almost immediately, partly because of the damn monitor. I got it because when she needed to go to the bathroom in the middle of the night, she really wanted to go physically to the bathroom, until it was too much for her. She did wear diapers. She welcomed them—unlike my father, who was incontinent and wouldn't wear them. They seemed to comfort my mother. The diaper was there if she had to go, if she had company, for instance. But she really didn't want to use it. The monitor was there because I really did want to help her with that, and I also wanted to hear if there was a distress call. But you could hear everything—her radio, her coughing, her snoring. I had never had a monitor when Brad was a baby, so I didn't know what could be transmitted.

"One morning, early, I was awakened by a baby's giggling. It was bizarre. I listened and listened and the baby kept giggling. Eventually, other voices started talking to the baby. When I went downstairs to see if we had company, I learned that my brother had turned off the transmitter in my mother's room because he was up, but the receiver in my room was still on. So I was getting reception from two doors away, where their baby monitor was up and running. That was jarring. I was ready to hear signs of distress and death and instead I found myself listening to the beginning of someone's life.

"This experience made a distinct impression on me. The whole process of trying to care for my mother at this point in her life seemed to include a lot of inappropriate infantilization. You had to buy things that had pictures of babies on them. I couldn't bring myself to buy a sipping cup with a picture of Big Bird on it for my mother's last few sips of water, but I didn't have time to waste shopping selectively. The cup I bought near the end had a cutesy bunch of balloons on it—that was the most neutral cup I could find in a hurry. A lot of the items we needed were not going to be used for a baby. It was a sort of slap in the face—she was dying, not being born. I didn't want my mother to be as jarred by the contrast as I was. I remember feeling really angry when I had to do this kind of shopping.

"At one point when I was changing her diapers, she said, 'How can you do this?' I answered, 'Well, you did it for me for a long time, why shouldn't I do it for you?'

"'But the outcome is so much better with a baby. You have something to look forward to with a baby.'

"'Well, it's easy to do,' I told her. And it *was* pretty easy to do, because she was so accepting of it. I was glad that she was more accepting than my father had been. I think it helped me to understand more fully that, yes, there are some parts of the dying process that resemble infancy. For some people there is dependence, the inability to continue physical self-care. I think that knowing that that is likely to be part of the picture will help me to accept this help even more willingly than my mother did, should I need it in my future. I wish it hadn't been so hard to come by this information—that the elderly, the dying, have problems with incontinence, and often. Even with all the ads on TV, our expectations are that incontinence is the exception, not the rule. Our cultural silence denies how it really is for lots of people. It would have helped me, it would have helped all of us, to expect to be managing urine and bowels in this situation, so that we could just do it and have more time and energy for working out other issues and problems. There are so many things that drain your stamina. These issues shouldn't have to."

"The weeks at the camp were an angry, tense time. A major part of the burden fell to Harris because I had to be out of town working for a week." When Harris spoke about this period, his emotions were still raw. "I felt like I was going to have a nervous breakdown, especially the week that Susie was away. I had Bernice and Susie's brother, James, and Brad to take care of. Susie had arranged for people to come to help get Bernice into her nightie, just to give her more dignity. I could have done that kind of thing, but I wouldn't have been comfortable dealing with her person, her body. Susie and I thought it would be more dignified for Bernice to have a woman coming in to help with as much of that as possible, so we had professional help set up. But Bernice could not stand to have anybody else taking care of her. She wanted it to be Susie or some-one else in the family. Every time the nurse's aide came, even before Susie went away, Bernice was extremely agitated and very mean to her.

"One morning during the week Susie was away, I heard the aide arrive around eight. We'd had a big storm the night before and I'd slept right through it. Evidently, Bernice had been calling me. I'd had the baby monitor on but hadn't heard her at all. Well, was she angry! I was already feeling bad, because one evening Susie's brother came up to me and handed me a check for $200. He wanted to pay me for taking care of Bernice. I said, 'James, I don't want this,' but he had already turned around and was gone. He was non compos mentis at this point, drinking from morning on. So I went in and talked to Bernice. I said, 'Bernice, I don't want this.' She said, 'Take the check.' This made me feel shitty.

"So the day after the storm, Bernice is bitching at the aide, just giv-ing her hell by the time I walk into the room. Then she says, 'And *you!*' and turns on me. I'd come in to ask what she wanted for breakfast, to make her pancakes, which is want she usually wanted. '*You* can just take that money and go on up the highway.' And I felt like doing it, leaving her there to die with James. Brad was there too; he heard all of this. That was what really upset me. She had no mercy. When she was in these agitated states, she was the meanest person alive. I think at the time I said, 'What do you want for breakfast?' or 'Come on, Bernice, ease up,' instead of exploding, which is what I wanted to do, but you can't hit a dying person."

Harris explained that Bernice was always seeking control. "The money thing was so typical—that was the only way they ever expressed their love to Susie—'We'll help you with the mortgage.' As long as you're doing that, you don't have to say all the emotional stuff that's wrapped somewhere deep inside you." As a result, Harris said, "I just really hadn't liked Bernice for a long time. I couldn't stand being around her and at times I really hated her. I thought she was mean anyway, and she was generally unpleasant toward me.

"But I got to feeling like caring for her, which I never thought that I would feel." Harris realized that there were benefits to his caretaking. "I felt more in touch with her than I'd ever been before. And I felt more accepted than I'd ever felt I would be. She allowed me to take care of her, so I figured that she thought I was part of the family after all. It was a form of acceptance that I didn't think I would have with her, and it happened because of this process of taking care of her when she couldn't take care of herself. I was glad that it ended on that positive note. That was important to me, that she died with me having some sympathy for her, some positive human feelings rather than the negative stuff I usually felt.

"A lot of it had to do with mercy. I don't know if I understood her better. I had always tried to understand that she had a lot of built-up anger and it wasn't really me, that she would have been just as mean to somebody else. But I always had so much anger at her, because of the pain that I thought I saw Susie suffering from. I was angrier at Bernice for the lack of emotional nurturance she gave to Susie than I was for her nastiness to me. I felt like I had some understanding of her, but I couldn't quite accept it before she was sick. I had more acceptance after I was feeling more sympathy for her, which I would have felt for any dying, sick person. I was more accepting of her mean side, her lacking side, her lacking as a mother, her lacking as a human. I was more accepting of it than I had been before. Caring for her helped me with that."

Life at the camp grew more and more stressful as Bernice got sicker, James drank more and the Russells got less and less sleep. Finally, in early August it was time to move Bernice to the Russells' home, before she would be unable to endure the trip.

Susan recalled, "We got her to New England in a small private plane. The plane trip took more than two hours and then it took another hour by ambulance to get her to our house. But it was fine because she was able to lie down the whole way. And she had a great trip. She was bright eyed and really excited when she got off the plane. She thanked the pilots and told them that she liked it so well that she'd never fly commercial again! And she was right, of course. This was the first of many double-entendres that Harris and I would experience over the course of the next few weeks. She was living in one world, but constantly referring to another world that none of us knew anything about.

"Judging by her reactions to this trip, she was really glad to be coming. I think she felt released from the situation at the camp and from my brother. I think it would have been too hard on both of them to be together for the final piece. So part of her felt really good when she got here.

"At the same time it was strange for her. We had decided to turn one of the rooms on the first floor into her room. I was trying to make the room comfortable to her, so I placed some family pictures on the end tables. She looked at them but didn't seem really comforted by them; in fact, she didn't really talk about them or things they reminded her of, as I thought she might. My idea was to make the room hers, but it was just a way station. She never really settled in. She spent the first night on the fold-out couch, and the next day we got a hospital bed. We had brought along her wheelchair too, and we were trying to get her in and out of that. We had thought that she would be able to sit up and have us move her about. But the wheelchair was just too labored an ordeal for her, so that never really worked either.

"She asked me on the second day, 'Am I bedridden?' I said, 'Well, I think you are.' I guess she hadn't been able to notice it so much at the camp, because it was her own place and moving even just from the porch to the couch, in her own space, she felt like she was up and around. At the camp she didn't associate living on the first floor or lying down with being bedridden. But then one day she wasn't in her own bed and the next, she was in a real hospital bed. I guess that was too obvious for her not to notice. And then she asked, 'Do you think I'm going to die?'

"I said, 'I think you are, eventually. But I don't think you're going to right now.'

"She went on, 'How do you think it's going to happen?'

"'I think you're going to be asleep. I don't think there is going to be any big trauma.'

"She asked why I thought so, and I said, 'Because the rest of you seems fine. I think that you're probably just going to go to sleep.' Well, then, the rest of the whole three weeks, did she sleep? No! Sleep avoidance was her major goal.

"When she did sleep, she would have these wild dreams where she was incredibly active. When I'd come down in the middle of the night to help her go to the bathroom, she'd talk to me about whatever dream she was in the middle of. One night she told me to watch out for the cow in the living room. She had already moved the horse out of the way but the cow was still there. And she'd laugh, and talk about what a great dream she was having and how busy she'd been. I looked forward to asking her what she had been dreaming about, so when I'd go down to help her, I'd ask her what she'd been doing for the past couple of hours. She would say, 'I've been selling shoes. There's a great pair of alligator shoes over there I saved for you,' or, 'I've made sandwiches for everybody and I'm washing windows.' She was enjoying herself and enjoyed telling me about it. And some of it was hysterically funny! It was all good fun, positive.

"Then, toward the last few days, it seemed like she was dreaming during her waking hours. The transition between when she was going in and out of these dreams became less and less clear, so that she would say, for instance, that Roseanne, the TV star, was in the other room, or that someone else was sitting over there and I should be careful not to sit down on her. And she announced that Dad was out playing golf and would be back shortly. And that Harris had made a tuna sandwich and left it on the counter, and she'd eaten it. That's why she wasn't hungry, and if Harris had wanted it he shouldn't have left it lying around. She told me all of this with eyes wide open, in the middle of the day, when she hadn't been out of bed at all, or eaten more than a bit of the ice cream that I'd fed her earlier. So there was a transition from her dreaming vividly at night, and being aware of doing so, to dreaming during the day and not knowing that what she was experiencing was not being experienced by anyone else.

"A couple of times she was very agitated. She wanted to get out of that bed in the worst way. She wanted to get her coat and her things and get to the airport. She was not comfortable. She would pull at her covers and thrash around a little, and say, 'I just gotta get out of this bed. I gotta get out, gotta get out.' I had a really hard time with this. Nothing I did seemed to help her relax. I was worried that she might actually try to get out of the bed and hurt herself, and had begun to think that she needed some tranquilizers."

But the prescription drug situation was about to turn into something of a nightmare. Susan's family doctor had agreed to supervise her mother's care, but he had never come to see her. Indeed, the way hospice works is that a specially trained nurse manages each case, visiting the patient and making assessments. It is understood that the hospice nurse is the expert at the scene, and the supervising physician usually prescribes drugs based on the nurse's recommendations. Susan felt the hospice care that her mother was receiving was excellent, and she trusted the nurse in charge. As Bernice's agitation grew, "the hospice nurse thought it was time to manage the pain medically. This is where we ran into trouble. The nurse couldn't convince the doctor to sign for the medication she thought was best," a narcotic administered through a skin patch.

The doctor was unfamiliar with the skin patch and instead prescribed Demerol, which is given orally. When Bernice was unable to swallow it without retching, the doctor insisted on an unheard-of alternative, "that we administer the Demerol rectally. Which is not the way one administers that drug—we looked it up. And we kept telling the doctor that it was having no effect." But even after examination of a diaper revealed that the pills were unabsorbed, the doctor stubbornly rejected the nurse's advice.

Susan was worried that her mother would get so uncomfortable that in order to get the necessary drug, Susan might have to take her to the emergency room. "And the minute you call the emergency room to get the drug, you have a whole other group of people to deal with in terms of showing them the living will, making sure that they are not right-to-lifers, and more and more and more. We had gotten all the way to 11:59 without messing up and suddenly there was a possibility that after all we had done, she might not get to die at home, comfortably, after all."

After two days of worry and frustration, Susan took drastic action. "I said, 'We have got to find another doctor right away. I've got to start medicating her with narcotics *now*, so that I'll get some sleep and she'll get some sleep. We don't know how long this is going to take and we can't go on like this, and I *don't* want to take her to the emergency room.'

"I removed my mother from the doctor's care. It wasn't easy, because in this rural area it is hard for anyone to find a doctor. All the practices are full; in fact, I had offered my own slot in the first doctor's practice to guarantee his care of my mother. I would not have the same leverage with a new doctor, and to make matters worse, this was all happening on the Thursday before Labor Day weekend, when the few doctors available were likely to be on vacation. And, we were in the eleventh hour. I could see the difficulty of taking on this case, not only because of how quickly things had progressed, but also because I was asking someone to pick up the pieces for a colleague whose judgment I had come to distrust. I was so frustrated while all of this was happening. I felt that instead of being able to spend time with my mother, I was busy managing her case, arguing with one doctor, trying to find a new one and running around trying to get the medication—drugstores don't deliver around here. I shouldn't have had to do that, and I resent it bitterly to this day.

"I did find a doctor who agreed to take the case and sign the nurse's order for a skin patch, but then none were available! They were so new to this area that the pharmacy at the hospital and the three drugstores in town didn't have any and couldn't get one until Friday afternoon. We would have to make do until then with a prescription for rectal morphine.

After we got the prescription for the morphine, we were racing to fill it before 5:00 P.M., because out here, if you don't get it by five o'clock, you don't get it. There are no twenty-four-hour pharmacies."

The morphine did help her mother, but administering it became another ordeal for Susan. "You have to play with these dosages at first, to be sure you're giving enough and not too much. The morphine took forty-five minutes to get into her system and then there was relief for forty-five minutes. For the dosage to be maintained at the correct level, I had to insert a suppository every two hours. If we'd had two or three days to regulate it, she might have been calmer and we might have been able to talk more, not be so worried about her symptoms. As it turned out, once we got her calmed down, she died within a day or so."

Already frustrated and exhausted, Susan would spend the next twenty-four hours administering morphine every two hours, staying awake and alert until each dose took effect, to make sure her mother did not attempt to get out of bed and hurt herself. "Those last days were the worst of it," she remembered.

At night, Harris could hear what was going on because of the monitor. "Bernice was saying things like, 'It's done. It's time to . . . ' It was that dreamlike talk, so a lot of it seemed incoherent. At times she seemed really fearful. But other times, she seemed to be realizing that this isn't so bad: 'I gotta go.' No one was in her room at this time. Most of the time she thought Susie was there. The general idea was that she was always preparing, or she became very agitated because things were not quite right. She said, 'This isn't so bad. The clocks are on the wall. I gotta see how much time we have. I have about five minutes.' This kind of conversation went on a little bit each night. This was before she was given the strong medication."

Harris continued: "I was very curious. I had no idea that this kind of stuff happened. I found it fascinating. It made up for all of the stress. I wouldn't have not gone through that process for anything. I'm really glad that I did, because I feel I know so much more about life, knowing the process of death. It's more meaningful to me somehow. I feel very enriched by the experience. I was able to put myself in the position of being the viewer of how the death process worked. Bernice's changes in mentality from this world to . . . not necessarily a fantasy world, but another world, were constant. She was always talking about people who weren't there, things that weren't there, and the way I saw it, her mind was preparing to not be in this world anymore. She was constantly preparing herself, for at least a week, probably more. She was very nervous about getting ready to go. It would have to be perfect when she went. That was the way Bernice was. She would have to have everything organized and then she would make this trip. But it was very hard for her and it was very hard for us, because she was always asking us to make these preparations that we weren't sure how to do. She was really uncomfortable. She thought that she should know how to do it—that there were rules to this thing and she didn't understand the rules."

As Susan related the events leading into Labor Day weekend, her narrative rambled, reflecting both her exhaustion and the liminality of helping someone who was less and less oriented to reality. "On Friday afternoon I was able to pick up the Duregesic patch. Basically, it would do what I had been doing manually every two hours, and in a bigger dose. With the rectal morphine I had to stay with my mother until it took effect, because she was so agitated that I thought she might try to get up and hurt herself. She was waffling back and forth between, 'If you give me any more of that you're going to kill me' and 'I gotta get on this plane.' It was like she knew that this was it, but she didn't want it to be it. And it was a struggle for me too because it was what I was trying to do, calm her down enough so she could depart, so to speak. This was another one of those double-entendres, another time when we were living in two worlds at the same time.

"During those evenings, if it was early, we could still converse. She was more off the wall in the middle of the night than she was during the day or early evening. On Thursday night we went in after supper and watched the news. She was very interested in a story about a foreign leader who had mysteriously disappeared and then returned on an airplane. And that's when she really started to talk about traveling. She wanted to know, did we have the tickets, did we have her purse, and where was her purse? She needed all three pairs of her glasses, she said, and if Harris would just get them off of the wall, that would be a great help.

"She thought that her glasses were somehow on the wall, and Harris looked at me and whispered, 'Where are they?' I said, 'Just pretend. Just get them.' And he would do that. He would go over to the wall, take them down, and say, 'Okay, Bernice, I've got them. I'll put them in your purse.' This happened over and over again.

"We felt tense about what was literal and what wasn't. You were sort of freaked out because you didn't know what to say, or just where the goddamned glasses were on the wall. But she needed them, and you wanted to be able to find them, even though you didn't know exactly where they were. It's just not something that you can cope with real easily. Especially with her asking for the same thing every few minutes.

"Our hospice nurse had told us that it was better not to try to correct her. That made me think about my dad. My mother had told me that before he died, he had been very disoriented in the hospital. He wanted his cigarettes and kept telling people to just go over to the kitchen drawer—he'd gesture across the room from his hospital bed—and get them. But they'd tell him that he couldn't smoke and that he was in the hospital anyway. I thought that correcting him was sort of disrespectful, almost like saying, 'You're a foolish old man who's dying and doesn't know any better.' But I have to admit that I wouldn't have felt okay about humoring a person who is clearly not experiencing time and space in the way that you are, if the hospice nurse hadn't talked to us about all of this. So with my mother we just gave her the glasses and were lucky enough to go to the right spot on the wall to get them.

"My mother also wanted to know how much money was in her wallet and what she was going to be wearing, in preparation for this trip. She also asked, 'Will you be on the plane?' and I answered, 'Yes, we'll all be on the plane, we'll all go together.' I didn't say to where because I wasn't sure we were talking about the same destination. We *would* all be going back to the city for her funeral, and she would be on the same plane, but I thought from the way she was talking that she had a sort of metaphysical destination in place, whereas I was talking about a real trip.

"She had been very concerned about the details of the funeral, even early in her illness. Months before, she had laid out exactly what she wanted to be buried in. It was a nightgown that my father had given her a very long time ago, a pretty peignoir set. She'd never worn it. Along with that she'd set aside a pair of white stockings and underwear and slippers. She had the whole thing planned. I remember that she had this uncanny sense about my getting those clothes sent from the city to the house.

"When our hospice nurse had visited the second time, she reassessed the situation and told me that things were moving faster than she had originally thought, and suggested that I call the funeral home to begin the preparations. I knew I had to call the city to ask a friend to send up the clothes that my mother had placed carefully in the back of her closet many months before. So I went upstairs to the other end of the house to make the call, and I purposefully closed the door behind me. When I returned downstairs, my mother asked me, 'How are you going to get the things you need?' We both knew that she meant the clothes, but she didn't say it. I told her I'd ask a friend to send them sometime, not letting on that I had just made the call. I was trying to play it as if it were some-thing I'd get around to, as if there were no urgency. But it just didn't go past her at all. She *knew*, even though I'm sure she couldn't possibly have overheard my conversation with the nurse or my phone call be-hind closed doors.

"I think that the funeral was in the background of her questions like, 'Do I have my purse? Do I have my money? Do I have my glasses? Do I have all of that stuff?' It was almost like she really wanted to be there. She wondered, 'How will we, I mean, you, have all those people in?' She was worried about after the funeral, what kinds of things people were going to eat. It was going to be sort of like a party, and she wanted to be there in the worst way. She was trying to get as much detail as she could, but she didn't want all of it. We were both appropriately vague. She'd say, 'Are we going on the plane together?' I'd say, 'Well, yeah, we'll be there,' meaning Harris and me. Then she'd ask, 'Well, what if the pilot doesn't know the way?' Our nurse had alerted us to think about what she could possibly mean when she said things that didn't make sense—for instance, a commercial pilot would know how to get where he had to go. That's when we thought of answering, 'Well, Dad will be there, and your father will be there, and Marion (her sister) will be there.' She said, 'Oh, yes, that's right. They'll be there. They'll be able to help us.' Harris mentioned her other sister, one against whom Bernice was still holding a grudge, and Bernice added hurriedly, 'Oh, but she'll be in a different section. She won't be with us.' We had to laugh. She didn't want to be reunited with just anyone! And then she asked Harris, 'How will I know what to do?' She kept asking Harris, 'How do I do this? I don't know how to do this.' And he said, 'It'll be okay. There's no right way to do it. You'll do it fine.'

"Our nurse kept saying, 'Find the thing that she's still having trouble with and give her permission to go.' That's the kind of thing that the nurse did: try to help families say what they needed to say. She explained that there was often something that needed to get said or done. So I kept leaning on my mother's every word. 'What is it, Bernice! What is it?' The only thing I can think of to this day is something she said after we had finally been able to get the patch, which really did seem to settle her down quite well. The new doctor was scheduled to see her, and we were waiting for him to arrive when she said, 'You know what I'm really worried about?' I thought, 'This is it, this is what is holding her back!' so it was all I could do not to shout, 'What is it? What is it?' so I could relieve her and she could go! She said, 'I'm worried about being exposed.'

"I had thought she meant right then, that she didn't want the doctor to see her in her diaper. So I said, 'Well, we won't expose you. We'll see that you're not exposed.' And I pulled up her blankets snug around her. It didn't hit me until later that she might have been talking about being embalmed and being exposed then. She was very conscious of what was going to be happening to her body and, in retrospect, I'm sure that was what was bothering her. She was a very private person when it came to physical things. She would have worried about that part, but she couldn't quite say it. She definitely wanted to be at her own funeral. She was trying to picture it all mentally before it happened, including the plane trip back to the city, and I think she knew that she was trying to see how her body would take that trip at the same time that she knew she would be taking another kind of trip altogether. It was wild.

"After we had the conversation about the plane and how she was ready and everything was all right, we saw on the news that there was going to be a bad storm soon. She commented, 'Oh, I won't be here for that.' And she wasn't. That same night we all noticed that she had some discharge from her mouth. It was a nasty color and when she saw it, she looked scared. We were all there, and I cleaned her face, and we kissed her good night. We had been fussing and fuming with the rectal morphine on Thursday night and Friday. The new doctor came to visit her at five that afternoon, soon after I had finally picked up the Duregesic patch. During his visit, my mother said, 'Well, I think this is it. I better go to the hospital.'

"He replied, 'Why do you want to go to the hospital? You have everything you need right here. You're doing great.' She said, 'Well it's just going to be too much for everyone.' The doctor was really great. He asked me in front of my mom, 'Is it too much for you?' I said no, and then he turned to my mother and said, 'You see, your daughter wants to do this. She can do it. You stay put.'

"We left the room and went into the kitchen. We were all sitting around the table and the Duregesic patch was starting to really do its thing. At one point my mother called to Harris and said, 'Where is she, where's Susie? Well, this is it. This is it.' I just couldn't come then because I was still talking to the doctor and the nurse about the effects of the patch. But by the time I did come, she had sunk into this deep sleep. Her breathing had become labored and throaty. That's pretty much how she was all night.

"I had been told to expect her to sleep, because of the medication, and that was what we were after. But when I heard her breathing the next morning, I got scared. I went in and saw a lot of brown liquid coming from her mouth and nose. I knew that what was happening was that she was drowning. The nurse called me early that morning to ask how she was. I said she was still with us, but not really, that she had sort of left the night before. The interesting thing was that she hadn't moved since the night before, but she was still breathing, and fairly regularly—it wasn't one of those breathing-every-two-minute things, like you hear about. She was definitely still breathing pretty normally.

"'Here's what you can do,' the nurse began. 'You can go and suction her and clean her up a little bit.' I was worried that if anyone else saw her, especially Brad, they might throw up, because she really did look pretty disgusting. But I really didn't want to suction her. And so the nurse said I could put a towel under her and wipe it up a little bit, just a little bit. But I was afraid I would wake her up and throw her back into agitation. I really didn't know what I wanted to do. The nurse said, 'You can also do nothing. If you don't remove the fluid, then she will certainly die soon and she will anyway. The tumor is pressing on the bile duct and everything is backing up because that's what happens—the lungs fill and the throat gets full and then you cannot take that next breath.' And that's when I thought, 'Isn't that what we want to happen? Why should I do anything?' Plus I was scared to death that I would wake her up.

"Of course the nurse knew that I probably wouldn't, but she said, 'Well, there is this thing you can do, if you want to do something.' The hospice mentality, I think, is trying to find out what the person wants to do and then helping them to do it. She explained how you can go into the mouth with a washcloth and get the stuff out and that it might make her a little more comfortable—if there was anything to be done to make her more comfortable. Even that was hard to know at that point, because there was no other sign. I was looking for other signs of her body dying. She was cold. She had begun to get cold from the bottom up. Cold. But her hands were not cold yet. So I put some more blankets on her and then I did clean her up a little bit because I didn't want anyone else to be totally freaked.

"Everybody wanted to look in on her that morning. When Brad got up, we opened leftover fortune cookies. The night before, after she had sunk into her deep sleep, a hospice volunteer had come over so that we were able to go out on the deck and have Chinese food. We had saved the fortune cookies, including one for my mother. We were going to give it to her the next morning. When we opened the fortune it said something really . . . what was it? I can't remember exactly but it was really appropriate, about taking a trip, and we put it under her pillow."

Brad remembered what the fortune had said. He had been playing Nintendo, he explained, when "Mom and I went in to see what her fortune was, and it was something like 'Great waters will carry you far,' and then I played Nintendo again."

The next time Susan went in to check on her mother, she thought she witnessed her mother's last breath. "It wasn't like she *took* her last breath, but rather that she let the last breath go. And she went out. And she was gone. I knew she had died right that minute. The next gurgle didn't come. There was no more noise after I had the sensation of this breath leaving, this exhalation. I thought it was amazing that I happened to be there. We'd put the fortune under her pillow, and Brad had gone back to the kitchen, and I just happened to be walking through the room again. I patted her and said, 'Well, good luck. You're on your way.'

"Our neighbor, who happens to be the county medical examiner, was at that moment walking down the road past our house on his way to get the mail. We had consulted him about my mom several times before. I didn't hesitate to lean out the door and say, 'Would you come in here for a moment? Just bear me out here. I think something just happened.' He came right over and quickly confirmed for me that my mother had just died.

"I 'saw' her death as a little wisp. The only other time I noticed anything was later at the funeral home. When the funeral director first came to the house, we sat down and talked. There was a lot of small talk, but he managed to confirm details about the arrangements, including the fact that Brad would not be traveling with us to the funeral; he would stay here with close friends so he wouldn't miss the first day of school. Then the funeral director asked if we wanted to see her before we flew to the city. I thought this was a great idea!

"I never would have thought of having a viewing here. We had known all along that the funeral parlor here would prepare the body and make the travel arrangements, but the funeral itself and the viewing we expected to be held in the city. I had been struck by how messy she was when she died, but until the funeral director asked that question, I hadn't realized that the thing that I wanted was to not have that deathbed picture in my mind until I got down to the city and saw her laid out. It never occurred to me to figure out how to deal with this for myself and, maybe more important, for Brad. Because Brad wasn't coming with us, he would have had the Saturday morning picture of her as his last one too, but for the funeral director's asking, 'Do you want to see her before you go?' I jumped at the chance.

"The next day we got dressed up and went over to the funeral home and had our own private time, just the three of us. That visit ended up being very helpful for all of us. It helped us put some closure on what we'd just been through, before meeting the next challenge of confronting my brother, family friends and the more formal public funeral. Brad took over all the things he wanted to put in the casket, and we felt much better than we had on Saturday. She had been so ugly on Saturday, but when we saw her on Sunday, she really did look fine. We talked with the funeral director about how he had fixed her up, especially that part of her face that had been discolored and misshapen. While we were there, I sensed her again hovering above, wispy-like, totally aerated. And then she just took off and went to the city. She was gone. Her spirit was, like, out of there. She was going to beat us to the city, as only she would."

"That night of the day she died—after we had the upset feelings about how messy it was and how difficult and sad it was when they took her body, in spite of feeling all of that—we also felt totally relieved. We opened a bottle of champagne and we actually felt euphoric that we had helped her in the way that she wanted to be helped. We kept her out of the fucking hospital."

As the Russells toasted themselves and Bernice, they "felt really good that we actually had achieved this goal. I think my mother had felt good, even though she hadn't been completely comfortable. I know she was feeling some pain. But one of those evenings when we were sitting there talking—even on those last few agitated days, she had some calm periods—she said to me, 'You know, I think this has really been wonderful. I think we're closer, and I really have appreciated it.' That was great! That was the most she could say to me in twenty-five years. I knew that she was making a bigger statement: that she could let me do it. But that she could even say *anything* was wonderful. So we felt great, even though we felt terrible."

Sad and exhausted but also gratified, Susan and Harris flew with Bernice's body to the city. James, grief-stricken, had already arrived. Bernice was laid to rest the day after Labor Day. The next day James returned to the camp and the Russells returned to New England. They had arranged for James to enter a residential, dual-diagnosis treatment program later that month in the city, after he closed up the camp.

But two weeks after Labor Day, on the day James was to return to the city, he failed to answer Susan's calls. She telephoned neighbors and asked them to check the camp. James was found lying on the floor, naked and unconscious. He was transported first to the local hospital, then to the city hospital—the same one where his father had practiced and died—more than four hours away. The diagnosis was kidney failure. Susan, only three weeks into her new job and ill with a virus, had to direct James's medical care by long-distance phone calls. He died within three days.

Harris said, "It feels calmer to talk about it now. When Bernice first died and then James died, I felt the need to talk about it constantly, to sort of assure myself that it had really happened, or to solidify in my mind that they were really gone. Particularly with James. I couldn't quite believe it. I wanted to go to the city and bury him right away. I was tired of the process and I wanted to get out of it. On the other hand, I was always wanting to be involved with it in some way. I felt a real need to be involved in the aftermath and to continue to experience it, even though at the same time I wanted it to all be over. I was really impatient to get back to my life, so I think I felt that if I could experience it with intensity over and over again, that would get rid of it. That's the way I was reacting to it."

Although James's death had been a shock, it had not been a great surprise for Harris. He mentioned a dream he had had at the camp while caring for Bernice. "I don't know if it was a premonition or not, but to me it was symbolic of what I expected to happen. I felt strongly that James was going to come to a very bad end, although I didn't know he would die. I just thought it was going to be something tragic. A lot of that came from seeing his actions, the way he was drinking and the way he was hopeless, just the sadness that I saw in him. I didn't think he would get the treatment he needed. I didn't think he would bring himself to do it. I didn't think he could. I had this dream that James comes down to the kitchen, and it's as if he's getting his whiskey bottle out of the cabinet to get a drink, but it seems like he doesn't have any whiskey. He starts rushing around. He has his long raincoat on, but he doesn't have any clothes on underneath. He's running out the front door and starting to run down the road and he's pissing all over himself—all over everything—because he's frantic to get some more whiskey. After I woke up, I saw this as being James' end, a sign of his demise."

In retrospect, it was interesting that in the dream, James was urinating all over himself, perhaps indicating a kidney problem. That James died of kidney failure reminded the Russells of Bernice's kidney cancer, and Brad remembered another variation on this theme. He described how in her last days, Bernice worried about plumbing problems in the house. Her own internal plumbing blocked, Bernice was convinced that the toilets in the house were overflowing. She mentioned it during one of their evening chats. Brad remembered that—like other times, when his Grammy talked to people who weren't there—"It was funny. It was hard not to make a funny face, hard not to laugh. She was saying the toilets were overrunning, overflowing. Mom told her that she had it under control, and Grammy kept saying, 'Are you sure, are you sure?' Stuff like that. When we left the room and finally got upstairs, then I could laugh."

Brad thought it was weird that his grandmother would talk about things that weren't real as well as things that were. "It was sort of hard to play along because you wouldn't know what to say. She said for Dad to get the glasses off the wall and he wondered where the glasses were on the wall. We said that we guessed he got them. She was asking for help and things, and she wasn't really where she thought she was. So you didn't really know what she wanted. You wouldn't know what to do."

Brad remembered playing outside a lot when they were at the camp, but that it was a hard time for his parents: "Mom went to California to do some work and then Daddy had to take care of three people, because James didn't really know how to do stuff because he was drinking a lot. I went to the store on my bike if Daddy needed something. Daddy said that I was the person who could help himself the most of the other people there.

"When Grammy was at our house, it was sort of like having a baby in the house because she would take up more attention. We've had babies in the house before, and people have to pay more attention to them because they knock stuff over." He admitted feeling "sort of jealous," because nobody could play with him like they used to, but, he went on to explain, "she needed it more than me, needed help more than me.

"And then we had to put Sparky to sleep because he was barking too much and he was scaring Grammy." This was an incident that neither Susan nor Harris had mentioned. Sparky, the Briggses' family dog, had always been troublesome, but as more strangers came to the house to visit Bernice—nurses, aides and neighbors—the dog took to perching on Bernice's bed, growling and barking. When James proved incapable of controlling the dog, the decision was made to put Sparky to sleep. Brad compared this to the death of his cat. "I knew it was right, but I was sort of, you know, sad because Sparky was, like, living and he was a thing— he was still alive. When our cat had something wrong—it was, like, feline cancer—she was just lying around and she kept having to go to the vet each week and it costed a lot of money and stuff. But Sparky wasn't sick."

Brad expressed how it was frightening to have "a person who's dying in your house. I just pretended that nothing was happening, except it was hard. You knew she was going to die there. It was scary. I didn't really want to go up the hall because she was in that room. I'd go by it in the daytime, but in the night, it was like sort of . . . I was scared. After she died, I was really scared, except now I'm not really scared anymore.

"I wasn't scared to talk with Grammy when Mom and Dad were there. I read to her, *Where the Sidewalk Ends* by Shel Silverstein. I'd read a short poem to her sometimes. She was, like, in a coma. She was sort of asleep with her eyes open, looking at you, but she couldn't move her hands or arms. I didn't think she could see me, and then all of a sudden she just woke up and said, 'What do you want?' She talked about people who were really dead, but she thought they were alive. I thought it was weird. It was hard to see her like that because I remembered how nice she was before.

"It was hard for Mom" when James died, "because James was the last person in her family." Brad understood that his uncle "got killed by drinking." He had known that his uncle was sick and in the hospital, but like his parents, had not expected James to die. "I wasn't surprised when Grammy died because I knew she was gonna die. I just felt sad. She had that dark fluid that came out and it was scary. She looked a lot better when she was in the funeral place. We went there and brought her stuff that was important to her. I made a picture for her—it was a fish. It went with the fortune, 'Great waters will carry you far.'" Brad smiled at this.

After the funeral Brad talked a lot with his parents about dying. "We would sit down at night and talk about the good things that we remembered about Grammy and Uncle James." To other children who might find themselves in a similar situation, Brad advised, "Talk about it a lot with your mom and dad, and if you're scared, talk about why you're scared. Maybe they can help you think about something different. So, to talk about it is probably the best thing to do."

Susan noted the difference between the deaths of her mother and her brother. "In my brother's case, there were no plans. My mother had planned. We had had a series of steps to carry out and we did them. But then poor James, the guy was transported two hundred miles to the city from their camp in an ambulance with no clothes on." At this point in her story, Harris's dream of James, naked under the raincoat, seemed especially meaningful.

She continued: "All his good clothes were at the camp, so there was nothing to bury him in. Nobody was available to go to their city apartment to get anything for him. I had known exactly what clothes my mother wanted, and where they were and who to call to send the exact items. I didn't even know where to bury James. I had to call an elderly aunt to find out about possible cemetery plots on my mother's side of the family. It was very different.

"We had known that James was not in good shape, but I didn't think he would die, and definitely not within three weeks of my mother. During the time she was at our house, he would call us or we would call him, sometimes several times a day, until she couldn't talk to him because she was too weak. Sometimes she had nothing to say anyway. It was upsetting to her to have nothing to say and to feel like she couldn't really carry on a conversation. The less able she was to communicate, the more worried James became. I would tell him that she needed a lot of rest. I didn't want to lie, but I didn't want to tell the truth about how hard it was, because that would have agonized him. I was trying to prepare him that one of these days . . . It was really hard, trying to negotiate those last days. I had called him that morning before she died and told him that she was still with us, and then called an hour later and said that she had just died. He couldn't understand that and I don't blame him. I had the same feeling when my dad died. I needed to know everything, exactly what had happened. If you're not there, you just don't know enough. I could appreciate James's confusion.

"The only premonition I had of his death was, of course, in retrospect. The day before my mother's funeral, he had changed over all of the beneficiaries on his insurance policies from Bernice to me. At the time, I didn't think anything of it because we were together and it seemed like a good time to do that. Over a year before, when Mother was first diagnosed, we had gone through his policies and he asked me to write down all of the numbers for him in a list form. It had been really hard for him to organize them because it meant acknowledging that she was actually going to be gone. So he didn't complete the task of changing the beneficiaries then, but he had them ready. Signing those policies was sort of his last competent act. They had been sitting on his desk the whole summer, waiting for his attention when he got back. That morning he had been drinking, and he was very distraught. We had to show him where to sign. Sometimes he didn't sign the way his name had been printed, but he managed and he put all of the policy changes in the mail that day.

"It was Labor Day. My mother's funeral was the next day, and Harris and I left the day after that. I was starting a new job, and Brad was two days into the new school year. We had to get back. We hoped that James would be comforted by being back at the camp, and that he'd get safely back to the city in a couple of weeks to begin his treatment.

"I remember he said, 'Well, if I . . . something happens to me, you really will have a nest egg.' I had said jokingly, 'Let's just try not to have any more deaths real soon. This is hard enough. We have our work cut out for us here, to keep going.'

"Harris and I had started to come down off this physical, almost knee-jerk reaction to crisis, but when James was hospitalized, we found out how quickly that system goes up again. The fact that we weren't physically with James didn't make it any less consuming of a death. In some ways it was more frustrating because I had to talk to the hospital people quite a lot, and I never got to talk to my brother. I talked to as many people who lived near the camp as I could, to try to learn what had happened to him and when and how, but I never talked directly to James, even while he was in the hospital. I was always trying to get through this cloud or enigma. I could never get to James. A couple of people saw him at the hospital—our family's minister, and their lawyer, who was a family friend. They told me that James was agitated, but we didn't know from what. It could have been the toxic substances from his kidney failure, or the alcohol, or the decompensation from not taking his psychotropic drugs for five days. We just didn't know what was going on. I never had a concrete view of all that happened. I saw exactly what happened to my mother. I saw her get colder from the feet up and then she, that wisp, went out her mouth, sort of like dit-dit-dit-dit-dit, *poof!* But with James, I didn't know what was going on.

"I think that in a way he had been preparing for this for a long time. He had messed himself up so much inside that he was sort of stacking the deck, so that any crisis that happened would do it. Being a nonviolent person, the only thing he could do was just shut down and make sure that the pumps wouldn't get going again. Literally. On some level I believe that he knew he was doing this, and that he couldn't do anything else. James just couldn't make the changes that he might have had to make if he were going to be able to get better and live by himself. So I think that he drank himself into a really big stupor, fell down, and could not get up for a long time. Then muscle toxins built up because he didn't move for so long. I gather that can happen within even twelve hours.

"I asked the doctors if they were sure that they could rule out a drug-alcohol interaction. By itself, his increased drinking was worrisome, but what I feared might happen was the possibility of a terrible drug interaction, because his medicine clearly had 'do not drink' written all over it. But the doctors said that there would have been different kinds of effects if it had been a drug-alcohol interaction. James probably drank himself to near unconsciousness, fell out of bed or on his way to the bathroom, and then lay inert for so long that muscle toxins built up and caused his kidneys to fail. His kidneys were not able to process that amount of toxicity. It was ironic that he died of kidney failure because, of course, my mother's illness was kidney cancer.

"On the day James died, I had called the hospital at eight in the morning, which I did every morning, to check in. He was about to be dialyzed for the first time. They said that he hadn't gone for the procedure yet, but that he was due to go any time. So I got off the phone, planning to call again later, but the doctor called me back soon after and said that James had thrown up and aspirated, inhaled vomit into his lungs. His heart had stopped and they had worked on him for twenty minutes. There was probably brain damage already. They were asking whether we wanted them to put James on life support.

"The night before, a friend of my parents—a physician who had helped us get my brother from the camp to the city hospital—had visited James, read his chart, and talked to the doctor assigned to James's case. When I had talked to the doctor in charge, a urologist, he had been primarily concerned with the kidneys: 'We've got to get these kidneys going.' But my parents' friend told me more about the rest of James's body, that it was ravaged. That made it easier to say 'no life support.' I don't think I could have made that decision just going by what the urologist said. He only focused on the kidneys, and without dialysis, James wouldn't have had any chance. If James had been put on life support after suffering cardiac arrest and probable brain damage, it wouldn't have taken him long to deteriorate. But why make him suffer?

"I had been preparing for my two o'clock class at the college. At noon I was scheduled for a site visit for a small grant that I had written. I was going to be very busy from around 11:30 that day on. After James died, I didn't know whether to go or not, to keep any of my appointments. But I decided I had to go because it's my character to do so; if I don't do things, I'm mentally not well. So I went. James died and I went, to the grant review and my class.

"The only piece of James that I could see was his sorrow and a realization that because Mother had died, his life was over too. I think that even through all the drinking, he could see that about himself, more clearly than even I could see it about him. I had hoped he'd be able to make it. But I think he knew he couldn't. He had some awareness of how bad it was. That piece of James was intact."

During James's hospitalization the doctor in charge had reported that James seemed to be all right—knew what day it was, who was president and so on—but James's visitors implied that he was in tough shape. "He was totally caustic to our lawyer, and it was his impression that James was very uncomfortable. He was connected to a lot of tubes. I see James as having been technologically assaulted, to be honest with you. But he even conquered that. He was not going to have any of it. He wasn't going to be revived.

"In some ways, I wish I had let James lie there in the camp a little longer before asking someone to go over, even though I knew something was terribly wrong when I couldn't reach him. Those days in the hospital must have been hard for him, and I could have spared him that if I'd waited a little longer.

"The neighbors who found James told me that he called for our father, he wanted to know where Dad was. But he didn't ask for anybody else. He told them that I was down in Florida for Harris's father's funeral, which was why I couldn't be there. When the minister asked me how Harris's father was, I replied, 'Fine.' We compared notes and realized that James was delusional. But we don't know which of the several possible causes was the operative one. James was delusional, but not in the way that my mother was. You could take no comfort from James's delusions.

"Their deaths are in no way comparable except that they died quite close together. Here's what it looked like to me: The three of them, who spent most of their lives together—my father, my mother and my brother—are still together, and I'm still the odd man out. I'm really glad in some ways because I am alive, but I have mixed feelings. You know, that's the way the family was and that's the way the family is and that's the way the family wasn't and isn't ever going to be. They're up there somewhere playing bridge and looking for a dummy. Even though they got me to be the fourth when I was little, quite literally—that's how I learned to play bridge—I would never play that role now. They want their fourth in bridge, but it's not going to be me, at least not any time soon."

For Harris, James's death was no less complicated. Harris had tried to like James, telling himself for years that "he's got an illness. I always tried to understand so hard so I could like my brother-in-law. And I couldn't do it. After he died, I would look for the relief and it wouldn't quite be there. It has been a very gradual thing to feel relief. We don't have to be his caretakers. Now I'm starting to feel that more and more.

"Then I felt that I should have more feelings about this loss. I started asking Susan a lot of questions about what James was like before he became ill. I decided it would be a good exercise for me to write a song about James, to think about what it might have been like. I would have liked to have had an older brother-in-law; I've never had an older brother, so what did I miss? I tried to express that. I have tried to make myself feel better about him, and I have tried hard. But I'm glad he's gone.

"I didn't really feel I could express all of that to Susan at the time. It was Susan's brother and she was sad, and I was sad for his life as well. That's the one thing I could say to her—I am sad that he had such a bad life, and I think we should be glad that he's not suffering. He was a miserable person."

During the following weeks, Susan recalled, "There were lots of details to attend to and there were things that kept annoying me throughout the aftermath of both deaths, like lawyer things. I would continue to get

Mother's mail, which was supposed to be sent directly to her lawyer. It would drive me up the wall. Why was I getting this stuff, why weren't people doing the right thing? People would say that it takes computers a long time, and so on. For months I would be jarred from whatever sense of calm I was having by little things like getting her mail. I would just get out of thinking about it for a little while and then something like that would happen and kick me off the track of feeling all right."

Susan remembered that "the only direct processing of this stuff or feeling like I was missing them or wanting to be in contact with them again was during this dream that I had. It happened in October, after the hospice held their yearly memorial service for the families and friends of anyone who had died that year. It was held in a church. You could light a candle for your person who died. They said you could light fifty candles if you wanted to think about and commemorate anyone at all. The nurses went up first and lit a candle for the people they had taken care of, and then lots of people from the audience went up. It was real touching. There were about 150 people there, all in various states of mourning. Some people's loved ones had just died; others had died almost a year ago. Even though I was so tired that I hadn't wanted to go, this made an impression on me. I had gone because I thought I should. I felt it was almost one of these annoying details to attend to. It felt like forced mourning. But I had to do this ritual, partly because the hospice care meant so much to me that I wanted to be supportive of the organization. Deep down, I thought it was the last thing I needed to do, but it turned out to be fine.

"As it turned out, the service was central in this dream I had, and probably prompted it. The actual service was sort of antiseptic and religious. In my dream, it was the same sort of deal, a large amphitheater setting, only my mother and my brother were both there; it wasn't entirely clear why the other members of the audience were there. In the amphitheater were hundreds of seats, all full, and people were milling about, talking as they do before a big performance. There was a stage up front, which was sort of like the auditorium at my old high school. I was wearing my first wedding dress—a big bridal gown. My brother was wearing his dark blue suit and looked very professional. He was busy walking back and forth attending to details related to the show, and then he went out to the lobby. He was probably not going to see the show, but that didn't seem to matter. It mattered that he got to take care of what he was doing, which he seemed to be happy about. The lights were flashing on and off, like they do when it's almost time for the show. All the other people kind of faded into the background and we turned our attention to the stage. Then the event assumed more of the quality of an exhibit, something you wouldn't see from your seat. You had to go up and look at the exhibit. Next, my mother and I made our way up to see these caskets on the stage.

"My mother was with me, holding on to my arm. She was in a little salmon-colored suit, short jacket, A-line skirt, complete with pillbox hat, which she may actually have worn at my first wedding. The first exhibit was James in his casket in his death pose—the one in the photographs that the funeral home sent me. He looked fine. But his being was out in the lobby taking care of business. The dead body was on stage. My mother liked that, James's casket.

"Then we moved to the next box, which was a snake exhibit, like the one at the city zoo behind glass. The box held many snakes, boa constrictors and cobras, living and breathing snakes. Nobody was freaked out. We were just a little puzzled by why they were there, because they had not been there earlier when the lights were flashing off and on. We commented on what a wonderful snake exhibit it was and then went right to the next exhibit. Next there were two caskets. We thought that was kind of odd but we were game. It was interesting. In the first casket was my mother as she had been laid out in her real casket, looking nice in her little peignoir, with all the little things we'd placed in there. My mother looked at this exhibit sort of quizzically, and then looked at the next casket. In this one, the view was of what was underneath, like in those The Way Things Work books, where the cover of something is taken off and you can see what's inside. In this casket she was lying on her side the way she used to sleep all the time, with both hands tucked up under her chin in a prayer-like posture. Her whole body was a skeleton but her face and hair were beautiful, as if she'd just been to the beauty shop. Her hair was perfect. And the mother on my arm who was looking at these exhibits with me said, 'Well, you did a good job. I didn't give you much to work with.'

"Then we moved on to the next box, which was their dog Sparky's casket. It was sort of like a Snoopy-type doghouse casket, only it's not a doghouse. It's a flat box. But Sparky was on his chain up on the top of it. Alive and perky. That's it. Then we went out. That was the end of the show. This dream seemed like they were saying, 'Okay, we want to see what happened. We're coming back to tell you that what you did was all right.' And I felt immensely relieved. I felt totally comforted. I felt really great after that dream. It was a good dream. It was nice to see her. She seemed fine, and James seemed much better than he had when he was alive.

"But I also felt a little strange after that dream: I had no idea why I was dressed in such an elaborate way and I didn't know what to make of the snakes. Those were two items that I just could not figure out. When I told a friend about the dream, she said it was fabulous. Didn't I know that snakes, because they shed their skins, are common symbols of regeneration, a new beginning? I didn't. And the wedding dress was a similar kind of symbol, of my being at the threshold, so to speak, of something new. And here my family was again, sort of giving me away to that new life without them. When I thought about it, all of that fit. That first wedding had been a really happy time for my whole family. My brother hadn't gotten sick yet."

After interviewing the Russells, we discovered another meaning for a dream of writhing snakes: "A symbol of the act or need to overcome a problem [and] of the tests we must pass before receiving initiation."[33] Like a funeral or a wedding, an initiation is a rite of passage, usually one in which the individual advances into maturity and knowledge. Thinking about the complicated, rich and sad history of Susan's family, it seemed that the deaths of her family members had indeed been an ordeal, a test that Susan had endured. In doing so, Susan had reached a new level of wisdom. What did Susan think of this interpretation of her dream? "Oh, yes," she said.

Notes

I Know That Every Single
Word I Say Is Being Listened to

Doctor Ted Parker

At age thirty-six, cancer specialist Ted Parker has been in private practice for only three years. His training included four years of college, four years of medical school, three years of a residency in internal medicine and a three-year fellowship in medical oncology (the study of tumors) and hematology (the study of blood and blood-producing organs). During those years he also moonlighted as a house officer at several hospitals and as an on-call physician at night in case of emergencies.

Ted is married and has two young daughters. As he welcomed us before the interview, the phone rang and he explained that he was on call that night. Ted took that call and two others during the course of the interview, but he proved to be adept at switching his attention back and forth as necessary. As he settled onto a living room sofa, Ted began by qualifying what many would consider the unique demands of his specialty.

"My work is . . . different. If you became a doctor for the experience of doing something and making the patient feel better and hearing the family thank you and tell you that you are a brilliant doctor, oncology is not the field to be in. Unfortunately, in oncology we are still looking for good

119

treatments, which is part of the stimulation of going into this field—that you're always looking to new frontiers and new ideas.

"Not all my patients die. Probably a third to up to half of the people I see are in fine health or have chronic problems that are not life-threatening. You *can* hit a home run in my field—I mean, I have some people who, I think, I cured of leukemia. But on a day-to-day basis, it's little victories—helping people by giving them less pain, or reducing their fears or, in some cases, helping them to die a less complicated or painful death—that are satisfying."

There are times, however, when Ted wonders what satisfaction he does get from this work. He recalled a party where he and a colleague listened as her spouse described his job in advertising and how much fun he has at work. "And she turned to me and said, 'I never really thought about it, but it must be nice to go to work and have fun.' I never have a fun day at work. I do get pleasure in everyday human contacts with colleagues and nurses, but a lot of time I am dealing with people who are dying and for whom this is the most important thing in their lives. I'm dealing with families that are going through a crisis, and along with that I see the dysfunction in the family. All the pathology comes out, and a lot of times it's directed at me. They have no one else to direct it at. Often, it's the children—they're just so unrealistic about what's going on, or the out-of-town children who come in and expect miracles, so I have to deal with a lot of anger, a lot of fear."

Ted continued: "You're dealing with the whole realm of human nature. You may deal with angry patients, although for the most part, the patients and the families I deal with are very nice. When people are faced with a malignancy, they become a little more philosophical, a little kinder, and they tend to make their complaints meaningful. You're not dealing with an athlete who injured his knee and suddenly is out of a big contract. I'm dealing with people who are faced with losing their lives and they tend to be nice and grateful. I sense that they appreciate the things that I try to do for them.

"Most of what I say to people is very serious, and I know that every single word I say is being listened to." One consequence of this is an underlying tension, because "I know that every single thing I say and every single thing I do can be thrown against me in a lawsuit. A lot of doctors complain about this but it is true, and it does not make it any easier."

Another difficulty of Ted's job is that "people, understandably, don't hear what you're telling them. They're in shock, so I tend to talk to people over and over. But then I may have to talk to out-of-town children who have had a rocky relationship with Mom or Dad and now all of a sudden they're flying in after ten years of separation and they're angry at *you* because you're saying that Mom or Dad is dying. Or, I may have a patient who has a malignancy because of years of heavy drinking or smoking, and has the underlying personality problems that lead to that. Then I have to deal with that. So those types of stresses contribute to my day.

"Also, on a daily basis, I see nightmares. It's one thing to deal with somebody who's eighty-five years old and now they have cancer. That's life; they've lived a full life. But quite often I deal with people my age or even younger who have cancer, who have young children. Honestly, in the course of one day, I see more tragedy than most people see in a lifetime. And I can't help but take that to *my* house and *my* family and think, 'Gee, what if this happens to them? What if this happens to me?' I'm often accused of thinking that everything is cancer, but I can't help that because I see a lot of complaints that seem benign on the surface that turn out to be something very, very serious. It colors how you look at life.

"Of course, the flip side happens too. I always tell patients that it's worth their while to come to me, because there are things that other people get excited about that I just don't think are that bad. On the other hand, there are things that I know deep down could really be something bad. By nature, I tend to be calm and a little detached, which serves me well in this field. But I can't help but come home and worry about my wife, Jenny, or the kids, any slight lump or ache or pain. Any little spot on their skin, I think, 'Oh my god, what if this is melanoma?' 'What if she has breast cancer?' Because I just know what the future can bring. It's very stressful.

"Doctors are often accused of being cold and detached and uncaring, and unfortunately, I have to be cold and detached to a certain extent.

I went to the funeral home of one patient, and I will never do that again because it made it a much more personal loss. This was a woman who was my age, and she got very attached to me and was calling me constantly. When I went to see her at the funeral home, it was an odd sensation to have the family thanking me and telling me how wonderful I am when my patient is lying there in the coffin. It also made it more like a friend who had passed away and that hurt. It was a much more personal experience than I really wanted to have. The next day my partner told me that when he started practicing, he did that too. He said, 'But you can't. You'll go crazy. You just cannot do that.'

"So, what I have to do is to walk a fine line between getting very involved with a patient and trying to get to know them and trying to understand their life, but at the same time keeping in mind that this is a stranger. Because, especially in the hospital, I'm going to walk into one person's room and into their tragedy, and then go right next door and enter a whole new tragedy. I just cannot get personally involved. Some internists who have known their patients for years go to their weddings and all that, but I just don't think in my field you can do that. Because you may end up dealing with losing this person, and you just have to keep that separation. I think you can do that and still be very personable with the family and be caring and be their friend. But once that person passes on, you have to put them behind you and move on to the next family and the next patient.

"I protect myself by keeping that distance. The trick is being able to bridge that distance so that patients realize that you care about them and that you are going to do everything you can to help them. I do know other oncologists who don't cross that bridge and are perceived as cold and uncaring, and maybe they are. You also see older oncologists start to lose that compassion or that caring, because they've seen too much and it's time to get out.

"Aside from the obvious—giving drugs or recommending procedures that will save their lives—the best thing I can offer people is my time and my attention. A certain percentage of my patients will be cured of their disease. It's important that I take the time to constantly remind and reassure them of that. There's another percentage of my patients that will have a chronic illness but could well live fairly long and reasonable lives. I have to reinforce that with them, and try to relax them when they see me, because they always think that I'm about to tell them something horrible. The third part of my practice is people who are, just by fate, terminal. They have an untreatable illness, they're going to die, and all I can do with them is to make their lives comfortable. Sometimes the best thing I can do is just sit there and listen to them.

"With families, it's my availability that's important. During office hours and my share of weekends and nights, I'm around if a family member wants to ask questions or has concerns. I'm more than happy to talk to families and explain everything that's going on. A lot of times I'll have a patient with four kids scattered in four parts of the country. Sooner or later, they are all going to want to talk to me, and they are all going to want to get the personal information. I just have to do that. I just have to be honest and let the family know what is going on so that they can make the appropriate decisions."

Ted believes that doing this work has changed him. "I'm definitely a lot older than my thirty-six years, because I've seen so many things that can happen. I used to be pretty happy-go-lucky, but now there are times when I feel like I'm a combat veteran. My sense of humor about things, the way I look at things—I can't help but be colored by what I do every day. It has taken away some of the innocence and joy in life.

"Probably it is preferable to go through life and not think about dying, or what happens when you die, because no one knows. So it is easier to just put it off and think, 'Well, I'm young, I don't have to think about this.' But people in my profession are forced to look at the fact that, yeah, people die all the time and you know it can happen at any time.

"It has also changed how I look at life. To get to where I am and to do what I did, I always had to delay gratification, to plan for the future and sacrifice to get where I wanted to go. But now I know that my life or anyone's life could change tomorrow. I could wake up tomorrow and suddenly feel a lump somewhere and my life would be completely different. Nowadays, if push comes to shove, I'm more in favor of enjoying the moment rather than saying, 'Gee, *next* year we'll do this.' You don't know how long you're on earth, so you might as well enjoy what time you have here. I've seen so many different things. I can recall some really tragic deaths, particularly parents with little kids. I remember one young man died of melanoma with a little eight- or nine-year-old daughter just lying on him, crying and crying. *That* I remember.

"One motivation going into this field was hearing or reading about people who have been to 'the other side,' or have seen the light and then have come back to earth. I haven't met anybody like that yet, but I have met people who clearly are ready to die, whether because of their religion or because they're just comfortable with death. It's not so much because they want the suffering to end; they just seem ready to die. I remember one older woman, a very strong woman, who at the end developed an acute leukemia that was intractable to treatment. All we could do was give her blood transfusions to support her. It was just going to be a matter of days or weeks before she had some type of overwhelming infection or bleeding episode that was going to cause her to die. She hung on long enough for her son to come in from some distant place to see her for the last time and talk with her, and she was actually in very good condition, very coherent and comfortable talking with him. Then the morning after he left, I came into the hospital room and she pulled me really close to her and she said, 'Now I want you to help me to die. I'm ready now.' She was very calm about it. She wanted me to use my judgment to help her die comfortably as fast as possible, and I have no problem with that at all.

"If you want to talk about that, I personally think Dr. Kevorkian is crazy. I have this conversation with a lot of patients. Dr. Kevorkian has gone beyond the pale. To a certain extent, I understand what he's espousing, but I think he's nuts. Part of the reason I say this is that I have helped many a person die and I don't make sure I'm on the six o'clock news talking about it, and I don't deposit the body outside the police headquarters. I think there are plenty of doctors out there who help patients die peacefully and don't make a big deal out of it. If you go out and take that one extra active step to kill somebody, and if you do that more than a few times, something has to change inside of you. I have a problem with Dr. Kevorkian. I think he's a dangerous person.

"I know I have probably helped thousands of people die, and I have no problem doing that—with increasing pain medicines as much as needed so they can rest comfortably, knowing full well they could just fall asleep and pass away; with rapidly facilitating someone coming off a respirator knowing full well they need it to stay alive, but that they're basically just going to be a vegetable stuck on the respirator. I make these decisions a lot, in full conversation and agreement with the family and whatever legal parameters we need to follow, but I have no problem helping people to die. If you don't have quality of life and you don't want to live like this, I understand that. The flip side is, if I have a patient who absolutely insists on everything being done, I will do everything they want. From my experience, I know how ugly that can be. But some people want to do everything possible, so we do everything possible.

"I have to think that helping people to die is more common in my field. I know certain specialties that are a lot less inclined to take a humane approach to a dying person. There are some physicians or some fields of medicine that have a very difficult time accepting this. But I've always had that philosophy, and everything I've seen in this field has made it easier for me to feel this way. But I do see doctors who have unrealistic attitudes about a dying patient. Unfortunately, I still meet oncologists who are very reluctant to give pain medicines, and I still see oncologists who, up to the very last minute, will push chemotherapy or do anything to keep the patient alive. I think they're in a distinct minority, but I do see them. And I can't understand it. Especially the pain medicine—I have a hard time understanding how any doctor, let alone an oncologist, can be hesitant to give someone pain medicine."

But Ted could not suggest a particular type of specialist who would be more likely to let patients dictate when the end should come. "It just comes down to the individual physician. Whatever the illness is, hopefully there are physicians in that area who are more reasonable than others."

Ted said that he sees his patients a good deal less now than he did five years ago, and that includes being present at their deaths. "You see more of that when you're a resident, because you're just on the floor all the time, in the hospital all the time, fourteen to eighteen hours a day. I saw quite a few people die as a resident, and I wouldn't describe it as beautiful. Certainly in emergency situations it's quite violent. To resuscitate a person, we do quite a bit to the human body: shocking them, chest compressions—and we break the ribs doing chest compressions—putting tubes in them, putting IV lines in them. It's actually very violent. Even when someone is just slowly passing away in their sleep, I wouldn't describe it as beautiful. I'd describe it as cold, ugly, kind of frightening. But it's interesting also in that when you see a dead person, a dead body, it is clearly not the person you were dealing with. It's a body. I was raised a Catholic. I'm not really a practicing Catholic right now and I'm not sure what my religious views are, but clearly I can see something that I almost could describe as a soul. Something has left that person. And yes, I'm sure it's the biochemistry of the brain and all that, but there's something gone, and it's odd. I have had circumstances where I was in there talking to a patient who actually looked fairly healthy, walked out of the room and two minutes later, the patient is dead. It's just odd, looking at that person and realizing a minute ago they were functional, and now they are no longer there. They went *somewhere*.

"These days I occasionally happen to be present when someone is dying, but I don't deal with it as intimately anymore. Maybe that goes back to how I protect myself. I've spent a few years being much more intimate with people dying and I've seen enough. The less I have to watch it, it's probably easier for me."

Ted's description of a typical day reveals the complexity of a modern medical practice. He sees those patients who come to his office or are in the several hospitals where he practices. But he is also responsible for patients in nursing homes, inpatient hospices or their own homes. "The bulk of it now is seeing people in the office. The way health care has changed, it's both by the direction of insurance companies and in my interest to see as many people and do as much in my office as I can. And people do fine. Ten years ago everyone got chemotherapy in the hospital. Now 90 percent of the chemotherapy is given in my office. So patients get the chemotherapy and go home to their own houses. We have much better medicines for nausea and pain these days, so people are quite comfortable and can live reasonably normal lives while they're getting treated. So I spend a lot of time in my office, where I mostly see people who are mobile and functional, living a fairly decent or close to normal life. Then at some point in the day I go to the hospital and see people there. If I'm in a hospital with an oncology floor, I start rounding, seeing twenty to thirty people, one after the other, who *are* sicker, whose illnesses are more life-threatening. I go in and examine them, talk to them, take care of immediate problems.

"It's during those rounds that I still occasionally happen to be present when someone is dying. If I come into a room and the person is dying and the family is there, I make sure that I take the time to talk to the family, address any questions or concerns, try to convey my sympathy. Even when they're strangers, I feel sorry for the family. It's a tough time and I do try to spend time there to help them. And there are times when I see a dying patient who looks uncomfortable and I get more involved, making sure they're getting enough medicines or giving them extra medicines.

"I refer a lot of patients to hospice and I supervise hospice patients, but not on site. I'm legally the physician of record for a lot of hospice patients, so the nurse can call me if there are problems. In hospice the nurses are much more involved, and it's really the visiting nurses and the hospital nurses who get to know the family intimately. They are the ones in the house with the dying patient, and a lot of what I do is over the phone. That's why when you establish a relationship with a good visiting nurse, you try to continue doing business with that person. Because this is someone who is representing you in the person's house, and you need to trust their judgment and what they're telling you, because a lot of this *is* going on over the phone. When nurses you trust and have good judgment and are intelligent tell you that someone's in pain, you believe it. When they tell you someone's having breathing problems and this is why, you believe it and respond appropriately. Unfortunately, that doesn't always happen. You get visiting nurses calling you who are panicking about the slightest thing, and then you just don't believe what they're telling you."

When that happens, Ted responds conservatively. "You always have the option of putting the patient in the hospital. A lot of times, families don't want to go to the hospital. People hate hospitals: They're worried about the cost, they're worried about how long it takes for something to get done, they're worried about the poor level of care, and they prefer to be at home. But if push comes to shove and you're not sure, you err on the side of caution, put the person in the hospital so you can see first-hand what's going on. Or, if they're not *that* sick you can have them come to the office so you can see them and make a judgment. And it *is* true: Experience is the best teacher. Usually, I can look at someone pretty quickly and get an accurate idea of what's going on."

Although Ted does not visit the homes where family members and other loved ones care for his patients, he consults with family members. He ventured an opinion of what motivates those who take on the burden of caretaking. "A certain amount of time, it's out of love; a certain amount of time, it's out of a sense of decency and obligation. Also, people are aware of the quality of care you often get in an institution such as a nursing home. Everyone is aware of stories of people who were ignored or even abused in nursing homes, and they don't want that to happen to their loved ones. Sometimes it's a financial consideration: They don't have insurance coverage to pay for the nursing home. That's usually not the problem with an inpatient hospice, but I'm sure finances can enter into it. I think it's mainly that they want to really help the person until the very end."

But Ted also feels that there are some families and loved ones who should not undertake caregiving. "I'm dealing with a very difficult case right now where a man who's divorced is living with this woman. They're in their sixties; she has her health problems and he has a terminal illness. He wants additional chemotherapy, which is going to be futile. He's not absolutely terminal yet, but he's not strong enough to take care of himself. And he wants to go back home and have his girlfriend take care of him, but she does not want to do it anymore. She's worried about her health and feels that she can't do it. They both tell their side of the story to me, and I tell them they have to talk to each other about this. But you get caught in this triangle that never ends. I agree with the woman: She is *not* in good health. There's no way she can give him adequate care. You run into situations like this and you run into families that, even with their best intentions, are not going to be around enough to give adequate patient care. Sick people need a lot of attention. They need help going to the bathroom, they need to be bathed, they need pain medicine. There are a lot of unpleasant things that happen to a sick, dying person. Some people just are not physically capable of handling that, or emotionally capable of handling that. Or, because of work and other family commitments, they don't have the time. Sometimes it's best for the patient's health that they are placed in an inpatient hospice or a nursing home.

"As for home care, I have a couple of friends who are hospice nurses, and the stories that they could tell you! There are a lot of odd people in this world. The circumstances that the visiting nurse comes into at the home are sometimes bizarre. Who's to say what's right and what's wrong, as long as the family and/or patient are happy, if they're getting adequate care or they're comfortable. You also run into the situation where the patient insists on going home, or the family insists on taking the patient home, and you know that they are not going to be capable of doing it. Maybe it sounds cold, but even though you know that they're going to end up coming right back, you let the patient go home. A few days later, they end up back in the hospital because they're dehydrated or they've been having pain or they're too weak. After that I think it's easier for them to accept, 'Okay, I can go to a nursing home.' Personally, I wouldn't want to go to a nursing home, so I can understand that people refuse our suggestions. But I think nursing homes are getting better. Because of insurance and business, more hospitals are trying to get involved in nursing homes. Every once in a while, on call at night, you'll get a call from a nursing home from a nurse who's had experience with a cancer patient and feels strongly that the patient is not getting adequate pain medication at the nursing home or something along those lines. But that's few and far between. I think more often than not these days, people get reasonable care in a nursing home."

Determining exactly where a patient is in the dying process can be problematic, said Ted. "What I almost universally tell patients is that they will know when they're dying. I have a hard time with the type of doctor who breezes into the room and says, 'You have 6.23 months left to live.' Because none of us knows. Too often, I see people who have been told that they have x number of months to live and now they have exceeded that. I don't think that's fair to that patient. The day before they're supposed to die, they must sit there thinking, 'Well, that's it. Tomorrow my time is up.' Quite a few people live well beyond what they were told they could expect."

But "if they're getting weaker and losing weight, it's clear" that the end is approaching. "There are certain things that I can tell from blood tests. If the kidneys are failing, certain liver enzymes are getting worse, you know that it's a matter of time. I think most people know when they're dying because they just feel weaker and weaker, sleep more, lose interest in everything, lose more and more of their appetite. It's just the general behavior. When they're pulling away from everybody, you can tell they're going to die. Certainly at the very end—the pattern of the patient's breathing, if they have a lot of fluid in their lungs, if they're totally comatose—obviously it's getting close. But even at that point, it depends on the age of the patient. If you have a young person who has a healthy heart but has metastatic cancer, they can remain comatose for quite some time. Sometimes it can drag out for quite a while. At that point all you can tell the family is, 'They are sick enough that anything can happen at any time.' Sometimes it can carry on for weeks. You always hope that that won't happen, but every once in a while you see it. It's tough on the family."

Although he has not had any patients "who have received some big message from above," Ted has noticed certain patterns in how dying people perceive their passage into death. "A lot of times, you hear elderly patients start talking to their mothers. I had one or two people tell me about a dream of a box underneath them. I have a feeling a lot of times that people know they're dying but don't want to talk to me about it, because they're afraid I'll come right out and say, 'Oh yes, you're definitely dying, you're going to be dead in two weeks.' You have to walk a fine line between how much you tell the patients and, in reverse, how much the patient is telling you. I'm sure patients don't tell me every symptom, for fear that I'm going to say, 'That's definitely a sign that you're worse off.' And a lot of people are private. I'm not sure that when *I'm* going through this that I'm going to say, 'Gee, doctor, I think I'm closer to death.' People prefer to keep things to themselves. I've had a lot of spouses tell me that their husband or wife told them something they didn't tell me, that they know they're dying. A lot of times people are aware that they're getting sicker but don't verbalize it. I don't see a clear checklist or orderly stages that people go through. Certainly some people are scared to death and do everything they can to avoid death, but the majority of my patients seem to accept it gradually and slowly.

"It also depends on what's going on in their personal lives. A lot of elderly persons who have already lost their spouses don't care. They just want to be sure they're not in pain. The younger ones tend to want to do everything possible. It's very tricky. There are a lot of things we can offer and with all the publicity these days, everyone knows about them, but the results are very questionable. I'm particularly thinking about bone marrow transplants for breast cancer. It's still very, very debatable if they're of any benefit, and yet the technology is there, it's very easy. Say you have a desperate thirty-five-year-old woman who wants to live, and she definitely wants a bone marrow transplant. What do you do? You know some people are clearly not going to benefit from it. The toxicity isn't as bad as it used to be, but it's going to cost a lot of money and you're putting them through an ordeal. You know it is not going to work, but the person wants that because they don't want to know the truth, and this is part of their bargaining with death. They want to do everything they can to fight it off, they're waiting for that miracle, and it's something we just have to handle in the best way possible.

"Death is the great unknown. I mean, who knows what happens? I have not met anyone yet who has had a near-death experience and come back and talked about it." Speculating about those patients who feel comfortable about dying, Ted thought "it's because of their religious beliefs. For others, it's a sense of fulfillment that they have lived their lives and done all they can. Particularly with the elderly, when they are no longer physically or mentally capable of doing what they like to do, it's just not worth being alive anymore; or that they don't want to have any pain. A lot of them just say they're so tired that they've had enough. It's probably comforting to say that the majority of the people I deal with don't seem to fear death. It's rare that you get the really desperate frightened person, which is a little reassuring. You even meet some young people who are very calm about what's going to happen. A lot of the older people just accept this as life. They're ready to pass on, to whatever may happen."

Although they are "totally anecdotal," said Ted, there are "old wives' tales" within the medical profession. "When you have an older person admitted around their birthday, it always makes you nervous. You think, 'This is it, they've come full circle.' When you see someone who has recently lost a spouse, it makes you very nervous, either because they've just given up or maybe they're destined to go at the same time. When people start talking about a deceased loved one, or talking about someone who's obviously not there, you get the sense that they're going to die. These are little things that make you nervous, unless you're expecting them to die.

"I have had people tell me that they know they're going to die, but I don't think I've had anyone say, 'I had a dream last night that God came down and told me that it's my turn to die today,' not anything along those lines. But I wouldn't expect people to tell me everything. If they're in the hospital sick and dying, I'm spending minutes with them; I'm not in there for three hours talking to them. I'm sure there are a lot of things that happen that I'm not aware of, that I'm not told about by the family or the patient. Perhaps if I spent more time asking people, I might be hearing more, but it comes back to what I say. I know that every little thing I'm saying is being interpreted. I try to not scare people. As their doctor, it's not best if I come in and say, 'So, have you had any visions of your death yet?'"

As for his own beliefs about what happens when we die, Ted said he has "no idea. I really don't. When I was in sixth grade in Catholic school, I thought about it a lot because of all the Catholic teaching. But you'll go crazy. Who knows what happens? I mean, if there's an afterlife and eternity and if there's a God. I've just accepted that you'll just never know this answer until you die. I'm comfortable with that. I just decided not to think about it.

"I've read some about religion, but right now I do not attend any type of religious ceremony. I'm not atheistic, I just don't know. If push comes to shove, do I pray to God? Sure. That's just something I haven't decided to figure out yet. But to firmly believe you know what happens when you die, that's just crazy, isn't it? It's the great unknown, no one knows. I guess if I had to vote, is there something beyond life, yes or no, I'd say yes. I just have to believe there's some reason for all this. But who knows?"

If Ted were to put together a survival kit for families going through the death of a loved one, he would include, "First, Valium, sedatives. I prescribe sedatives to family members if they want them. I have no problem helping people with that. However, I think anti-depressants are too liberally prescribed for people with terminal illnesses. It's *appropriate* to be depressed under these circumstances.

"Second, I'd tell families to talk about it. I'm not a touchy-feely type of person, but it is very beneficial for people to talk about things—with the patient or with each other. There are a lot of conflicts, and there are things that need to be resolved or else you're going to torture yourself for the rest of your life wishing you had spoken to the person about that.

"From the standpoint of a doctor, what would help is for families to find a doctor who they can trust and believe in, and not play games with that doctor. Especially if there are multiple family members, it is best that either one person represent the family or that everyone is there at the same time as much as possible. Because I juggle a bunch of patients, I cannot say the exact same words to every family member." This can lead to confusion and more phone calls as family members struggle to reconcile their impressions of what each has been told.

In addition, Ted recommended, "Try not to develop a hostile relationship with a doctor. I understand that a lot of people don't like doctors and are unhappy about the cost of health care, but you need to find a doctor who you trust and who you are going to listen to. Too often I see people going to too many doctors and getting too many opinions. You go to ten doctors, you're going to get ten opinions. Instead, find one person who's going to give you health advice and tell you what's going on medically. Then just put your family into that person's hands and trust what they say. If you start getting different opinions and going to different centers and challenging every little thing, it's going to become a nightmare. Every doctor knows he or she can be sued by every single person they talk to. So the doctor is naturally going to get defensive and that's just bad.

"Also, keep in mind that the most important thing is the patient. Whatever problems you may have, that person dying right now has bigger problems and don't lose sight of that. Find out what your health insurance policy is and is not going to cover. Find out about coverage for hospice, for nursing-home visits, for supplies, for medications—just so there are no surprises at the last second."

Because Ted is frequently on call, he suggested that families and patients "try to have problems taken care of as much as possible during the week, during office hours. Don't ignore something until the middle of the night. Too often we get phone calls at 3:00 A.M. about something we can do nothing about, so we say, 'Well, go to the hospital.' Then they're pissed about that. And if people wait until Sunday night to get their narcotics refilled and there's no pharmacy open, they can't get their narcotic. Things like that. I know there's a lot on the person's mind, but try to look ahead and head off problems before they happen.

"Don't hesitate to voice your opinion and talk about what's concerning you with health care providers, but you have to respect that those people have a job to do and that they can't spend their entire lives with just you and your family. Too often in the hospital, the family is at the nursing station every five seconds wanting this, wanting that, demanding this, demanding that, 'I want to talk to the doctor right now,' this and that. Either everyone gets so nervous that they overtreat the person, or they get so ticked off that they just naturally start to avoid them. Either way, you're hurting yourself. If you just let the medical staff direct you through this, you'll be better off. If you have religious feelings, let them help bring you peace of mind.

"But I don't think there's any way you can prepare anyone for taking care of someone who's dying. It's just one big, horrible nightmare. Your life has changed, nothing is going to go right. Gilda Radner, who died of cancer, wrote a book called *It's Always Something*. It *is* always something when someone's dying. Things are falling apart. Things don't always go right and things don't always go well and there's just no way to prepare for what's going to happen.

"It's a nightmare for people who are losing a loved one. Or they're dealing with someone who's been a pain his or her whole life and now they've got to take care of that person. It's not infrequent for me to take care of a man who's been a very abusive spouse, and now he's sick and dying and he's expecting his wife to do everything to help. Some people have lived a full life and they're ready to die, but even then it's not pleasant. The person's dying. It's frightening, it's a big mystery. They can be uncomfortable, they can be short of breath, they can be in pain, they can smell. The body is great when it works, but when it doesn't work, it can be really pretty disgusting.

"I am always asked why I am an oncologist. I honestly feel that this is what I was meant to do. My personality is detached enough that although it gets to me sometimes, I can handle it better than other people. I'm a very confident person but I'm not an egomaniac, so when my patient dies, I can deal with it and still feel that I'm helping people a lot.

"I first got started in oncology because I became very interested in DNA and how it controls everything about life. And that's the basics of cancer. It's amazing how the most minute change in DNA can ultimately cause a person to suffer a terrible death and the family to fall apart. It's just a single change of one sugar or one amino acid that can cause all this. That's pretty amazing."

Ironically, treating patients means that Ted cannot spend much time on the research end of his field. "Unfortunately, these days I'm getting further and further from the basic science. It's exponentially increasing and it's hard for me to read it. I keep up enough to know what they're talking about, but these are academic issues, whereas I see this stuff in the real world every day."

Although Ted characterized current treatment methods as "very crude—we kill everything and hope the good guys win and come back"—Ted expects that slowly "we're turning cancer into a chronic illness like diabetes." He pointed out that AIDS may well become a "chronic viral infection," but he does not think that "we're ever going to hit a home run" and develop a vaccination or cure for cancer. With the exceptions of smoking, exposure to radiation and some genetic factors, "we don't know what causes cancer." We do know that "usually it's the side effects of cancer that kill—malnutrition, infection, blood clots, heart attacks." There's much uncertainty, but Ted believes that "good, healthy habits" are probably preventive—"exercising, eating well, not smoking."

Ted's father is a lawyer, and together they embody the classic contention between doctors and lawyers. Most doctors regard lawyers as an abomination, according to Ted, and malpractice suits are a constant threat to every physician. But his father will point out that lawyers are necessary because doctors don't police themselves well. Ted had to agree that there are bad doctors. "They're out there, and it's embarrassing." Ted said that he encounters them especially in rural areas and in the Veteran's Administration system. "Everyone knows people who shouldn't have graduated from medical school. But once you're in, you're in. They're not going to toss you out halfway through, when you've got $50,000 in loans and can sue them." He recalled an instance when he and other residents tried to take action against an incompetent superior but with unsatisfactory results. He also described one doctor who is so obviously weird that even his physical appearance is bizarre. He would never see such a doctor twice and suggested to others, "If you think someone's a nut, don't bother to see him or her again."

Health Maintenance Organizations (HMOs) may help in this regard, as they seem more selective. Although Ted has many reservations about managed care, it does appear that it will help to prevent some of the worst incompetence. "Medicine *can* do a better job."

Ted surmised that about half of his patients try alternative treatments, but he is "very skeptical" of these claims. Although he and other conventional doctors tell clients, "I'll be honest with you," he doubts that alternative practitioners do. If someone with a terminal illness wants to meditate or drink green tea, Ted does not protest, but patients should not have the same expectations of these measures as they have of his treatments. "I'm a physical scientist. What I do to a patient I can do everywhere in the world and get the same effects."

Sometimes the work is discouraging, Ted reflected, when "I think, 'Why am I doing this? I'm just making money by giving people drugs that don't work.' But I know it's not true. There are clearly malignancies with which we have solid proof that what we do makes a difference. There are other cancers for which what we do doesn't make a difference, and I'll be honest about that. It's a weird area to work in. But see, I look at hospice nurses and think, how can *they* do that?"

Ted then described the difference between "what nurses do and I do. I probably deal with ten times as many patients as they deal with at once. I have everyone calling me, everyone wanting this, wanting that, sign this, be here, go there. I cover four or five hospitals. That's my burden, whereas the hospice nurses have to watch the very personal things. They're my buffer from the ultimate reality.

"In private practice I deal with people all the time. That's what I do. And I really don't mind talking to patients. I feel sorry for these people. At least the people I deal with have legitimate reasons to complain to me. When my patients say, 'I really hurt,' or 'I'm really tired,' or 'I'd really like to have a taste for food,' I know there's a reason for it. Those are real things and they are real people. I don't mind talking about that, trying to help them." The irony is that when Ted is off duty, "I'm often accused of being antisocial, but I deal with so many people all day long!

"I'm like the infantry, seeing the reality of what happens all the time. Then there's academic oncology, which is a whole different world. These people rarely see patients, and they travel to a lot of nice meetings and sit up there and talk about the future and all the new cures and advances. A year later we realize these advances don't work, but the academic oncologists don't deal with that part. 'Oh, it doesn't work? Well we have a new cure over here.' So that keeps *them* going. But then, they might spend thirty years chasing some theory and then suddenly they're fifty-five years old and they realize they've been chasing a total crock. They've wasted their entire lives on research that doesn't work. At least I know there are a certain number of people I've helped. There are some people I've made feel better, and some people I've cured.

"I have this one lung cancer patient, a really nice guy. In the operating room they hit more cancer than was apparent in the x-rays and they just closed him back up; basically he was doomed. Chemotherapy is not that successful with this type of cancer, so we gave him radiation and a little chemotherapy. It's been three and a half years now, and he has no evidence of lung cancer. It shrank and disappeared. Every oncologist has a certain number of these patients—they just have had a fortunate response, and he's one of them. I know this patient likes me and I like seeing him. He keeps coming back to visit me, but just once I would like him to say, 'Boy, you're brilliant! You saved my life!' He's never said that.

"I have seen some people where I'd have to say that what happened to them is a miracle. Not many, but you certainly remember those. One lady had a lymphoma that was widespread and had resisted all treatment. She was turned down for a bone marrow transplant, and we sent her home to die. She was really beat up from all the chemo, and we just said, 'Don't try to come to the office, we'll handle stuff over the phone.' We sent her home with IV nutrition and IV pain medicines. She figured she was going to die soon, and we got her in good enough shape to go on this final trip she wanted to go on. After that, she would come in occasionally, if she had a cold or was nauseated or some other minor problem. About a year later I finally said, 'You know, not to be cold here, but we sent you home to die and you're not dead.' We sent her off for x-rays and all her lymphoma was gone, completely gone. Rare disease, rare case of lymphoma, maybe some kind of an immune mechanism, who knows? She moved to another state, she went to nursing school, and the last time I talked to her, she was fine. She said that she has had a lot of friends praying for her, so I've asked her to mention me once in a while. She knows somebody!"

Notes

139

You Only Get to Die Once—
You Should Get to Do It
Decently

Jim Viviano

Jim Viviano, a clinical psychologist, and Don Belmont, a psychiatrist, had lived together as a couple for over ten years when Jim met Alex Lesko, a bartender. Troubled by unresolved conflicts with Don and knowing himself to be monogamous by nature, Jim moved out of their house, settled into his own apartment, and began dating Alex.

But during the following two years, first Don and then Alex learned that they were HIV positive. This grave news would lead to a situation in which what began as a classic romantic triangle became one of tolerance, need and endurance. When Don's health began to deteriorate, Jim moved back to the house to take care of him. Don was a highly respected physician who wanted no one—including his family—to know the nature of his illness, and Jim was determined to honor these wishes. Neither could abide the prospect of Don's death being minimized, as "just another fag dying of AIDS." Although today AIDS has spread far beyond the confines of the gay community, at the time of their crisis, the AIDS epidemic was characterized by anti-homosexual moralizing and victim-blaming.

Don's decline was precipitous, taking less than three months. Jim worked hard to attend to Don, to maintain his own work schedule and to keep Don's secret. When Alex's symptoms began to grow serious only six weeks after Don's death, Jim became his primary support as well. By the time Alex died a year later, Jim found himself manifesting symptoms of an emotional breakdown and began seeing a psychoanalyst. We met with Jim a year after Alex's death, and the healing has been ongoing.

The recent deaths of his partners had made Jim reflect as he never had before on the death of his mother. When Jim was seven, his mother, pregnant with her seventh child, was diagnosed with cancer. She died in childbirth. Jim began by explaining the effect of his mother's illness on his adult experience.

"I had assumed for much of my life that, being Catholic, my mother had made the decision to save the child and not herself." It was many years before Jim understood that "it wouldn't have made any difference anyway, so she decided to proceed with the pregnancy, trying to live long enough to deliver the baby.

"She would spend months in the hospital and then come home for months because there was nothing more they could do. Our house was two stories and she was confined to my parents' bedroom suite. The door was always closed, but you would often hear moaning and screaming, sounds of agony coming from behind the door. Whenever we would hear those sounds, Dad or my grandmother, who had come to stay with us and who was my mother's primary caretaker, would go running upstairs and disappear behind the door. The door would close again and ultimately the sounds would stop. There was always this mystery about what was going on behind the door.

"We would only see my mother during those periods when they would bring her in or out of the house on a gurney. But I always knew she was up there. Even as a kid, I thought how isolated that was. All of us were downstairs, and I knew she was in this one room way up at the top of the house, alone, dying, which, I think, really did play a major role in the way I handled things with Don and Alex. I was determined that they were not going to do this alone in the way I felt that she had. Neither one of them was going to be pushed off into a room and left alone."

Throughout an angry adolescence and for years afterward, Jim blamed his father for his mother's pregnancy and for what he believed was the "inappropriate religious decision" that led to her early death. But when, at age thirty-seven, Jim cared for Don as he died, Jim realized that his father had also been thirty-seven when his wife had died. "I felt I was retracing my father's footsteps," he said, then vocalized the theme music of the *Twilight Zone*. "I got into these magical thoughts like, 'This is what you get for not having any sympathy for your father. You were doomed to relive his life. You have been so unempathetic to what his life must have been like that you were going to have the same experience.'"

Since Don's death, Jim and his father have undergone a "dramatic change in our relationship. It's as if my eyes were opened, and it's only now that I can really understand. I only lost my lover; he lost his wife and three kids by that same age. It has radically changed things for us. We've never explicitly discussed it, but implicitly I think that he understands that there's nothing like the experience to make you understand."

Jim continued: "There was this horrible period of constant death when I was a kid." Two of Jim's siblings had died before he was born. Asked about his birth order, he had to chronicle the family births repeatedly to figure it out. He had been fifth of the seven children born, and the third of the four survivors. "The last death was the child that my mother did manage to deliver before she died, Michael. He was not doing well from the outset. But what complicated that further was that my father refused to pick the baby up from the hospital. When the hospital said, 'Look, we can't keep this baby here forever,' my father said, 'I don't want the baby, keep the baby.' It was my grandparents who retrieved the baby and brought it home. He was quite ill and did not live very long past that, so I never had a chance to attach. It was only a few months later. In part, the baby's death was attributed to a failure to thrive. He was a weak child and there was just so little available for him that he died. But again, for Dad, in retrospect I can't imagine what that would be like."

It seemed that Jim had experienced a great deal of death at a very young age. But, he explained, "that all happened in a flurry. By the time I'd reached my eighth birthday, there was this incredible reprieve." And for the next thirty years, "death took a holiday. There were no more significant deaths" until those of Don and Alex. "My favorite line these days is, 'Denial ain't just a river in Egypt.' It was as if, for all those years, death was this distant thing. It just stopped happening. The family moved on, and there was no more of it after that."

As much as he knew what was coming, Jim was still "floored when it happened." Even during Don's illness, although both men knew he was not getting better, "we didn't address it." And at first, things went slowly. It was not until two years after learning that he was HIV positive that "Don's hand began to give him trouble." Don was an accomplished pianist who "loved playing classical music. It was at the end of February that he began complaining, 'I can't control my left hand.' He got a consult" and the conclusion was that this was "some stroke type of thing, but no big deal. He could still use it, it's just that he couldn't control it to play. It distressed Don so much that he dragged me out to buy a brand-new baby grand piano. It was this counterphobic response, like, 'No, I'm not going to lose this, and I'll show you I'm not going to lose this; I'm gonna buy a new piano.'"

Within a few weeks, "he began to lose control of his left arm, but Don was a bit of a symptomizer, and I kept dismissing this. But by mid-March he was saying, 'Something is wrong. I want you to go away with me.' He wanted to go to Europe, and I wouldn't do it. I had just finished an internship. I didn't have the money to go; he wanted to pay but I couldn't accept it from him." They were able to manage a trip to Florida, and during that period Don "just kept repeating, 'Something is wrong, something is wrong.' We got back from Florida and I started my new job on April 1." Ten days later, "we were in a neighborhood restaurant. We had ordered and Don stood up from the table and began pacing back and forth in the dining room.

"I said, 'Donald, sit down. What is wrong with you?' He got very agitated. 'I don't know but I don't feel right.' I said, 'Oh, please don't start this here. Settle down.' He kept pacing around and got more and more agitated, and then he lit up a cigarette. 'I can't sit down. I can't tell you why. I feel very strange. I want to get out of here right now.'"

Jim told Don to go to the car while he paid the check for meals that had not yet been brought to them. He found Don sitting on the curb next to the car, begging to be taken home. But when Don "got up off the curb, he fell back. He couldn't get his balance. He would reach for the door and he would glide off from the door handle. I finally got him in his car and drove him back to the house, and he couldn't make his legs go. It was as if he forgot how to walk. He was reaching out and couldn't tell where anything was. He was totally spatially disoriented. I thought, 'Holy shit! There really is something wrong.' I got him through the front door and he let out this moan, fell to the floor and had this explosive vomiting attack. He was lying on the floor, and in between the retching, he was telling me, 'I don't know what's wrong. I've just lost control of my body.' His eyes were terrified. But he was able to speak, he was cognizant and he was self-monitoring. I could see the physician in him kicking in. He was doing systems checks, reporting to me: 'My coordination is off, my spatial ability is gone, I don't feel as if I have any voluntary muscle control anymore. My breathing is erratic. I don't know what this is.'"

Jim helped Don into bed and went back downstairs. "I just started cleaning up, not knowing what to do. I'd always relied on Don for this kind of stuff. So I walked back upstairs and I sat on the edge of the bed and said, 'How are you doing?' He said, 'Less stimulation is helping. Keep the lights off, keep the sound down . . . ' He said that breezes felt very odd, so I closed the windows; we turned off the lights, we sat in the dark with no motion, no sound." Although the quiet was helping Don, he told Jim, "I can't sense anything anymore. It's as if everything in my body is doing new things and I don't know any of them." Jim offered to take him to the hospital, but Don was emphatic: "No! I don't want to go to the hospital. Just stay here with me—just stay here."

Jim stayed until after Don had fallen asleep, then went home and called Alex at 2:00 A.M. "Something's going on with Don; I can't figure it out. I'm going to go to bed and then go over in the morning and see how he is. It seems better if I'm not bothering him." Jim was able to shower and get to sleep, but woke abruptly at six and rushed back to Don's. Don was still asleep, but when he woke, he still felt strange. He concluded, "I think we better go to the emergency room." It would prove to be a frustrating trip. Don was able to walk better than he could the night before and didn't seem especially compromised. When asked about what happened, Don could only answer, "I don't know. I threw up and I fell down." The attending physician was unimpressed and wanted to send him home.

Jim recalled, "I kept telling these guys, 'This is not what Don is like. He's flatter than usual. He's not as alert. He's got this crooked smile.' But mostly I couldn't organize myself anymore. Panic was beginning to rise." Then a doctor who had started medical school the year Don graduated happened to pass by and recognize him.

"He said, 'Dr. Belmont, what are you doing here?' I gave this real cross, 'Who are you?' He said, 'I'm the director of emergency medicine.'

"I said, 'Could you please help me? I can't seem to convey to anyone that something's going on.' I listed several things, and the doctor did some quick checks and asked, 'Don, what do you think is going on?' Don said, 'I feel very strange.' So they decided to do a CT scan."

The test revealed that Don had suffered a stroke, but an atypical one. "They found damage to huge areas of the cortex but nothing that involved any of the voluntary reflexes or muscles. For some reason this had not affected his speech, his vision or any of his motor movements. Over the course of the day, they came up with this model of what had happened: The virus had become active in the cortex and was literally just chomp, chomp, chomp, chomping away."

After this trip to the hospital, Jim and Don underwent a role reversal. Jim realized that he would have to be Don's medical interpreter and advocate. "Don was one of these people who was born to be a doctor. I felt like I had to be that kind of a doctor for him, because he wasn't going to be able to do this for himself. I was going to have to be the advocate of a physician in a world of physicians. I was so frustrated."

Paralyzed on one side, Don was unable to care for himself after leaving the hospital. Jim moved into Don's house to take care of him. "I brought him home and things were very hard, but we were laboring along. I knew he wasn't getting better, he knew he wasn't getting better, but we didn't address it. We developed all these routines. What we would do for him to stand up was hilarious. I'd get him sitting on the side of the bed, and then I'd sit next to him. Then he'd link his arm around me and I'd stand up and we became this unit. We would literally walk around like that. My hand around his waist and his arm around my neck, and we would walk into the kitchen or we would go upstairs. It was as if he was using my body and coordination to move his body. And that's how I handled it from April 11th up until the time he died" six weeks later.

During those weeks, Jim found himself "doing this insane schedule. Thank God I worked fifteen minutes away from the house. Initially, Don didn't want nurses in the house." There was a visiting nurse who came every few days to check on Don's progress, but the day-to-day caretaking was left entirely to Jim. "Internally I was very angry, because it left a whole lot more work for me, but I was determined to respect every wish Don had. 'You don't want nurses, we won't do nurses.' But that meant that I was getting up at five and six o'clock in the morning to get ready for work, to then get him out of bed, clean him up, get him dressed, get him downstairs, get him fed and set up on the couch for the day. Because I was going to work, I had to anticipate anything that might happen between the time I left and the time I was going to come home. I'd put the phone within reach, even though I knew he wasn't going to answer it. I would make sure there were fluids there, that the TV remotes were near his hand, there was paper, there was a book. I'd get him all set up, then I'd leave and go flying into work.

"We were just beginning a new project and I was very much in the role of the primary coordinator, the same role I was in at home. Everybody at work was waiting to start the day till I showed up. So I go to work and say, 'Do this, do this, do this, do this.' I would then call home, use the secret ring, ask 'What do you want for lunch?' and spend thirty minutes on the phone going, 'Yes, you do have to eat. What is it that you want? You name it, I'll get it for you.' And it could be anything. And then I would run off and get that and take it home, feed him, clean him up again, get him settled in for the afternoon, and go back to work, 'Do this, do this, do this, do this,' leave at four o'clock, get home, what do you want for dinner, do dinner, clean him up after dinner, get everything set up, go back into the office, try to get a couple of hours alone to do things, go back home, and then the whole bedtime process started. It was day after day after day after day. I kept thinking, objectively, 'I wonder how long you can do this.' It was as if I was totally detached."

Jim managed to keep it up, eventually getting "into the rhythm of it. I set up the house so that things were easy. It reminded me of a mother with a new baby, where you learn to keep things right there." And Jim was able to "develop little delightful games" with Don. "It was so humiliating for him to be so incapacitated, I had to find ways to play." For example, showering, drying and dressing a paralyzed man was not easy, but "there was a whole routine." After the shower, "I would lay a big towel down on the bed and flop him down on it. I'd throw a towel over his face and he would throw his arms up, and I'd spray deodorant on him and then we would start working with clothes. We made a little game out of it."

During one lunchtime break, Don asked to get cleaned up, so Jim got him upstairs and into the shower. But afterward, something went wrong. "That day he was lying back on the bed, and I was laughing, going 'Okay, here we go.' I threw the towel over his face and all of a sudden, he wrenched, he just contracted, incredibly. And he looked at me so long. He looked floored. Lying there wrenching, then he started looking terrified, and he couldn't speak to me. 'Don, what's happening?' He couldn't speak, and I kept seeing everything contracting, contracting, and I'm thinking, 'What the fuck is going on?' and then I went, '*Seizure*. He's having a seizure, oh God.' So I just held him down and I said, 'Don, it's okay, I'm here, it's okay, I'm here.' And I kept thinking, 'What do you do? You don't put a spoon in their mouth, you don't hold their tongue down, I don't have anything that would work as a relaxant.' I physically held him down and finally the seizure stopped. He was trembling, scared, half-laughing, half-screaming at me, 'How can you say everything's all right? How could you say to me everything's all right? Everything is not all right!' And we just started laughing. I said, 'I have no idea what that was.' Don said, 'I don't know either—it was the strangest feeling I ever had.' I said, 'I can only assume it was a seizure.' 'You know,' he said, 'years as a doctor, I never knew this is what a seizure is like.'"

Jim continued: "There would be moments where this learning, which had made Don this tremendous physician, would go on. Almost as if he was going to have an opportunity to use this." For Jim, this incident would serve as an excellent example of the denial factor in his care-taking. He called work and told them that he wouldn't be back that day, then told Don, "'I should take you to the hospital.' Don said, 'I don't want to go to the hospital, don't take me to the hospital.' I asked, 'Do you think you're going to be okay?'" The seizure "had come out of no-where, we didn't know if it was going to happen again, we didn't know what to expect. So we kind of sat around all afternoon trying not to think about the fact that this might happen again at any moment."

That evening the visiting nurse was scheduled to come. When Jim told her that he thought Don might have had a seizure that day, she rushed into action. "She goes flying upstairs, whips out her little light, and she's flicking it in his eyes, and she comes out of the bedroom and asks, 'Why didn't you go to the hospital?' I said, 'He didn't want to go.' She just looked at me and said, 'Do you understand what's going on? His left pupil is fixed and dilated, he has no feeling on the left side of his body. Now I'm getting no reflex from here . . . ' She's ticking off all these things, as if to say, 'You idiot, put it together.'

"She took me downstairs and asked if the doctor had explained to me what was going on. I said, 'Well, yeah.' She said, 'You do understand that he's terminal.' 'Well, yeah,' but it was this real naive, 'Well-yeah-but-not-now' kind of thing. And what she conveyed to me was, 'Today could well have been it, and you were in no way prepared for this.' She's looking at me dumbfounded; it was like reality checking in with me: Do you know he's dying? Do you know that it really is close?

"It hit me then, but then Don went into the hospital. He was there a week, they discharged him, I brought him home, and again, death took a holiday. Okay, we fixed that, now we're on Dilantin, the seizures are under control. Yeah, you've had a massive stroke; yeah, the CT scan shows three quarters of your brain is now wasted."

The HIV virus was destroying Don's brain. "They would let me go into the CT room to watch the scan. I had a lot of medical knowledge from Don and as the scans were coming out, I could remember where the shadow was before. I remember thinking, the shadow is bigger. I knew it was moving. The seizures were an indication that the virus was hitting major autonomic centers and causing massive dysfunction throughout his body. System after system was going. Ultimately, what he died from was intractable seizures, because his brain stem literally died."

After this second hospitalization, Jim would have more help. Don's doctor refused to release him until nursing care was arranged. He could not allow his patient to be left unattended for hours every day, but if he hadn't insisted, "honest to God, we would have tried it again." But the extra help caused some problems too. The nurses were insisting that "'he's got to have some kind of a bowel movement.' I was ragging on him, 'Look, this has gotta happen somehow; they're going to take you in and they're going to try to remove some kind of obstruction.' I argued with him incessantly in the last month about eating and the bathroom. He felt so humiliated and so infantilized in so many ways. He would get so angry, he'd go, 'Look, it's not gonna happen.' Actually, what was happening was that the muscular control in his colon was going because the brain center had been killed."

The time from Don's second hospitalization until his death was only twelve days, but to Jim it seemed much longer. We asked how he had known when death was near. "Three days before Don died, he changed. He got real quiet, he got real inaccessible and he would just lie in bed. I had rearranged the house and he had been downstairs much of the time. There was a pull-out sofa in the living room that was always open. We didn't have a bathroom on the first floor, so I had gotten this portable commode, got a room divider and set up this little bathroom for him downstairs, and for weeks he never stayed upstairs. But then he asked to go upstairs. He got very quiet and he began to drift a lot more. He had shifting levels of consciousness. There would be long periods of time when he would be talking to me and would literally drift off. I'd be sitting there thinking, 'What the hell is going on?' and then he would snap back in.

"'What happened?' he'd ask.

"'I think you fell asleep.'

"'Oh. What were we doing?'

"'We were just sitting here talking.'

"'Okay.'

"I'd reorient him and we'd talk a little more. It got to be longer and longer periods that he'd drift off like that and I'd sit there watching and wondering, 'What is going on inside?' I asked him about that and he said that it was real confused, a jumble of images and memories. Sometimes he would feel like he was still talking to me. It would be conversations from before but it would be as if it were happening again." During those three days, Jim remembered, "I was sure we were getting pretty close to the end, but again, I had no idea how long it could go on and I didn't care; I just wanted it to go on. I didn't care if he was there just fifteen minutes a day, I just wanted it to go on.

"He died on a Friday afternoon at five o'clock. I had gotten really tired Wednesday night taking care of him. He was really worried about incontinence. That Wednesday night, when he would drift off, he kept feeling as if he was going to urinate. We had this bedside urinal and he kept making me hold it for him. Then he would drift off, but as soon as I would move the urinal he would come back around and yell at me that it wasn't there. I finally said, 'Don, look, I'm so tired that I don't care. If you wet the bed, you wet the bed. I'll deal with that. It's easier than sitting here for hours holding this thing for you.' I was really tired, and aware of feeling really tired and aware of feeling angry with him and I didn't like feeling angry with him, but I was just worn. I knew at that point I had hit the wall.

"So we both finally dozed off and Thursday morning—he was always more alert in the morning—and that morning he didn't roust, and he wasn't moving and he wasn't talking." Jim got up and started to get ready for work, looking in on Don periodically. "While I was standing there tying my tie and looking at him, I finally went over to the side of the bed and said, 'Do you want me to stay home from work today?' and he said, 'Yeah, I do, I want you to stay home.'

"That terrified me, because he never asked for anything like that. And he didn't even ask for it, but it was just quick, the minute I offered it. That morning, as soon as I agreed to stay home, he was back. We talked, the cats came upstairs, we were playing games with them. He was lucid. We watched a whole TV show together. It was the first time I had sat with him for thirty minutes and we didn't have to attend to something.

It was this real delightful morning. By lunch time he said, 'I'm really tired.' I asked, 'Why don't you get some sleep?' 'I don't really want to, but I'm really tired.' He fell asleep and he woke up at about five o'clock, writhing in pain.

"'My head is killing me, give me something, my head is killing me . . . it hurts, it hurts!' That's all he kept saying, 'It hurts, it hurts.' I got on the phone and started screaming at Stan, Don's doctor. 'You get something over here; I'm not going to sit here and watch this go on.' Stan sends over liquid codeine. I'm looking at this bottle thinking, 'Right, this'll be wonderful.' I said, 'They gave me codeine, Don.'

"'Codeine is not gonna work!'

"I said, 'Let's try it.' And I started pumping this codeine down him and it just wasn't working."

This was a new challenge for Jim, because Don had never been in pain during the course of his illness. "Then Don started getting nauseated. He couldn't keep the codeine down, and his head hurt and he was vomiting." At this point Jim was unable to reach the doctor and could only speak with his answering service. "I was so angry with Stan. I could have killed him. I kept calling his service and screaming, 'You get that motherfucker on the phone and you have him call me and you have him call me *now*. I don't want any goddamned delays.' I found his home number in the phone book, and I was calling his home and leaving messages on the machine, 'Stan, I don't care where you are, I don't care what time it is, if you get this message, get back to me, I *will* be here. I *will* be waiting for your call.'"

When the nurse came on duty at nine that night, "she took one look at Don and went, 'We've got to do something to help.' I said, 'I know! I know!' Like, thank you for the validation. Yes, we've got to do something to help him. 'They will not listen to me, will you please try?'" She called her supervisors, telling them, "'Listen, things are really bad here, you had better get something over here, get hold of his doctor.' I'm listening and all of a sudden—y'know, when people are dying, voices drop. It's funny. The man was damned near unconscious and now they're whispering. I'm sitting there going, 'There is no reason for that, I know exactly what you're saying. He may not hear you, but I'm no fool.' And her tone got much more emphatic, and her words got stronger: 'Look, things *are* bad here, we need some help.'"

When they finally reached Don's doctor, he informed the nurses that he was "not ready" to start morphine or Demerol. When the charge nurse conveyed this information to Jim, he exploded. "What are you, worried he's going to be addicted? *I'll* sign. Give me something to sign, I don't care! What are you waiting for?!' Her answer—'it's too soon'— threw me because I was getting prepared and all of a sudden they were saying, 'We don't want to do this last-ditch thing.'" Jim told the nurse, "Look, all I can tell you is, he's in pain and this codeine is not working. He's nauseated and every time he comes to consciousness all he talks about is the pain. I don't want this to go on." Jim spent Thursday night at Don's side. "From ten o'clock that night until about six o'clock the next morning, he was probably only conscious for an hour. The rest of the time—thank God—he was somewhere else. Everything was getting increasingly disorganized." But when Don did regain consciousness, "he knew who I was, he knew where he was, and he knew what was going on.

"The next morning, I woke up and rolled over and he was lying there with his eyes open. I said, 'Don, are you okay?' and he smiled and said, 'Yeah.' I noticed that his lips were cracked and his mouth was all dry, and they had showed me how you need to keep them moist. I sat there with a cup, pulling water up into a straw and dropping it down into his mouth. Then I would take this little sponge thing they gave me and wet his lips and his teeth. I was doing this and thinking, 'God, he looks miserable,' and the heart-breaking moment through this whole thing is, he says, 'Thank you.'"

Jim thought, "Oh God, you're lying here dying and the last thing you're doing is thanking people for just wetting your mouth. Not 'Save me, stop this, make this over.' It was 'thank you' for doing this thing. I left the room at that point and stormed around the house going, 'Sons of bitches, I'm going to kill them if I ever get my hands on them. This is crazy; this is not going to go on. I'm not going to do this all day long again. No more!'

"I started calling Stan's service at six-fifteen in the morning. At seven o'clock he finally called." It had been more than twelve hours, "and he finally returned the call. I just ripped in to him. I said, 'I am so angry with you! He is miserable. I promised him there would be no pain. I promised him it would not be this way. You will not provide me with what I need. If I have to take him out of your care, I am willing to do this. I am thoroughly dissatisfied. If you will not do this I will find someone who will.'"

But Stan told him, "Jim, I don't want to go to these last-ditch measures. I want to save some of these things." Jim recalled bitterly, "To this day, I don't know what the hell he was waiting to see." When Nicole, the day nurse, came around nine that morning, to find Jim "changing the bed for about the fifth time in twenty-four hours," she announced, "'This is ludicrous,' and got on the phone. 'Get a hold of Stan, tell him things are not good here, and I want to speak to him.' Stan calls the nurse back and she's going, 'Stan, we're getting there.' This was the first time I'd heard it. That Friday morning about ten o'clock, I heard them say the words 'getting there.' I love the euphemisms."

As Jim watched the nurse on the phone, Don suddenly "wrenched again in bed and started shaking violently. He started convulsing all over again. Nicole says, 'I've got a problem here, I've got to go right now!' and she threw the phone down and came running over. We hung a new bag of Dilantin, we put a needle into his arm, we got him back, we got him relaxed, held him for ten minutes, and then he doubled up again and started wrenching again. She got on the phone and said, 'I need help out here, I can't control him anymore.' They started sending over bags and bags of liquid Valium. Finally. At noon we started dripping liquid Valium into him continuously."

At this point, Jim made a big decision. He called Don's parents. Don was their only child, and not only did they not know that he had AIDS, they did not know that Don was gay. "He had made me swear that I would not involve his family, that I would protect his mom. His mother and his father did not know he was dying. They knew he had had a stroke, they knew he wasn't doing well, they knew he had to go in the hospital, that he had developed seizures, they knew things did not look good, but no one had ever said to them, 'Your son is dying.' But Don's stand was, 'I don't want them to know. I don't want them to go through this hell.' So I had said okay. Well, at noon, when they were hanging

Valium and Dilantin, I knew it was close to the end. I sat there for a minute and I thought, 'I can't do this to them,' and I got on the phone to his mother."

Don's parents lived upstate, about four hours away. "I said, 'Look, Don isn't doing very well, I think you need to get down here.' And she froze. I could literally picture her. I said, 'Take your time, be careful. I don't want you to go running out of the house, but you need to get down here as quickly as you can. Is there somebody who can bring you down? Are Walter and Martha'—they're relatives—'are Walter and Martha around? Can they bring you down?' They said, 'Yes, we'll get hold of Walter and Martha.' I said, 'Okay, everything's okay now, so take your time, but get down here.' I got off the phone and thought, 'How is this going to play out?' And then I put his family out of my head."

Throughout the long afternoon, Jim found it "agonizing" to be around Don but even worse not to be. The nurses "would tell me to go take a break, go someplace else. And I would go downstairs and pace back and forth. Alex had come to sit with me—Alex was the only person I had let into the house while Don was dying. I was frantic, absolutely frantic. I kept pacing back and forth and then I would go back upstairs. And the nurses would say, 'Didn't I tell you to take a break?'"

Jim paused in his story to relate an incident that seemed to characterize his relationship with the nurses. A few nights earlier, he and Alex "had been smoking—I feel so guilty about this—we'd been smoking dope. The nurse in charge of Don's care came over. We butted out the joint and I'm trying to clear the room, and I just felt so guilty that I had gotten high. It was wrong, wrong. The nurse went upstairs to check on Don, came downstairs and said, 'Everything's fine, he's resting comfortably.' And then she smiled and asked, 'Have you been getting Don high?' 'No, no! No ma'am, no, no, honest to God.' She said, 'It might not be a bad idea. Do you think he'd like to get high?' 'I don't know. He seems disinterested in so many things.'

"She shrugged and said, 'It can't hurt at this point. If he wants to and it helps in any way, God knows, do it.'" This was Don's main caretaker, the nurse who coordinated all the other nurses. They were not part of a hospice, but were affiliated with a special AIDS program. "The nurses were very supportive. They were always saying, 'You're doing a great job, you're doing all the right things.' But I was floored that night. 'Why don't you get him high?' I was amazed, but hey, what the hell, it was helping me.

"So the afternoon that he was dying I came downstairs and I was pacing and pacing. Alex looked up at one point and said, 'Would it help to smoke?' I told him, 'I don't know what would help. All I know is that I feel more disorganized in my head than I've ever felt in my life.' It was total chaos in my head. I knew that Don was dying but I couldn't let my mind be clear enough to absorb what I knew, so I just kept myself real confused. There were all these things that had to be attended to. There were things to do, things to do. At one point I was standing on the steps and I said, 'As hard as it is to be up there with him, it's even harder to be away from him, because then I don't know what's going on. I'd rather be there and know what's going on than be away from him.' I went back upstairs and after that I didn't leave the room."

At five in the evening, the nursing shift was due to change. Nicole, who had been there since the morning, had to leave to pick her children up from daycare, but her replacement was late. Disgustedly, Jim said, "Go, all of you get the hell out of my life, just get the hell out of here. Just leave us alone." He listened as Nicole phoned in her report: "'It's not looking good, I really don't think it's much longer.' And while she's on the phone, Don has another violent seizure. She turned around and I said, 'Nicole, please, don't do anything. I'm asking you, just as a person, let it go this time.' She said into the phone, 'Look, he's seizing again, I don't know what's happening, I've got to go.' She turned around and started intubation. And as she was intubating him, it was apparent to both of us that he was in the final . . . wrenching . . . throes."

"So . . . Don died and I'll never forget, I was sitting there holding him, and the nurse must have thought I had completely lost my mind, but I used to tease him. When I first got him his computer and he was worried that he'd erased the disk, or broken something, usually I'd take a quick look at it and be able to assess that it was really simple. I would give him one of these Dad-chastising looks and say our favorite little phrase: 'Oh,

Donald, what have you done?' Then I would smile, and he would know that it wasn't so bad. And that was the last thing I said to him, as soon as he died. 'Oh, Donald, what have you done this time?' It was like, 'I can't fix this. I can't make this any different.' The nurse looked at me and kind of nodded her head.

"I left the room and went downstairs and everybody's trailing after me and hovering, hovering, and I'm saying, 'Please, get away from me. Really, just give me a minute.' I went in the dining room and I remember going, 'This can't be it. This just can't be it. It can't be that simple, it can't be over. What will I do now, I mean, literally? What do I do, what comes next, what happens next?' I was lost in that running around in my head, and all of a sudden, Alex looked out the front door and said, 'Oh my God! I think Don's parents are here!'

"Honest to God, I really do like to think of myself as something of a scientist, but I have to admit . . . Don did not want his mother to see him in the final throes of dying, he just didn't want her to see that. He died and they pulled into the driveway five minutes later. It was one of those things, almost as if somehow in this dream-like consciousness, Don was aware that with every passing minute, his parents were getting closer." Jim had not mentioned calling them to Don and yet, the timing seemed exquisite. He tells himself, "It's merely coincidence. One tries to impose structure where there is no structure. And certainly the thoughts were much crazier then, but still I have to believe that Don wanted this over before his parents got there, and somehow knew—I can't tell you how— that they were on their way and that this had to be over with before they got there." That Don hadn't been "conscious enough for me to convey to him" that his parents were coming that afternoon "makes it all that more magical.

"Sure enough, I go to the front door, and here are his parents coming up the sidewalk. I turned to Nicole, the nurse who had to go get her children from daycare, and point blank said to her, 'How do you tell a mother that her only child is dead?' knowing that this is a question that cannot be answered." But it was Alex who "just kicked into action." Although not generally a "terribly competent type of guy," he was the one who was able to think in Jim's moment of panic. He addressed the nurses, "Is the upstairs cleaned up? Is he under a blanket or something?" As soon as they finished upstairs, Alex announced that he was going next door. He said, "'Let me know what you need' and shooed everybody else out of the house.

"So the Belmonts are coming in and they're laughing. I met them on the front porch and said, 'I have some bad news.' Um, and it's, whoa, master of the understatement here. Y'know? And they ask, 'Oh, did he have to go back into the hospital?' Okay, so I've got to gauge this. Bad news would be if he had to go back into the hospital. I said, 'Nooooo.' And then Mrs. Belmont came by me and started going up the stairs. I ran up and blocked her. 'You can't go up there!' She asked, 'Why?' Then I said, 'Listen, I don't know how to tell you this, um, Donald died this afternoon.' And she hit the floor. Literally, she just fell on the steps, and her husband was at the bottom of the steps and braced her up and looked at me like, 'You must be joking.'" All Jim could do was say, over and over, "'I'm so sorry. I'm so sorry, I don't know what to say . . . '" It turned out that all she was doing was running upstairs to use the bathroom. If I had just waited, the woman could have had a chance to go use the bathroom, we could have sat down in a civilized manner, but I froze. I thought, 'She's gonna go up and see him lying there, and she's gonna freak out.' She was only going to use the bathroom. I thought, 'Oh, what an ass! What an ass!' But she would have walked right into the whole scene. I knew I couldn't let her, but I felt like such a jerk!

"It got ludicrous at that point. She looked for a hold on the stairs and Mr. Belmont was saying 'No,' and I was saying 'Yes.' He asked, 'How did this happen?' These strange questions: How did it happen? There's no answer to this question. They're looking at me like, 'You fool, you were here, how did this happen? How did he die?' And I'm thinking, 'Well, he got sick and then he died.' The most stupid answers were coming; everything feels so stupid at a moment like that. Everything pales. Words seem stupid, things that go on in life seem stupid. Everything seems—I guess more than stupid—everything feels empty. I kept saying, 'I'm so sorry, I'm so sorry.' I know part of that 'I'm so sorry' was, I was supposed to stop this. If I'd taken care of him, this wouldn't have happened. I did something wrong, there was something I should have done,

I should have known something to stop this.

"Then we went upstairs and we went into one of the bedrooms. Walter and Martha stayed down in the living room, looking like deer caught in headlights. The questions were tumbling out. 'What the hell's been going on? Nobody told us this was happening. Why didn't he tell us?' I told them, 'Don had shut everybody out. He wouldn't let people come see him.'

"'Why wouldn't he let us see him? What went wrong? What did his doctor say? Did you call the doctor?' Did you call the doctor?—as if we could undo this now, call the doctor. 'Look, there's nothing to undo. Look, Don had made me promise.'"

Jim shook his head at the recollection, and the necessity of his having to avoid telling the Belmonts the truth. "Don extracted all kinds of promises. He had said, 'I don't want mine to turn into another smutty AIDS death. One more fag dies from AIDS, that's what people will say. I can't stand that. I don't want my parents to be going around town with people saying, *That's the couple whose son, that fag, died from AIDS.*'" Jim had promised to do everything he could, but the moment of truth was upon him. In the next moments, there were several hurdles Jim had to jump in order to keep his promise and Don's secret.

Once a death has occurred, along with family concerns, there are legal ramifications and medical facts to impart. Jim recounted his urgent conversation with Stan, Don's doctor, that afternoon. "'I have to report it Jim,' Stan told me.

"'I understand that you have to report it, but I also know there are ways to handle this.'

"'What do you want me to put on the death certificate?'

"'I'm not asking you to lie, but I know there's a way you can hide this.' So, he listed three causes of death: intractable seizures, leukoencephalopathy (which is what it's called when the AIDS virus is eating the cortex, killing the brain cells) and a third cause that was not related to AIDS.

"Stan said, 'This is as far as I can go. Any educated person—any medical doctor, any coroner, any funeral person—is going to know that the leukoencephalopathy means that he was HIV positive and that he died from AIDS. But it has no meaning to a family member or anything like that. That's the best I can do.' I said, 'Thank you, thank you, thank you.'"

The next hurdle was even more challenging for Jim. Don had never expressed any particular wishes for his remains, and "we had finally agreed that for the both of us, we didn't care. I promised him that whatever his family wanted was fine." The Belmonts announced, "We want to take Sonny home." Their plans for a funeral in the remote community where Don grew up meant a call to a small-town mortician. Jim arranged a conference call with Stan, the funeral director and himself.

"I was listening on the conference call and the funeral director said, 'Did he have AIDS?' Stan said, 'I'm not sure why you're asking me that question.'

"'Because it's a state requirement that I know.'

"Stan answered, 'You should handle every death with precautionary measures. There should be standard procedures for handling every body.'"

But the funeral director persisted. "'It's state law, I have to know.'

"Stan said, 'He did die of leukoencephalopathy,' and the funeral director said, 'Okay.' Stan added, 'This is of great concern to the family.'

"The funeral director said, 'I understand.' And thank God, knock wood, toss salt, there's never been a squeak, a rumor, even hearsay. This man was tremendous. This funeral director in this tiny, tiny town has never once violated that."

Finally, Jim felt that he had to say something to Don's parents. "I went back upstairs to talk to them and said, 'Look there's something you are going to have to know, because I don't want you to be broadsided. When Don was in the hospital, they found out that he was HIV positive.'

"They said, 'We don't want this reported.' I told them, 'I'm doing the best I can about that, but there are limits. The doctor and I are doing everything we can to control it, but I can't ask the doctor to break laws.'

"Then they turned to me and said, 'How do you think he got AIDS?'

"I was saying, 'Gee, um . . . ' and his mother said, 'He must have stuck himself with a needle at the hospital. That must be it.' And I said,

'Probably so.' And we all agreed that Don must have stuck himself with a needle at the hospital and that's how he got AIDS."

When Don's mother asked to see her son, Jim said, "'Just give me a minute and then you can go in.' I went in the room and shoved all the medical stuff out of the way, got rid of the pole, got rid of all the bags, put him in bed, put his pajama top on, pulled the blankets up, and laid him back on the pillows. Then I came back out and said, 'Okay, you can go in.'

"She came in and said, 'He's just asleep!'

"'Well, that would be a wonderful thing, but . . . ' Profound, profound sleep. I said, 'It does look that way.'

"And she said, 'I'm so glad. He looks like he's really peacefully asleep.'

"'I'm glad that's how it feels to you, because I know that's how he'd want you to feel about it.'"

The Belmonts remained with Jim a very short time. "They left the house thirty minutes after he died—they couldn't stand it. And so there was me, the two cats and Don. I was exhausted, I was frazzled, I was confused and I was getting kind of silly. I found myself laughing out loud and then covering my mouth. I couldn't believe his parents had come and gone. They knew he was dead. Someone was coming to pick up the body, and I was sitting on the couch going, 'Okay, they're going to come to take the body away, and Saturday I'm going to go up and we're going to bury him, okay.' Then it would be, 'Did I park the car? Are the cats fed?' Just a crazy flow of consciousness. Then that all started slowing down. I'm sitting there thinking that this is bizarre, to sit here knowing that he's lying upstairs in bed, in our bed, dead. I crept partway up the stairs and peeked into the bedroom to see if he was there and, sure enough, he hadn't moved! I went back downstairs thinking, 'You should want to be upstairs with him.' But I didn't want to be around the body, so I sat downstairs and waited and in a little while the doorbell rang. I looked outside and there was this tastefully gray van in the driveway, with these men in very tasteful suits and this bag tucked under their arm. Blue. It was bizarre, like, 'We came to pick up the package.' They came in the house and asked, 'Is there somewhere you could go for a few minutes?'

"I said, 'What?' and I'm thinking, 'I, I have been holding this man while he was retching, I have told his parents. Nothing, nothing you guys are gonna do is going to top my day, trust me. You could dance him down the stairs doing a tango, and it would not faze me at this point.' I said, 'I'm not going anywhere.'

"They go upstairs and come down and they have this bag. There are lumps in this bag and I'm trying to figure out what position he's in, in this bag. There's his head, I could see his feet. There's no gurney or anything, so this bag is sagging and there's two handles on each end and they're walking out. I think, 'They're gonna bang his head on the stairs.' I stood there watching them ditch this bag into the van, and I'm thinking, 'This should be getting through somehow.' I'm clawing at it, to get something. And I'm thinking, 'Why am I watching this so dispassionately?' But if I had access to all of this, I'd lose it."

After the funeral home staff left, Alex called and suggested that Jim get out of the house, but Jim declined. "'I just want to be here alone.' The house had been our fortress. Don had not allowed anyone to come into the house during his entire illness. He wouldn't take calls, he wouldn't let anybody in the house. He was so embarrassed that he had lost his capacity and been paralyzed, and that he had this drooping face and he drooled and couldn't control his arm. He would not allow anyone near him." There would be resentment and rage about this afterward, as friends held Jim responsible for Don's isolation. Fortunately, the colleague with whom Don shared his practice had insisted on coming to the house and was able to confirm that seclusion was explicitly Don's wish. "If it had been only me knowing, it would have been much harder." In any event, that night Jim wanted to remain secluded in the fortress.

"I stayed there hoping that, if he's going to ever come to me, it'll be tonight." But along with Jim's hope came fear. "There was only one bed in the house, the one that Don died in," so Jim decided to sleep on the couch. "I had turned out all the lights in the house, and I felt like he *wasn't* gone, he's going to come back. And I thought, 'I'm afraid.' Then I went, 'No! Fight back the terror.' If there's going to be a chance of contact, I wanted to embrace it, run into the storm, go with it.

"Nothing ever happened. Nothing really. There were dreams, typical dreams, and maybe I'm minimizing them because I also had them after my mother died. Typical dreams of Don coming back, that he wasn't dead, that things were normal, but no messages, no parting gifts. I think I didn't need that because our parting had been so complete before he ever died. There was too much that was real to hold on to. Most people who deal with death in that way still need something. They're trying to fabricate it through these experiences. I don't think that there was anything left that I needed at the time he died."

But lying there that first night, Jim recalled a conversation he had had with Don near the end, about fear. One night, Don had told him, "'My biggest concern is that after I'm gone, you're going to be afraid. I don't want you to be afraid.' I think that he was saying, 'I don't want this to contribute to how timid you are about the whole world to begin with.' He'd always said, 'I wish you weren't so timid. That's the one thing I wish you would change.' And since Don's death, I think I've become really aggressive. In fact, it's *no*, I'm not going to be timid, I'm not going to be afraid, I'm not going to let all this throw me. I'm going to grab life by the throat. I'm not going to be beaten by this thing."

But it would not be easy. For a long while after Don's death, Jim would feel horror at "the gross stuff that goes on in death. The hardest part was getting rid of the ugly images of the violent processes that go on in the final throes. You're not disgusted at the time, but I was worried that all I would remember of Don were the ugly things that his body did at the end." Jim recalled the day when he tried to summon some good memories of Don and could not. The "whole process of being ill and dying had so overwritten everything that I had this panic." He mentioned this to a neighbor when she stopped by, and she reassured him that the bad memories would eventually go away and the good ones would return. This was how it went for her when her husband died. "She knew so precisely what I was talking about. She said, 'Trust me.' I said, 'I have to.' She said, 'In time, in time.' And she was right. Now I have to actively think about the ugly parts."

But another fear proved to be groundless: that Don's illness would be exposed. "Honest to God, I don't know how it's been kept so quiet, but there's never been a peep. It was just that Dr. Belmont had died of a stroke. Anyone with any medical background could put this together, but it was never spoken. They read the memo, it said stroke, that was the party line. I think that reflects the kind of respect that Don had commanded. That's pretty much the way it's always stayed. I have to say, I take some pride in having protected him, because that was of real concern to him. We'd both seen how so many friends' deaths had been minimized: 'Well, it was AIDS.' The simplification that makes it less important."

Jim reflected that Don's colleagues and associates knew the truth, but they kept the information to themselves because they knew that's how Don wanted it. "Don was very loved and respected. Even doctors who didn't know him somehow knew of him. Don was one of those gifted people. He graduated from high school early, flew through college in three years, went through medical college in three more years, got his M.D. at the earliest possible age, was chief resident and was director of inpatient services at a nationally prominent institution. On top of these achievements, Don was thought of as a nice person, somebody who people liked to talk to, and who other doctors came to with their family problems. By the time he died, Don had become only a doctor's doctor. He only treated other psychiatrists. This was understood and had to be absolutely confidential. If he ran into them in other settings, you never would have known what he knew about them or that he knew they were incredibly stressed. He treated people with such dignity and respect that I think everybody felt like it was the perfect opportunity to reciprocate. It was as if everybody internally had taken this vow of silence."

Jim wished that Don could have known about this loyalty. It would have been a "major reward" because it seemed to reflect Don's own character. "His big thing was, 'All you have to learn is to treat people with dignity and respect.' It took him ten years to learn this lesson for himself. It didn't matter if it was a waiter, a cashier in a store, a colleague at work, or Albert Einstein himself. They all deserved simple dignity and respect. That's what Don stood for and people responded to it. It was his power in treating people."

Jim decided to remain in Don's house and buy it from the estate. Only six weeks after Don's death, Jim's friend Alex contracted pneumonia, and Jim was pressed back into caretaking. He reflected on the differences between the two men, and their deaths.

"Alex is a whole different story from Don." Although Don and Jim had not lived together for the four years prior to Don's death, they had "grown up together" and felt as if they had been married. Furthermore, Jim explained, "I drew on Don's strength, but that was exactly the reverse of Alex. Alex was so much like a child, and I was always clearly the adult in that relationship. So the whole experience of caring for Alex and the experience of his death was very different." A substantial reason was that "Don was prepared to die, and Alex did not want to. It was a real difference, even in the process of watching them die." Don was thirty-nine when he died; Alex was thirty-five.

"Don had a healthy respect for death. It's inevitable, there is no way you're going to cheat death. But Alex was quite frightened of dying and he was never able to admit it. He had a sense of aloneness in death. And it's true: No matter how many people are around you, you really do die alone. To Alex, that was the most frightening aspect. He was a dependent kind of guy and relied on others for validation of himself or his sense of worth. Don was much more autonomous. He had developed a sense of his own integrity and sense of being. Don wasn't looking forward to dying, but he wasn't afraid of it. What worried me most about Don was his resignation."

Jim felt that Don's resignation may have "expedited the whole process" and even wondered for a while if Don's decline had been accelerated because Don himself "embraced it and went with the flow of it." Now, in retrospect, Jim could argue that Don "contracted a more fast-moving level of virus" because Don accepted it, whereas Alex suffered "a long, slow, tedious, process.

"Alex started with the wasting syndrome, losing weight, and the development of fibrosis in his musculature, slowly losing strength. He went through torturous treatments." He took AZT orally until its side effects became dangerous. It was replaced by "DDI, which is incredibly toxic and is miserable to take. He was constantly nauseated and ill."

Eventually, Alex couldn't take DDI orally anymore and so needed daily injections in the stomach and abdomen.

Initially, Jim would give Alex the injections because Alex "was terrified of needles. Every night we would have to double him over to find enough of a roll of fat to get the injections in. Night after night we had to go through this terrible ritual of doing this injection. He would dread it and put it off for hours. We got into huge battles because I told him that his refusal to learn how to use injections was a way to guarantee that I would stay engaged with him. He was concerned about me abandoning him, and he knew I wouldn't leave him needing his injections. He became very angry but finally overcame his needle phobia and started being able to give himself his own injections. Then he began to develop scar tissue in his abdomen and he had to inject himself on the inside of his thighs, and he started developing scar tissue there. Then there were no more fat deposits to be found anywhere on Alex's body for the injections. It was the most painful, slow, miserable process.

"I'm convinced that the protracted nature of Alex's illness was because he was constantly terrified of dying. And yet, he was still alive. I used to talk to him about it, encouraging him. I would say, 'If you can just hang on, they could develop some technique or drug that could just split the virus off of your cells and flush it from your body. If you can hang on that long, maybe some day that will be developed.' And he would say, 'Talk to me about that. Tell me that's possible.'"

Alex had had his first bout of pneumonia a few weeks after Don died. In fact, "he was in the same hospital room that Don had been in. Room 412. I hate the room. He was in the hospital for seven days, then restricted to the first floor of his house. There were nurses in for over a month and he recovered to the level where he was able to function on his own. He got so much better that by Christmas he was looking good again. But in February he started developing fevers of a nonspecific origin, and by March he had painful shingles all over his body. It started coming fast and furious after that, up until the time he died, on July 15. It was one thing after another, as it had been all along."

This prolonged caretaking was hard on Jim. "I felt like I let go of one body and picked up the other." He explained that this was true even before Don's decline, for Jim had been helping Alex with his early symptoms. "When he had first started the AZT, he was having lots of rashes and I was putting creams on and charting his medications and making sure he took them and went to his doctor's appointments. Stan would give us his blood levels and we would chart them. Then Don became very ill and Alex kind of melted into the background. Actually, he did quite well during that period. It was almost as if he rallied in the face of Don's sickness."

When Don died, Alex "became very sick very soon thereafter. With his hospitalization and slow recovery, Jim didn't have time to think. "I just kicked back into my take-care-of-Don mode." Alex asked if he could come recover with Jim at Don's house, and "I didn't think about it. I just took care of him. I set up the house, got the nurses, took care of medications. I didn't think about what I was feeling or what I needed or anything.

"It wasn't until Alex started getting better that Don's death started hitting me. By Christmas, Alex was pretty much stable and emotionally I was a wreck. It was the first Christmas without Don and I was in battle with Alex because . . . I knew he was dying. It was like, 'I can't do this again, I'm not ready to do this again. I can't give up another one like this.' And I was aware of actively pushing Alex away. I put so much distance in between us that by that Christmas, Alex went away alone.

"I remember I felt so bad. He turned to me and said, 'You know, I can't do anything right anymore. No matter what I do with you, for you, to you, about you, it's never right.' I said, 'This isn't you, this is me. I'm having a real hard time with Don's death.' I never said to him, 'And I'm horrified at the thought that you're going to die too.' Because I was seeing him get so sick. He was absolutely skeletal. And I knew it couldn't be too long."

Months earlier, Alex had worried that Jim was killing himself by all that he was doing to take care of Don. Jim had told Alex then, "'I have no right in this. The man is dying. You only get to die once—you should get to do it decently.' And the following spring, before Alex died, my own voice came back to me and said, 'Whether you're ready to deal with him dying or not, this is what he's in the throes of. You have got to do every-thing possible to make this easy for him. Even if you can't tolerate being around him, you're going to have to find a way to do this.' And that's actually what happened."

Jim described how he "struggled along" over the winter and into the spring, but "then I hit the wall." On the anniversary of Don's stroke, Jim was at work and "became very distressed, very disorganized, much the same state I was in the day Don had died. I couldn't pull myself together. The most distressing thing to happen to me is to not have control, and I was in my office and couldn't pull myself together." He went to his boss and told him, "I've got to leave. I can't tell you where I'm going, but I can't stay here." He left work and made a call to an analyst. This doctor had been recommended years ago by Don, but Jim had never followed up. But this day, he knew that he needed help, and fast. Within a week, he had an appointment.

Now, over a year since Jim had begun seeing a psychiatrist, he could say that psychotherapy had not only provided him with the balance he felt he was losing, but it had made the past "a rich experience for me, because I've literally spent a year of my life kind of understanding this. It took a year of some pretty intense treatment to really get the whole thing in perspective. And in the middle of that, Alex died. I thank God that I was in analysis at the time that Alex died."

When we asked how talking about these events now differs from how it was then, Jim answered intently, "It's organized now." But at the time, "It was utter chaos in my head. I couldn't make sense out of this. It was just a jumble.

"My best friend, Sara, helped me get through a lot of it. I remember turning to her one night and saying, 'I must be terribly, terribly evil.' She said, 'What!? How did you arrive at this? Take me back, take me through this—how did you get to this?'

"I said, 'Only the good die young, and clearly I've been chosen not to die young, which is an indication that I must be evil. But what could I have possibly done to warrant this? What horrendous deed or misdeed could I have done to warrant this kind of punishment, Sara? What did I do to deserve it?'"

Sara told Jim, "'Nobody deserves this. It's miserable what's happened to you, but I don't see this as punishment meted out to you.' But I was so desperate that I was getting into these absolutely crazy models. I remember saying in my first session with this analyst that I must be terribly evil, that I need to be destroyed. And he looked at me and went, 'Whoa, whoa,' and started asking me whether I would agree to psychological testing, which scared me."

Jim had to convince the analyst that, as a professional who knew not only the tests but also the testers, the idea would be a waste of time and money. "Later, in analytic rhetoric, he commented on how suspicious he had been at the sheer degree of my disorganization when I had first come into his office. I felt totally passive in the world and I had no control, no ability to structure my experience. I had told him that I felt like I was on this raging freight train that was hurtling forward into time.

"The world became surreal to me. I would walk around and the most common things didn't make sense anymore. I would stand there and study the process of us all lining up in grocery stores to buy groceries, and I wanted to turn to other people and go, 'Does this seem odd to you? We all line up and buy groceries like this?' And it was that confusion, that chaos, that finally led me to go into treatment because I couldn't tolerate it anymore. I couldn't make order out of things in life."

Shortly before our interview, Jim happened to stop at a traffic light and "noticed that there was an ambulance in this driveway. Coming out of the house were two paramedics, one at each end of a gurney, and they were rolling out this fragile-looking old man with this blanket up and some kind of a mask over his face. Then my attention immediately went to the little old lady hustling out of the house behind them. Closing and locking the door, she had her husband's coat over her arm, and she had her purse and all these things in her hands and she was running to kind of catch up with them. She became my total focus. I wondered if she was thinking, 'Is this it? Is this the time it's gonna happen?' I wondered if she was having that cold terror I used to have every time something would change in Don's or Alex's medical status and I would think, 'Oh my God, is this it?' Because the problem was that with Alex, I didn't know when we were at the end. With Don, I had this creeping sense it was coming, but with Alex it totally broadsided me."

The end of May had marked the anniversary of Don's death, and Jim accompanied Don's parents to the gravesite to unveil the tombstone. Then Jim experienced "some really bad problems in June" and so for the Fourth of July, he decided that he needed to "get the hell out of town." He phoned the island where he and Don had vacationed every summer and was able to secure a room for a week. "It was absolutely rejuvenating. There were all these memories about Don, but it was all of life at its most vital. I remembered him tanned. I remembered him on the beach. I remembered us sailing. And there were these birds everywhere, sea terns. They have these little sprouts that come up on the side of their heads and they look kind of geeky. I used to laugh and tease Don that he kind of resembled one of these sea terns.

"The big event of that vacation happened while I was sitting on the beach one day. It was dark and cloudy and stormy and the waves were crashing. And this overwhelming feeling of sadness came over me, and I sat there sobbing on this beautiful beach, all alone. I ended up talking out loud. I remember saying, 'Donald, I can't hold on to you any longer. I've got to let go. I love you, but if I hold on any longer, I'm not going to be able to go on.' And I had this real sense of relief in doing that. It was almost as if I had gone back to 'our' place to bury him."

That night Jim called Alex and told him how "this catharsis had really worked," and how beautiful the island was and how he wished that Alex could be there with him. Then Alex both surprised and disturbed Jim by making reservations to join him on the island at once. "Talking to you on the phone the last few days, it's like I've got you back," Alex told him. Jim said, "Well, this is wonderful, but how are you doing? Don't pull any punches." It turned out that Alex was in bed with a fever. Jim protested, "Do not come here. There are no medical services. I'm using a bike to get around. There are no cars available. If you got ill, we'd be screwed. I couldn't even get you to a doctor. Do not come."

Alex "was really hurt by this and he got very angry and we had a huge argument and ended up slamming down the phone." When Jim got home, he didn't call Alex right away. He wanted to wait until the anger had cooled. But the next evening, a mutual friend called Jim and told him, "Alex is not feeling well and he's asking for you. He wants you. He won't let anybody else help. He won't call you himself because he's too proud, but he wants you badly." When Jim explained that it was likely that his going to visit Alex might further aggravate him, the friend said, "I'd feel more comfortable if you stopped over."

"I went down to Alex's and he was sitting in his bedroom, cross-legged on the couch, panting. I said, 'Alex, what's wrong?' He said, 'I can't get my breath.' I went over and turned on the light. He was chalky gray and his eyelids and hairline were completely blue. I thought, 'Oh my God, he's anoxemic! No wonder he's panting, he has no oxygen in his blood!' I turned the light back off and dialed his doctor's number."

Although Alex had just seen the doctor two days earlier, the doctor's advice to Jim was, "If you're concerned, take him to the emergency room." Alex "hated going to the hospital," and Jim was prepared for a fight, but Alex was surprisingly compliant when Jim suggested they go.

"'But first,' he said, 'lie down with me on the bed and hug me before we go to the hospital.' I said, 'Okay.' I helped him get up and we went to the bed and lay down. He had this big sleigh bed and we would love to kind of spoon for hours and just lie there and talk and talk. He said 'Just hold me for a few minutes.'" Jim did but Alex told him shortly, "I can't breathe. Maybe we'd better go to the hospital."

"So I got him in the car, got to the hospital, brought a wheelchair out, took him in the hospital, brought up his name, who his doctor was and everything, and they said, 'Okay.' Nobody seemed really alarmed. They took him in and hooked him up and found out that his oxygen saturation level was below seventy: He was on the verge of cardiac arrest from oxygen deprivation and an increased heart rate.

"They said, 'The problem is that he is so exhausted from fighting to get air that he's going to fall asleep, and once he does, he's going to asphyxiate. We have to do something now. He's either going to have cardiac arrest or he's going to asphyxiate in his sleep. We need to intubate him but we have to warn you that if we do, he may never be able to come off the ventilator again. What would you like us to do?'

"I'm sitting there in my shorts, tanned and having taken one shower since I got home from vacation and I'm going, 'No, no, this can't be. It's three-thirty in the morning.' And they're saying, 'We need you to make decisions. Should we medicate him, so we can intubate him, get his oxygen saturation up, and prevent him from going into cardiac arrest?'

"'But you're telling me that he would live the rest of his life on a ventilator?'

"'That's a distinct possibility.'

"'Hold on, hold on.' I laugh, literally, and say, 'Hold on. He's been okay.'

"'Look, we need to make decisions fast, because he's on the verge of cardiac arrest.'

I went in to talk to Alex, and he was on the verge of unconsciousness from oxygen deprivation. They could not get clear decisions from him. He kept saying, 'I don't want to suffer, I don't want it to drag out. Please don't let it drag out.'

"Finally I said, 'Look, it's three-thirty in the morning. I'm not going to make these decisions. You talk to his fuckin' family, I'm not doing it again. I just did this. I'm not doing this again. His family is doing this this time.'"

But Jim had misgivings immediately. Alex's closest relative was a sister who lived on the outskirts of town. Jim thought, 'I'm not calling his sister in the middle of the night and alarming her. She's got two little kids, her husband's out of town. This is no way to present it to her, in the middle of the night . . . ' The hospital staff are saying, 'We're going to have to intubate him. We're going to have to do it. Will you sign for it?'

"I signed for the intubation, and they raced him down to the intensive care unit and medicated him literally into a coma so that they could get the tube down his throat. And he never woke from that. Four days later he died, in a coma, after his mother arrived. And I'm standing there the whole time going, 'No! Wait a minute. He was just going to fly to the seashore.' It was one week to the day that he was going to fly to the island that he was intubated and dying on this respirator. I was totally floored. As protracted as his illness had been, I had no concept that we were anywhere near that."

Recalling Alex's last day, Jim remembered being "intrigued and appalled watching the physical process of Don dying. I found myself standing next to Alex and gauging how dead he was by watching the same processes. It was: 'He's dropping hair, he's getting closer; he's starting to push fluids back out, he's getting closer; he's starting to push dark fluids, he's getting closer.' I was standing in this real dispassionate way, thinking, 'This is happening, now we're closer.' I tracked it the whole time. I watched him and was astounded. I stood there blankly when he died."

After that, "the nurses herded the family and all of us into this little area. We could go see him one at a time, and the family let me go in and have some time with him alone. I came back out and everybody was working themselves up into a kind of emotional frenzy. And in the midst of this, I stood up and put both my hands down on the table and said, 'I've got to call my office.' And I walked out of the room and I went to the phone, dialed my office and said, 'What's going on at the office, who's called and everything?'"

After being updated by his staff and reporting to them about Alex's death, Jim returned to the waiting area, where someone remarked, "Is your office at least still there for you?" This struck home with Jim. He hadn't realized it, but he had "needed to be able to hold on to something that's not going to be going away anytime. I distinctly remember, 'I've got to call my office. I know it will be there. My secretary will be there. She'll have messages for me. I know it will be business as usual. I've got to call my office.' I needed something to be normal, to be routine. You know?

"After that the whole world became surreal. Processes became so odd to me. I'd stand there and think, 'Did we not do it this way before? It seems different, doesn't it?' I had no one to talk to. Because Don and Alex had so totally filled my life for that period of time, there was no one else. My friend Sara was the only person—I remember becoming intensely dependent on her for a period of time. But otherwise, I was aware of how much had been drained out of my life. That there were these two major relationships that had totally absorbed my waking hours, and all of a sudden there was all this time. I'd wonder, 'What did I used to do with all this time?' Well, I'd go to Alex's or I'd go to Don's."

When we asked, "What do you think happens when we die?" Jim gave a long and thoughtful answer: "That's something that really has changed since the time Don died. We were all post-hippies. Don and I used to hang out with this group, and of course we were all tripping in the sixties and the seventies. Then we would talk about this great cosmic oneness. We believed that there was this transfer from matter to energy, and we all joined this large, undefinable, energy source. That was all well and good when we were tripping and before we were faced with death. Faced with death, Don found himself wondering what the experience of being in the state of death was going to be like. For me it took on a whole other importance," Jim confided. "I found myself grasping the concept that there must be life after death."

It was not long after Don's death that Jim saw the movie *Ghost*. He found it "very sad, but it leaves you with a good feeling. It leaves you feeling optimistic that those who are dead do continue to exist in some form. Not totally available, but not totally removed. And the other thing was the one line: 'You take all the love with you.' That became very important to me. But more important was the belief that I would get an opportunity to talk to Don again. Because that was the one thing I kept negotiating for after he was dead. I would give everything for five more minutes with him, and the belief that he would be made available to me again after I was dead kept me going for a long time because it didn't mean total and utter abandonment. And at some point it was going to happen."

But these comforting thoughts were disrupted by a friend who "didn't realize the kind of import" his ideas would have for Jim. This friend posed the question one day, "Don't you think it's the ultimate narcissism to believe in life after death? It's easy for us to believe that a dog dies and that's it, there's no more conscious experience. A cat dies, it's the same thing. But all of a sudden when it comes to us, it's got to be different because we're these thinking creatures. It's totally narcissistic. When man dies, that's it. The brain stops firing, there's no more experience, there's just blackness. There's not even a sense of emptiness because there's nothing more. Consciousness ends."

Jim was "absolutely floored. I wrestled with this big time and thought,

'He's right.' And that started wrenching this hope away from me that I would ever have the opportunity to speak with or be in contact with Don in some way again. But that caused another subtle shift. I began to think that immortality is really what happens when you're dearly loved and you're incorporated into those people that you've left behind. Then that part of you that is incorporated in them is then incorporated into others. Immortality is really that incorporation of your self into the living. And then I became very committed to perpetuating life: what Don had given me, and particularly what Alex had taught me. Alex was one of the most gentle, generous people I had ever known. I had a whole new commitment to being gentle and generous. No more harshness anymore, in Alex's spirit and Alex's honor. I will become the best of what he was and I will become the best of what Don was. And I will pass that on and then when I die and people say, 'Gee, Jim Viviano was a gentle, kind guy,' it will be Don and Alex as well being passed on.

"This commitment enriches the quality of life. It makes you think very seriously about what's important, what it is that you want to pass on. Knowing Don and knowing Alex has made me a much better person. Now I have this duty to reflect that in my own life, to convey that to other people.

"But I do have to say, I still have this hope. Sometimes I have dreams that I've died and Alex and Don are both waiting there for me. Or we are in this place—wherever that is—where we can connect again. They're always cognizant of all that's occurred in their absence, and there's no more pettiness, no more animosity between us. They're welcoming me, smiling, slapping me on the back going, 'Well, you finally made it. We've been waiting around for you. What the hell was going on in 1996 when you did this and this? Aww, never mind. C'mon, we've got a lot to do now. Let's get going and catch up.'"

We asked Jim what has helped him to come to terms with these deaths. His answer was short and to the point: "Basically, treatment. Because I am a psychologist, I've been trained in psychology. I turn to it—not religion, not family. The thought of turning to family didn't seem reasonable. Religion was out from the beginning. I turned to what my religion was: psychology. To look for answers there."

Was there anything that Jim would have done differently? "I don't really feel that I had a lot of choices. If there's a time in your life when you should get what you want, to have control of it, it should be death if nothing else. I wanted these men to at least have the kind of death and the style of death that they wanted. So I wouldn't have done anything different."

What advice would Jim give someone going through a situation like his? He responded facetiously, "Refuse. Turn, run, do not walk, from the situation!" But then he grew serious. He explained that he had not given much thought to himself. "My focus was much more on the person who is dying." But he did recall giving advice to Alex's sister. "I talked to her about pacing herself. About knowing her limits, knowing what she could fix and what she couldn't fix. Not losing perspective, such as believing you can stop this, that you can make it not happen, that it's your responsibility somehow." In fact, giving this advice had helped Jim to manage his own equilibrium. His recommendation to her to "walk away from it for a little while, because you go back into it that much more refreshed" helped Jim to do the same.

He continued with more advice: "Don't beat yourself up. It's a waste of energy and serves neither you nor the person who's dying. You can't stop it. It's going to happen. The worst thing I did to myself was that for months afterwards, I beat myself up. If only I'd done something different, if only I'd known something different, I could have made this not happen. And that was just self-mutilation. There was no point to that."

Jim compared the most helpful approach to learning karate. "I found that the more I went with the force and motion, the more it flowed. To resist it, to try to stop it, to try to control it, to try to make it to be different just caused greater tension. Accept it, it's going to happen. Try to go with the process as much as you can, while not taking any burden of responsibility for it for yourself. You can't be responsible for someone else's death. Because they're dying, you can't die too. You can't live their death for them. And everybody does ultimately die alone. You're not going to die with them."

How had these experiences changed Jim? "I'm much better about not getting bogged down in trivialities. When I was wrapped up in taking care of these guys while they were dying, I was struck by how many unimportant things there are that fill life day by day. I just didn't get absorbed in them again." He described a friend who was recently castigating himself for missing out on an investment opportunity. Jim told him, "You missed an opportunity to make some money for Christ's sake; life didn't end. It was only money and it was only one opportunity. God willing, it will happen again. I can't get wrapped up in that kind of stuff anymore. So I think these experiences have made me more patient too."

But "the most critical change" for Jim was his realization about immortality, "this concept of keeping the best parts of the relationship with the person alive in you. It has given me a commitment to perpetuate those aspects of Don and Alex that I treasured so. From Don, I learned that a little dignity and respect go a long way. And from Alex, I learned that to be generous and kind is little enough to do and a tremendous contribution to people around you. I have a commitment now to live those four things: dignity, respect, kindness and generosity. That's how I can make them immortal. That's what I want to pass on, and when I pass it on, I want it understood that it's not just me—it came from them as well."

Notes

⁓

Amiably Going Along with the Human Drama

Home Health Care Aide Richard T. Murray

Lean and graying, Richard T. Murray is a cordial middle-age man with an infectious enthusiasm for discussing spiritual principles and meditative practices. He is interesting on the subject of caring for terminal patients, and he is interested in their passage. For anyone who has been through the challenge of finding and hiring reliable and compassionate aides, Richard would be a godsend. He seemed to be an illustration of Zen master Philip Kapleau's advisory:

> Any health care professional who takes up meditation on a regular, daily basis will begin to find themself not only better able to relate to the dying patient, but also with greater energy, strength and emotional resources. . . . He or she will then be able to know what to do with a dying patient even when medical intervention is no longer useful.[34]

We visited Richard at his workplace, the home of an elderly stroke victim, Jack, who greeted us from his wheelchair before being helped to bed for his afternoon nap. We then interviewed Richard in a sun-filled den, where, he explained, he often meditated while his client slept. Quiet and solitude are important benefits of his occupation, he explained in a soft Texas accent.

178

"Actually I'm on kind of a paid monastic leave, where I can read and meditate, call people on the phone and have visitors in a very free way. This is really helpful to me. The time is too cluttered to sit down and write a book or an article, but in terms of meditation, reading, talking to people, it gets to be very enjoyable. So typically, in this job, my friend Jack will go to sleep at 7:00 P.M., and then I'm pretty much free. Usually I'm up till 1:00 A.M., visiting or meditating or reading, and then asleep until 6:00 A.M. I wake myself up so I have two hours of meditation and reading before he wakes up. So I start the day right, and in recent months this has become important to me, getting into a commitment for the day, an initial contact with a sense of bliss and peace and significance."

Now in his fifties, Richard has done this work for six years. He estimated that he had cared for perhaps two dozen terminally ill patients, and had been present for the actual deaths of a quarter of those. The ages of his clients ranged "generally from thirty to eighty or ninety, the whole range; AIDS patients, quite often, are thirty to forty, some even younger."

It is satisfying to Richard to be "on the front line in unexpected situations, where I'm sent in with virtually no preparation. It can be a very wealthy home, a very poor home, and so I have to deal with things in a very fresh way, and be helpful on a lot of levels, from rearranging furniture so that a sickroom will work better and more friends can come and visit comfortably; to giving people baths and helping them to have bowel movements and making sure they don't get skin breakdown and bedsores; to counseling the client and family members in all kinds of ways, generally rather subtle ways. My main contribution is just to be happy myself."

Happiness, to Richard, is crucial; it is a centering that helps him to maintain quality in his work and his life. "I am seeing what happens to people who are seventy, eighty and ninety when they don't have a spiritual preparation and aren't very aware that they create their own experience. That's pretty dreary, and it's really instructive to me to see what's available if I don't get it together in a very fundamental way right now. So I really like that sort of contact with reality.

"Often, over the months and years, there's a lot of boring empty time, and then there are moments of unusually deep significance and contact where I know that I'm being extremely, extremely helpful."

Besides boredom, Richard said, there are other drawbacks to the job. "I would like to make quite a bit more money than I do." This current assignment is a welcome exception, "where I'm making $600 a week. The price is that I'm here twenty-four hours a day, five days a week. But I had been making $300, $320 a week, for years, and that's with a sixty-hour week, a lot of night shifts, a lot of separation from my wife and family, and a lot of erratic sleep schedules. It's not so bad—usually at night I only wake up a few times, and maybe not even that, so I tend to want night shifts. I would like to be financially able to afford to do just three nights a week. That would be thirty-six hours, and I would feel like a free man. Sixty hours really eats into my time for being at home, for starting other projects, and that's been a problem for years."

Yet he feels that "everything has a sort of double edge. Like when I have trouble with my wife, it's really helpful to be scheduled away from her, so we can forget how to have trouble together. So she gets to be more in charge of her own process, and I do too. It makes for a constant rediscovery and reconnection between us."

As for job stress, Richard does not experience "any grief or a sense of loss," although he is affected by the suffering he witnesses. For example, he described a gay couple he had cared for who were both dying of AIDS. "These were Washington, D.C., people, business people, real estate people, authors of history. I thoroughly enjoyed them.

"They'd been together for fifteen years, and they were both deathly sick, side by side in each bed in a million-dollar home. They were in their late forties and both of their mothers were there, in their early eighties, wonderful, competent, lovely ladies. And I'd go there a few nights a week and be there from 10:00 P.M. until 8:00 A.M. and wake up several times because they would be having this terrible diarrhea. I would have to help them, and empty the potty and maybe clean up the floor, half-asleep myself. They were *so* sick. It was uncommonly pathetic because they were side-by-side sick."

Richard added that at the end, the couple "reached the point of awareness where they decided to quit fighting it and quit taking their medicines. And then suddenly one of them died in the morning, and then the other one died at night the same day. There was a nice story in the paper about it, very open about them being gay, and commenting on the remarkable way in which they died."

There can be other kinds of stress for Richard when a client is suffering. For example, one patient "had cancer for eight years and was getting really bored with it. He just quit eating, and he wanted me to get him his pills so he could kill himself. But I refused go to the bathroom to do it, and his wife refused to do it, so he was stuck with people who wouldn't give him the pills. I wanted to. It was the right thing to do. But my professional role wouldn't allow it. All the agencies would come down on me and I would not be able to get work. So that was a close call. I still wish I'd found a way to get those pills to him. Because it was stupid for him to spend two months not eating and getting weaker and weaker. He looked just like someone in a concentration camp. He got to the point where he couldn't talk and all I did with him was give him a bed bath and meditate."

Taking up this work required very little training. "You take a very simple class and get a certificate. You learn totally by experience, by trial and error. I've generally done things right the first time. One difficult thing was a heavy man with liver cancer, and I'd have to get him into a wheelchair so he could use the bathroom. It was the wrong decision, he should have had a bedpan. I couldn't control him and he ended up on the floor of the bathroom at two in the morning, and he was real hard to move but somehow I got my hands around him, facing him, and just lifted him right up and got him in his chair and back into his bed again. It was real clumsy, though nothing bad came of it. That's one of the definite hazards, hurting your back moving people around, or having people fall and hurt themselves."

Richard shared some of the techniques he has developed on the job. "When I do bed baths, I put the patient on something that's waterproof, like plastic garbage bags, and I get really big towels and make them pretty hot. I cover the patient all up with hot towels, and keep changing them for a while, and rub them around a little bit. And that's the bed bath. It's extremely relaxing and soothing. You have to be careful not to overheat people, but they just love it. Another thing that's really good is to rub the face and neck and rub the top of the head. Sometimes I do that. Not always—it depends on what can help them relax. But any time I touch a client, I'm always being loving. I'm always caressing them, squeezing them, appreciating them as I'm helping them move around."

He continued: "There's never an impersonal touch in my process. If I'm wiping their bottom, I wipe it a lot. I get it really clean and then I put on cream. It's very, very important to keep that region clean. It's a totally neutral thing to me now. I used to say, 'Shit and piss are my bread and butter.' After a while, you're desensitized to the genitals, the body, all the things there are phobias about in this culture." Richard has developed a "completely neutral" acceptance of the body, "of what's going on and what will help," without "resistance."

"Another thing I've done occasionally with clients is, I take them in my arms. There was one gay man, about twenty-five, who was really very weak, and I just spent hours holding him in my arms. It just seemed like the most natural thing to do. One evening I got in the bed and scooped him up and held him. And then I went home at midnight—it was very stormy—and he died within a few hours."

Reflecting on his own losses led Richard to recount his personal encounters with death and dying, and later, with higher consciousness. "I grew up in east Texas. My father died when I was nineteen, in 1962 right after I finished my sophomore year far away from home. He had a heart attack and died just like that, lying upside down on the couch taking nose drops. Very unexpected, and I was in Boston having a summer job after my second year at Massachusetts Institute of Technology, where I was studying physics. I took the news really calmly and flew back to Texas, my first time on a jet plane. And I went through the funeral and the family hanging together, and then went back to MIT. And I didn't really have grief or tears. There was something in me that wasn't troubled. It wasn't like being completely dead to my feelings or being repressed.

"Right after my father's death was the Cuban Missile Crisis, and there was a real sense of common danger that was undeniable. I had a very strong commitment that no matter what, I was not going to help design bombs or participate in this insanity in any way." In 1962, this was an uncommon sentiment for an MIT student.

Although his father had been a chemist and Richard had intended to be a physicist, he had trouble keeping up with the rigorous science work at MIT, "principally because I had a head injury when I was ten and that's affected my memory. I'm a little bit dyslexic. I'm very poor at languages or remembering words to songs. I have poor physical coordination and my social skills aren't sharp. I miss a lot that's going on and people operate around me more quickly than I can track. So I tend to go into the background and watch and listen carefully, and then interject creatively when I feel it's safe. So I was a real good nerd, growing up in east Texas and being the high school atheist and being socially isolated. Then I got to MIT and *everyone* was like me!

"For the next couple of years, I worked hard at MIT doing anything I wanted, which was to take courses in history, economics and psychology, history of science, and try to figure out what was going on in the world. There was the sense that World War III was just going to take us all away anyway. My father had been very keenly aware of that. He once said at the kitchen table, 'If there's a World War III, I can't see how we can possibly survive.' I believed him.

"I'd been reading about World War III ever since I fell on my head in the fifth grade, because after that I started reading adult books. I conjecture that I had a near-death experience. I don't remember it. I was knocked out. But I certainly became more introverted and more deep, more creative, and a lot more separate from the world around me after that experience. I spent two weeks in the hospital, and my photographs show a distinct kind of lifeless quality in my face after that. I understand now that it's common for head injury victims to have trouble with languages, communication, social skills, coordination and short memory of details. But I was a real crybaby until ninth grade, when I got into some kind of consciousness where I would just stare everyone down, because I was ready to kill them. As clumsy as I was, there'd be big trouble if they tried to attack me physically, and no one ever did after that.

"I was really concerned about death after junior high school, reading about Hiroshima and the Nazi death camps. I was scared of death. I remember my dad was signing us up for life insurance. In case I died, there'd be a thousand dollars to bury me. I was physically upset at this. This dread swept over me, and I suspect he felt it too. Another time we had a collie that was too big for our yard, and my dad and I took it to the vet to be put to sleep. This was my dad's choice, for me to witness this for some reason, watching the life fade out of my dog's eyes."

Richard's mother's approach to death was not much help to him. "Her quality was very gloomy. There was a family tradition of pain and fear and grief about death and a stiffness about the expression of these feelings. So death was a real issue for me, and I didn't have any direct handle on some way to deal with it until I started reading books on Zen Buddhism and on altered states of consciousness. Aldous Huxley was at MIT in 1960 when I went there, and he was the first enlightened teacher I'd ever met."

Huxley was a pioneer in describing altered states of consciousness— his *Doors of Perception*, first published in 1954, became a classic text— and attending Huxley's lectures was a turning point for Richard. He was further propelled by the "big shock, John F. Kennedy's death. A year after my dad's death, JFK was killed. It was an incredible event that had a planet-wide shock. I think it was the beginning of what we call the New Age. Everything came loose after that day. Suddenly the Beatles were singing, and '63 was when the mescaline and LSD experiments at Harvard began. My friend at a Unitarian youth group came in one Sunday looking really spaced, and I didn't know what that was. He was saying he'd had this experiment with mescaline at Harvard, and it had taken him a very long time to get across the river on the subway, and the advertisements looked incredibly beautiful to him."

Boston during the early sixties was the very nexus of what would later be called the "consciousness revolution." Richard recalls, "That was the first breath of it, in 1963–64. It was very exciting to me when I finally got some dope in early 1967 and started smoking it with the intention of discovering high consciousness, and it worked. I'd read Zen paperbacks and have these incredible mystical illuminations for ninety minutes and then fall back into the munchies. At the same time, I started going to these wonderful encounter groups and began to come alive as a person in a whole new way. It was just a tremendous period for me, a breaking out of school, out of books and into living experiences." Although Richard completed a master's degree in psychology at Boston University, he went to work as a night security guard and would thereafter devote his life to exploring deep dimensions of consciousness. To this day, he has continued his practices reading esoteric literature, meditating and applying his insights to everyday living.

Understanding Richard's history, especially his study of Zen Buddhism and psychology, brings insight into his style of caretaking. He believes that his greatest contribution to patients is that "I'm present in a way that doesn't need anything from them, that's very approving, very gentle, very accepting, and with a lot of trust in what's going on. So I'm not trying to fix them or change them or hold them to this level, and I'm not trying to push them off. I do a lot to stay in a very deep state myself and to stay happy in myself, and I do whatever I can to make their lives easy and pleasant. And they slip off in my presence. Quite often I can say things like, 'Well, just let go. There isn't any problem. This is natural. This is the time to just totally let go, don't fight anything.' And that's very, very, very helpful when the moment is right. Quite often after that, they'll be gone in a day."

Richard tells his clients, "It's like going to sleep, or, if you're starting to have lots of strange memories, and they seem super real and you start to lose track of what's real and where you are, that's fine. You don't need to know what's going on, you don't need to understand it. It's totally safe to let go. And if you want to ask someone for help, if you meet any old friends, or Jesus, or anyone, just ask them for help and go to the party with them. If someone comes up in a taxi and says, 'Hey, hop in, we're going to a party,' go."

Richard reflected on his contribution to patients' families. "I give them a lot of approval. 'You're doing the right thing. Your feelings are valid. It's okay to feel upset and emotional and tired, frustrated, helpless.'

And I demonstrate to them how to talk about letting go. How to say goodbye, tell their parent or brother to let go, and it really works. People pick up on it and with just a little bit of encouragement, they'll start doing this. And everyone in the game, everyone who is in the house will start picking up on, 'Sure, it's time to let go. Sure, I love you; sure, we'll miss you, but it's time for you to go now, it's time now.' And everyone starts to come from this direct intuitive knowing that, in fact, it's fine. So, there's very little grief and hysteria and fighting against the inevitable. So, I'm sort of teaching by example. I'm the safe neutral person who doesn't make any trouble and who listens to everyone, and who comes up with helpful suggestions on a lot of levels."

Doing this work has changed Richard. "I've become much more robust in my inner spirituality," he explained. "And I've seen a lot of strange and miraculous events happen. I've had the satisfaction of *knowing* I've been there at critical moments for people and have been very, very helpful in fact, no doubt about it."

Richard then recounted a recent case that concerned "a lady who was quite ill, in her seventies, and she was quite a strong person, a real feisty old lady. When I met her she was weak, and there were embarrassing, literally shitty things wrong with her, and she was puffy and not very attractive, but she was radiant and cheerful. So I said, 'Do you remember your dreams?' If I ask that question, then they know I'll listen to any weird story." Richard has learned that this is a natural way to steer the conversation toward spiritual experience.

In this instance, "I found out that when she was in her early twenties, she had been in a coma for three weeks. I said, 'Wow, that's fantastic, what do you remember from that experience?' And she remembered the heavenly realm, and the stones that were like jewels, and the decision to come back, and then her present understanding that, 'Well, there's nothing to be afraid of.' She'd told very few people about it, so I was able to do what's called validation. 'That was absolutely real, lots of people have it, that's the way it really is and you're going to go there again.' So then I was called away to other cases, and I came back two months later and she was much weaker, but now she was in the middle of the house, in the living room, in a hospital bed. This is always a good sign. When patients set themselves up in the middle of the house, to share life with everyone rather than being hidden away in a back bedroom, it's a good sign because everyone is handling it in a very open way.

"Her dog would sit up on her chest and bark at her, and everyone was involved. There were brothers and sisters there, and one sister was still an active social worker at the age of eighty. We were watching this dreary TV murder drama for two hours. I just sat by the patient, because I could see that she was getting quite weak, and getting to the stage where she was looking without her eyes moving. That's a key thing, when the eyes get kind of dark and look without moving, without blinking, almost without seeing." When that happens, said Richard, a patient is very close to death, "probably actually spending their time in other realities and just checking back into their body once in a while. So I held her right hand, and her sister came over after this show ended and held her left hand. I said some things like, 'Well, you can let go now. Don't fight it anymore. You're going to be fine.' And her sister said the same thing—a very intelligent, willful and uptight lady, but she did the same thing, really earnestly and gently. The other brothers and sisters came over and everyone was clustered around the bed as if by unspoken agreement."

Seeing that she might have gone on like that for days, Richard asked the family, "'How does she feel about using the word *Jesus?*' Everyone said, 'No, she doesn't like to have any truck with religion.' But at that moment, her mouth fell open and her false teeth fell out. I watched this and I took out the teeth." Although the family had not noticed, she had stopped breathing. "She had died just at that moment when I had said, 'Jesus.'

"But also at that moment, I was watching her face, which had been getting more and more radiant. I could see her essential spiritual self shining through this old face. It got much more intense at the point of death, and it continued for another forty-five minutes or so. I said to everyone what I always say if I get the chance: 'Hey, let's not make any phone calls, let's not run around, let's just sit here and talk about her and appreciate this event.' And everyone said, 'Fine.' I find that my leadership is just to mention things. That's really how it always goes. So I sat and watched this light changing and deepening in her. She was still present in a body that was gone, and then suddenly the face looked totally vacant and inert and primitive. I'd never been through the process with that much clarity. The radiance in and around her face persisted for forty-five minutes and went through some modulations and subtle deepenings, and then really clicked out rather quickly."

To those who choose to go through the dying experience with another person, Richard offered: "Everyone knows that something very significant is going on. Obviously the client, and the mates, and the close friends and the helper, are all aware that it's profound. In our culture it's a very mysterious process; there are a lot of superstitions about it, a lot of almost completely mistaken views. A typical view is that something bad is going on. Another mistaken view is that you have to control it, or understand it. There is relatively profound ignorance about the fact that everyone's minds are joined, that everyone can trust their intuitions, trust their hunches about what's going on and how to communicate. There are also notions that God is distant or judgmental or rejecting or inaccessible, rather than being the infinity within each of us. It's just incredible, the misunderstanding that's in our culture.

"Even people who have had near-death experiences—they have something that is really profound and yet it's not very developed. They know basically there's nothing to fear, they've made contact with a wider realm of identity, but that's still not the same as having a deep understanding that they can work with thoughtfully; or having a consistent meditative practice to deepen and expand their explorations, or teach it to other people. Probably the best common thing that people know about is asking Jesus for help, the idea that something loves them, approves of them, will guide them. That seems to be a broadly shared archetype."

Richard believes that those who come to the bedside when death is near will have a spiritual experience. "When a person dies, they are literally making a fundamental expansion into a higher level of identity. To a certain extent, they are meeting a god realized. And that's very contagious, everyone shares in it. So when my dad died, for instance, everyone in the family had something profound touch them, something unspoken, and everyone got a lot of energy. Their lives developed and accelerated in pretty healthy ways. When President Kennedy died, that happened to the country and the whole world. That's what's behind the old practice of sacrifice, of animals and of people, and even of sacrifice of people in war. All this dying sort of opens up the barriers between different levels of reality, and so the traffic flows both ways. When someone in the family dies, everyone in the family gets an effusion of certain aspects of that person's competence, because we're all one mind."

Although this standpoint may seem too esoteric for many, for Richard, "this is all stuff I take for granted. It's a demonstration of the spiritual healing principle of the infinite way." Richard then described a very influential source. "Joel Goldsmith, a man who lived from 1892 to 1964, wrote a book called *The Infinite Way* in 1946. His point was that if you learn to open sufficiently, to make an inner-God contact, with a sense of presence and peace, as you go about your worldly affairs, you'll notice each day that things work out very well and often not according to plan. In fact, all kinds of problems disappear rather mysteriously, whether financial, personal relationship or physical healing. And people who come into contact with you also experience a healing. It's not always a peaceful resolution that happens to yourself and others, but it's always a resolution that speeds the process of realization itself. In other words, people get what they need in order to come into a more profound awakening. They may sometimes fall into a troubled experience, but it's one that leads to a lot more growth, and overall there's a big saving of pain."

This is the paradigm from which Richard performs his duties. It includes spiritual as well as physical care. He described how he applies his approach to the tasks at hand: "The spiritual healer has to be totally unconcerned about history, diagnosis, treatments, symptoms and outcomes, but rather he or she must abide in the direct experience of the whole infinite, which is right here where we are. It's a very gentle, silent awareness, and you just amiably go along with whatever is happening on the level of human drama, doing commonsense things, and overall you see this tremendous cooperation in all elements of the situation and mysterious positive outcomes."

We asked Richard to generalize about what types of individuals are able to weather the home-death experience. His only reservation was "families where people are extremely dysfunctional, like out-and-out schizophrenia, or alcoholism." Otherwise, "I've seen everyone handle it really well. I highly recommend it." He added the caution that "there needs to be sufficient support because generally the family goes through a lot of trouble taking care of an ill member. They stretch themselves way beyond any sane limits, and they don't know how to ask for help from friends and agencies. They often make really primitive mistakes when anyone who has any knowledge could come in and show them how to do things, like diet and changing bedding and treating pain, and also giving up trying to make the patient recover. So family members get to be very tired. Their whole life is disrupted. They feel very helpless, very guilty, very ashamed, and it's very moving on all kinds of levels. Also, when a person is dying, he or she is starting to cross the boundaries a lot, so there's a psychic field in the house that's different. Strange things happen and this goes on for a long time before the actual death. So there's a tremendous turning over of the soil in everyone.

"I've known families that specialized in this. There was the young man with AIDS in his brother's house, and this family had already seen two grandparents and an aunt through the death process over the preceding fifteen years. And everyone in the family was pretty competent— the twelve-year-old, and the eighteen-year-old, and the father and the wife—they already knew and understood a lot. They had matured enormously as a family. It had been given to them."

Richard continued: "One of the first things I try to find out is whether people in the family have been through this before. A lot of people have been intimately involved with a parent or a family member or a friend who has died. I think that is really beneficial, because you come away from that experience with a fundamental loss of fear. You have met the most undesirable thing that can be dreamed of—in our level of creativity, the death of someone's body, the loss of someone—and experienced its fundamental normalcy, even harmlessness, the significance in it."

Richard also explained how he determines exactly where a client is in the dying process. "The real obvious marker is their physical condition. Have they stopped eating, do they sleep a lot, are they trying to make things happen or are they fundamentally just letting each day unfold in its own way? Are they still talking a lot about getting well or going on trips and stuff like that?" And there are more advanced markers, physically. "They are really not eating and hardly swallowing pills and hardly even drinking. Their eyes aren't moving—their eyes will be open, staring blankly into space. Another sign is if they gurgle a little, their lungs are filling up with fluid."

But there is more to it than physical markers, insisted Richard. "The instant I sit down with a person, almost always I take them by the hand and I look them in the eyes and say, 'Hi, my name is Richard.' By that point, I've already learned just about everything I need to know. I suppose I pick up a lot just psychically." Often, as death approaches, Richard doesn't "have to say a thing to people to grease the skids for them. If there's a quiet moment, I'll say, 'Let go,' and I mean it. I know what I'm saying." Having experienced transcendent consciousness through meditation, Richard has "learned how to let go. So my pronouncement has power."

Richard has noticed certain patterns in how dying people cope with their passages in the dying process. Since he began this work, he said, it seems that people have become "more honest, they're more in charge, they want to be at home, they want to control the amount of pain medication they take. They decide whether they're going to eat or not, whether they're going to take medicine or not. The client has quite a lot more control now and quite a bit more willingness to just let go and die. And to talk about it openly. 'I'm tired of this going on and I want it to be finished.' And I think there's very little fear of being punished or judged by God."

When patients do experience fear, it's because "they're losing control, they look ugly, they can't do anything that's fun, like eat and have sex and run around, and it's very, very strange. In our culture, people are almost entirely outer focused and they're overbusy. They have very little inner development, so the illness and death process is for most people the only experience with a lot of free time, no responsibilities, prolonged vacation, surrender, being babied, being touched, being emotional, people caring for them, having to depend on others, being radically bored for days, weeks, months and years. It's also a time of confronting really deep issues, like what is life and what is death and what's life all about. And they can't escape anymore, except maybe into television or possibly into over-medication. But dying is really an amazing process for people. It really balances out the deficiencies in our culture," especially the lack of custom and time for self-examination and reflection.

"Another thing is, a lot of people feel profoundly guilty and ashamed, and so they're getting the punishment that they believe they need. They feel, 'Well okay, this is the worst that can happen and I'm getting what I deserve so now I can relax and be okay.' Like the most terrifying thing has finally come upon you and snatched you up in its jaws. Once you're really in it, it's not so bad. It's just day by day."

When clients feel comfortable about their dying, said Richard, it has a lot to do with their own experience of the mystical, of transcending ordinary consciousness. Usually "it's because they've already had a spiritual awakening, or they've had an out-of-body experience, a near-death experience, or they've had someone who has died come back and appear and say, 'I'm fine.' That's a very common story. I run into that a few times a year. I'll ask, 'Has anyone you've known ever died? Did you ever dream about them, or did something happen?' And they'll say, 'Yeah, I woke up and there they were at the foot of my bed just shining with blue light, with a big grin, saying, 'I'm just fine, Sally.'"

Richard reflected on his own psychic or intuitive experiences in relation to the dying, and he offered several vivid examples. The first occurred years ago during a hospital visit to a co-worker, an alcoholic who was very ill from liver failure. "As I was by his bed talking to him, I saw him shine with a characteristic blue light, which is what happens when I have an intense spiritual connection with someone." Richard did not mention this to anyone, and later that night at home, he dreamed of a man being poisoned and then later walking around "just fine. The next day, I discovered my co-worker had died. I made a connection with my dream. I think that dream was about his experience of dying."

Another example occurred during the first months that Richard worked as a home health aide, when he cared for a "very sweet" Presbyterian minister for six twelve-hour days. Though dying of lung cancer, this client "was totally rational. I would give him a bed bath and hang out with him and his wife. They told me about their lives and their children, including one who had died as a law enforcement officer. They never knew whether it was a suicide or he'd been killed. There's kind of a healing quality to these discussions, because I said things like, 'Well, you know he did what he wanted to do, he had the kind of life he needed to have. It was a success. He did die, but that wasn't really a failure, that was the kind of life he had to lead, to live on the edge like that. And it's not your fault, you didn't do anything wrong. He was who he really was.' And they got that."

Then one noontime, shortly after Richard had given his patient a bed bath, one of the couple's sons arrived and took his mother shopping. The minister was sitting up in bed as Richard sat at the foot, tuning and listening to the radio. "There was this program about Spanish culture and a folk story from New Mexico about a woman who kills her children. As a ghost she goes around wailing, and the kids are supposed to be scared and not run around at night. It's a classical folktale, and then this incredible, uncanny wail came out of the radio we were fiddling with."

Although neither Richard nor the minister spoke, the sound was penetrating. Within moments, there was "this funny kind of gurgling sound and it was his breathing. I looked up at him and he looked at me. I went closer and he said, 'Call the doctor.' That happened to be his last bit of air, because his lungs were filling. I dialed 911 and notified the authorities, and meanwhile I could see he was sort of jumping in his bed. When I went close to see him, he was just staring straight ahead and there was still a pulse in his neck, but I knew he was leaving. And I broke into a sweat, bending over there and looking right into his face, and from deep, deep, deep in the middle of me, the word "Christ" came up. Just Christ. That was the only prayer that I could say at that moment. Just the word. And the pulse stopped. He was just sitting there with his eyes wide open, gone.

"At the same moment, there was a knock on the door. It was my wife, coming over for the first time ever to bring me my lunch that I'd forgotten. The next moment, two ambulance crews arrived. The next moment after that, my boss arrived, because her beeper had gone off and she was nearby. Then the minister's doctor arrived because he was in the area and *his* beeper had gone off. We were all gathered there as the ambulance people put him on the floor, and then the doctor said, 'Oh well, don't bother trying to bring him back.' And so they left him alone, put him back in bed, and then I just washed him. Just a half an hour after I'd given him a bed bath, I washed up all this blood and changed the bed. When his wife and son came back, he was all clean and she got to come in and cry and say goodbye and all that. It was just amazing, the orchestration. Within sixty seconds of my saying 'Christ,' everyone arrived to take care of the situation."

This story prompted Richard to recount what he considers his most clear and deliberate experience of deep spiritual work with a client. The patient, a retired high school principal, had already "learned to meditate and he'd studied some spiritual teachings. I would go over every week and spend an hour meditating with him and his family. He was one of those guys who sat in a chair in the middle of the house, day and night. His name was Harry, a very friendly man, lots of spunk and play. I encouraged him in my ways of letting go in the meditation, and we would just go into these profound silences together for an hour every week. Then we'd talk to other people in his family and eat and have a good old time. I'd visit for about three hours every week; they paid for an hour. That was fine. One day when I showed up, he raised his head and said, 'I'm getting weaker.' I said, 'Well, don't fight it, you know what to do, just let go, you'll be fine.' He said, 'I'm glad *you* think so, Richard.'" Richard laughed at the recollection. "He had that kind of wit."

Two nights later, "on a Saturday morning, I had a strange dream. I was in the garage and the door was open, and this big box made of thick metal walls was grinding without wheels into the garage. *KRRRRG*. I watched it come to a halt in front of me, and then it silently cracked open. These big pieces of metal just fell open. It was empty, an immense box as big as the garage. And dead silence. I woke up and thought, 'Now that was weird. It must mean that Harry died.' Within a few minutes, Harry's wife called me. He had died about the same time as my dream, and so peacefully that she thought that he had just gone to sleep. And the previous day had been very relaxed and happy and he was talking about a lot of people that other people couldn't see."

Richard interpreted the dream: "It was the theme of something rigid breaking open; the stillness; and something coming home, like a car getting parked in a garage. There was a lot of light as well. And the breaking of the rigid structures of this realm, something that just cracks open into space and light and silence. It was a very impersonal dream, which suited his intelligence, and the kind of space I shared with him—a very empty space of complete peace and bliss."

Sometimes, Richard's patients have volunteered to share their psychic experiences. One octogenarian told him about an accident that had occurred fifty years earlier. "He'd been an oil worker, and his arm got caught in a cable and got ripped right out. He had an out-of-body experience, spiraling higher and higher into this very beautiful western landscape with beautiful ranches and healthy cows. He was never afraid of dying after that." Richard validated the old man's experience, telling him, "That's all real, that's what happens."

Richard also tells his clients, "Whatever's happening, if you see some kind of light or situation or person, go straight ahead into the very middle of it." He believes, "That's a very helpful general rule. Just go right ahead into the middle of anything that comes up. If there's a yellow light, go right in the middle of the light. The color doesn't matter. The principle is to go forth voluntarily, right straight forward into things. Because basically it's always one's own production. You only make contact with yourself.

"I think death is quite complex and subtle, because in fact we are right now in the middle of infinite multidimensional realities, second by second, which are constantly fluctuating. A lot of the time we aren't here right now. We only spend a small fraction of our waking day in the body, in this place, playing the games on this level. Almost every moment we are somewhere else as well. And I call that the principle of 'already above.' Both sides of every situation are going on at once."

If Richard could put together a survival kit for family members experiencing the dying of a loved one at home, first and foremost he would include music. "I'd give them about ten tapes of people like John Aston, and other music like the Emperor Concerto, extremely beautiful, holy, high, playful, loving music. I'd put in quite a variety of religious pictures and icons. The Virgin of Guadalupe is excellent. Jesus and the Buddha and other characters. And I expect a videotape of a movie like *Resurrection* or *Terms of Endearment,* really true, spiritual, human movies. Of course, tapes and videos about near-death experiences and spiritual experience. And a lot of information on how to enjoy simple foods like blender drinks that are real easy to get down and nourishing. There's a lot of stuff about physical care that's helpful to know, just as simple as buying diapers, and skin patches that deliver the pain killer with no hassle. Put a patch on and you're covered for three days. There's no need for there to be any pain. There still needs to be a lot more available to educate people about meditation and prayer that they can hear and accept and work with."

It seems providential that Richard found a way to apply his spiritual beliefs and practices through a vocation where the need is so great. He confided that although he might seem unusual, he is not unique. In his town, Richard is sought after. "Fortunately, there are plenty of people in home care administration who are glad to have oddballs like me, because they know what we're really doing. So I'm supported very well by my bosses, and always have been."

Notes

I Guess I Was Meant to Be a Caretaker

Jeanine Strong

A forty-year-old African American, Jeanine Strong is the executive director of a human services agency in a small city. She is divorced with two teenage daughters, and lives with her partner, Arthur, who has grown children of his own. In addition, Jeanine is close to her parents and siblings and maintains a warm and caring relationship with members of her staff. Indeed, her sense of family seems to extend well into the community she serves.

It was as a boss and mentor that Jeanine first came to know Sharon Thornton, an outgoing African-American lesbian with a special gift for working with young people. When Sharon was diagnosed with breast cancer, all her friends and colleagues were called upon to help, but no one did for Sharon what Jeanine did. Jeanine took Sharon into her home during Sharon's last weeks of life. This act was complicated by a series of recent losses in Arthur's family and the sudden arrival of his three small grandchildren, who came to live with Jeanine and Arthur as Sharon was dying. Jeanine's is a complex and sometimes astonishing story of endurance, generosity and compassion. She began it by describing her family.

∼

"I have a daughter who's a senior in high school and one who's a sopho-more, and I have a partner whose name is Arthur. And then we have had three little ones living with us—a four-year-old, a three-year-old and a two-year-old. Arthur is their biological grandfather. Their father was stabbed two years ago and subsequently died. But they didn't live with their father. The reason that we have them is because they were removed from their mother by the Department of Social Services. So we are doing relative foster care. They ended up coming to us at the same time that Sharon was at the house."

She shook her head and laughed. "I tell people I should put a sign on the house that says, 'Jeanine's Rest Home—All Ages Welcome.' We have a small three-bedroom house. Because my oldest daughter goes to a board-ing school, her room was empty. So the three boys were upstairs in the spare room, and Sharon was stationed in the living room on the couch.

"I couldn't believe the timing of it. But I look back and think that it was fate or maybe God bringing the boys to us. Having three little ones there helped alleviate some of the tension and the distress that we were all under due to Sharon's illness. In the mornings it was a challenge get-ting them all off. Arthur had to be up and out of the house by five-thirty for work, and my daughter would get up for school and leave about seven-thirty. I'd get up and get the boys ready and fed, and then Sharon would station them in the living room with the TV, and she would keep an eye on them while I got dressed. So even though it was totally crazy, it was also helpful with all that we were going through. Little kids are a hand-ful, but they are also a great joy."

As Jeanine recounted her acquaintance with Sharon, it was clear that she was still processing Sharon's death, which had occurred five months earlier. Her tense repeatedly shifted from present to past, as often hap-pens when survivors speak of those who have recently died: "Sharon is, has been an employee of mine since she came to work for the agency six years ago. I've been executive director of the agency for eight years.

"The agency is a resource for underrepresented populations, which includes people of color, single heads of households, low-income people who are needing assistance around employment or discrimination kinds of things. We are probably the only truly multicultural organization in town, in terms of the makeup of the staff. On staff we have African Americans, we have some Latino people, we have an Asian woman, we have people who are gay, we have white people." Jeanine first got to know Sharon when she contacted the agency for help with a problem she was having on the job. "When a position came open here at the agency, Sharon left that job and started working here. She was an employee who came to be a very good friend. In her words, I was her second mother, even though we're just three years apart. . . . Sharon was an out lesbian and had been one for a long time, very proud of her identity, and a very caring person. She helped a lot of people, sometimes to the exclusion of taking care of herself. She was very friendly, very forthright. One of the things that I probably helped her with was learning how to be tactful and still get her point across." Jeanine smiled.

"I didn't know much about her family, initially." Jeanine explained that Sharon had grown up in a nearby town but did not have a close relationship with her family. Her parents divorced when Sharon was three. "Sharon's mother is a Jehovah's Witness. Sharon was the oldest, so she had a lot of responsibility for helping to raise her brother and sisters. I think things had occurred in her childhood, unpleasant things. It was not what I would consider a close family. At the age of sixteen Sharon went to live with the mother of one of her friends, who was like a mother to her."

Jeanine continued: "I would say that I come from a close family. I was fortunate to grow up in a household that had both my parents. My father was a professor and my mother worked in the administration office of the college. Because of the work that my father did, we were exposed to a lot of different people. A lot of the grad students were international students, and it was a rare holiday when it would be just immediate family. There was always somebody else there for as long as I can remember. I have an older brother and two younger sisters, and all but one of us lives here in town now. We get together at holidays, we go places together, we talk with each other on a regular basis. To me, that's what a close family is."

When Jeanine first separated from her husband, she had a baby and a toddler. Her family is the reason that she stayed in the area. "I really wanted my daughters to know their grandparents and be friends with them, and to have a close, loving relationship. I knew that my daughters would need a good, strong male role model, and I knew that I would need a lot of support as a single mother starting from step one—actually, below step one. I've never regretted that I've stayed here, because I got a lot of support. If it wasn't for my parents and for my brother and my sisters, I don't know where I would be. I still have that same support today, so sometimes it's hard for me to have a good understanding of how families are not close.

"Sharon came to town when she was nineteen, and her friends here became her family. When she joined the staff at the agency, we became in many ways her immediate family. It's a close staff. There are many people who have been there for a long time, and that's one of the things I like about it. I appreciate it as a single parent. My kids started participating in the programs at the agency when they were four years old, and there were people working there then who still work at the agency today. Especially nowadays, when so many kids may not have the support of their immediate families, extended or surrogate families are really important. My kids and many other kids in the community know that if something were to happen—whether it's something at school or in the neighborhood, whether it's major or little—here's a place that I can go and somebody's going to help me.

"Sharon would say all the time that the agency was her family. I was a mentor to her, a good friend. We spoke outside of work on the telephone. We didn't hang out though. I was 'friend' but also 'boss.' We would talk, and I knew a lot about her personal life. I would counsel her about that or just be supportive. She gave me a lot of support as well."

The difference in their sexual orientations was never a problem said Jeanine. "It was not an issue for me at all, because my very best friend, Celeste, is a male who lives as a female. I met her the year after I graduated from high school and my mother was horrified, because that was not something that she knew about. You know, coming from the South, and then cultural things—African Americans have a phobia around these issues. So I've helped my parents, my mother particularly, to be accepting of differences in sexual orientation. Now Celeste is a part of our family.

"Sharon worked with teenagers, and what a support, what a role model for them! They really loved her. She would help them and they would feel free to call her after hours. Whether it had something to do with school or fighting with parents or siblings or boyfriends, whatever it was, she was there. She put her heart and soul into her work, into her kids, as she called them. 'These are my kids,' she would say."

Although Sharon's job at the agency did not pay much, she supplemented her income with two part-time jobs. "She liked nice things. She leased a very nice sports car. She lived by herself and had a very nice apartment. She always dressed well." Sharon worked cleaning houses in the mornings, so it was unusual when she called the agency one morning in the spring. Jeanine's secretary telegraphed trouble, personally coming into Jeanine's office to tell her to take Sharon's call: "Sharon's on the phone, something's wrong."

"I get on the phone and I'm like, 'Sharon, what's up?' She is just crying. She can barely get the words out. She says, 'I have cancer' and I was just shocked, and sort of disbelieving." Although Jeanine had known that Sharon had noticed a lump beneath her armpit, no one was worried, in part because Sharon "was very health conscious. She used a lot of holistic medicine. She really believed in that. She lifted weights. At one point, before she got ill, she was training to become a female body builder." Later, Jeanine learned that months before the diagnosis, Sharon had treated the lump "with some homeopathic stuff. It didn't work, so she went to the doctor. He sent her to a surgeon. At the time they thought that it was just a cyst, no big deal. Then Sharon had a biopsy. The day I got the phone call was the day she got the results.

"When Sharon said, 'I have cancer,' all this stuff was going through my head, but I knew I needed to get her calmed down. She just got this news, she's by herself, she's sobbing. So I said, 'Where are you, Sharon?' She hung up. She was just in such a state. Then I ran upstairs to her supervisor and we tried to get phone numbers. I called her best friend, Maggie, and called her partner at the time, Lynne. Finally, Lynne called me back and said, 'I'm with her.' She'd helped Sharon get calmed down.

"Sharon came by later that day. She told me they thought it was breast cancer, even though this lump had been in the armpit. She was devastated, of course. There was the whole thing of, 'Why me? How could this happen? I don't smoke. I'm health conscious. I lift weights. I eat right.' She was the one who was always telling the rest of us what you should do, how to exercise, those kinds of things. She was just weak with despair. In our staff's usual style, we rallied around her. Because of what they found in the biopsy, they figured there might be more, so they scheduled surgery. I went to the hospital while Sharon had surgery. I brought her this little angel and was there when she came out of surgery. I met her mother and her younger sister. Maggie was there, and Lynne. Maggie had been Sharon's lover for seventeen years and now they were best friends."

For Jeanine, this was the starting point of being on hand for Sharon during her fifteen months of treatment, including chemotherapy and radiation. Informing their co-workers was going to be hard. Jeanine said, "Sharon, you need to tell the staff. First of all, it's a small staff. People are going to know. People are going to wonder why you aren't here. Or, what's going on? Your hair's going to start falling out. Let's talk." So Sharon came to a staff meeting and as the time got closer, she leaned over and she said to me, 'I just can't do it. Will you tell them?' Then she got up and left.

"I was the one who told the staff that Sharon had breast cancer. I told them that she was having a difficult time and she didn't want to talk about it. I told them, 'Give her a hug, tell her you love her, be supportive, but don't ask any questions unless she wants to talk.' They were all stunned but of course rallied around her." However, it was not always easy to help. Sharon "was a very private person and she didn't want to feel like she was a bother. She was so independent. I told her, 'You shouldn't be going to the doctor by yourself,' because it was really hard on her. 'I will work with the staff, we'll get a schedule together so that each time you go, you'll have support.'" But Sharon rejected this plan. "No, no, no. I'll take care of it," she insisted to Jeanine.

Then one day Jeanine got a call from Lucy, an elderly member of the agency's board who had been at the oncologist's office at the same time that Sharon was there. "Bless her heart, here Lucy was dying of lung cancer and she was concerned about Sharon, because Sharon was there by herself and she was in a real emotional state. She had sort of broken down. So I called up Sharon and I read her the riot act, because I wasn't going to baby her. She needed that, and she didn't want to be babied. I said, 'Stop acting nutty. Get yourself together and let's figure this out.' Then she started having somebody go with her, and sometimes I went with her. Maggie would be the main one to go."

It soon became evident to Jeanine that Sharon's current partner, Lynne, was a problem. "This part is really difficult for me," Jeanine said. At the time that Sharon found out about the cancer, she had been going out with Lynne for several months. They met when Lynne was with her boyfriend, the father of her son; they were all friends. "The little boy was in the agency's after-school program." Then Lynne's boyfriend left town, "and ultimately this relationship developed between Sharon and Lynne.

"I might as well just be real honest here. Lynne is a self-centered bitch. It became obvious fairly quickly that this was a one-sided relationship. I can't tell you the number of times that Sharon would be crying and have to leave work early or come in late because of all this turmoil around Lynne. Sharon had very quickly fallen deeply in love. When she fell for somebody, she would fall very, very hard and really give and give. For some reason, Sharon was always attracted to bisexual women and then would get hurt because they would end up going back with the male. In some respects, I think it was for her this power thing. It always caused her heartbreak and it would always drag on and she would be miserable. I saw that begin to happen with Lynne—Sharon's buying her stuff, she's paying for the little boy's daycare, she's paying the girl's rent. Lynne had a full-time secretarial job, not that she made a whole lot of money, but come on here. The picture became clear for all of us. The whole staff, everybody, knew what was going on.

"Sharon would ask my opinion and I'd kind of slap her up. I'd be honest with her, and I wasn't going to beat around the bush. But I'd also tell her, 'This is your life. You wanted to know how I feel and I told you. Now you gotta do what you gotta do. But don't whine and moan. Don't ask me can you go home early. Tell that girl to stop calling here.' Because Lynne would call Sharon five times a day. If Lynne wasn't calling Sharon, Sharon was calling Lynne. It really was impacting her work. A couple of times I had to really put on the boss hat. Eventually, Sharon accepted that although she and Lynne had started out strong and did truly care for one another, Lynne was not ready to commit to her."

When Sharon's cancer was diagnosed, "all of us"—Jeanine, the staff and Maggie—expected that Lynne would be at Sharon's side, that "Lynne was really going to rally around Sharon. It didn't happen. Anger started to build up in all of us. Lynne did not even go to chemotherapy with her." To make matters even worse, Maggie was Lynne's boss. In fact, Lynne had gotten her job with Maggie through Jeanine. "So now I felt bad for Maggie, because here she was upset with Lynne but she had to look at her every day because she was her secretary. Maggie was the one who took Sharon to chemo all the time. The few times that she couldn't, I would go."

Sharon's mother was no help during this period either. Although she came for the surgery, she did not come back to assist with the chemotherapy and radiation treatments, although she lived only thirty-five miles away. "She would call Sharon on the phone, but that was about it. Now you have to understand their relationship. Sharon rarely went home to visit. If she did, she would spend maybe an hour and after that she was ready to go. Her mother is one of these people who doesn't know how to show love in a positive way. Everything is, 'This is wrong, this is wrong, why don't you do this?' Nagging all the time and making snide comments. Of course, she was never happy about Sharon's being a lesbian, although she was as accepting as she could be of Maggie, because they were together for so long."

During those fifteen months losses were mounting at the agency. Lucy, the elderly board member, died of lung cancer over the winter, and the following spring, there was an unexpected tragedy. Jerry, a young man on the staff who had grown up with the agency, lost his four-month-old son to SIDS, sudden infant death syndrome. "Lucy's death and baby Joshua's death affected all of us, but for Sharon I think also it was: *Death*. You know what I mean? She knew she had cancer, and I think there was even more fear in her."

When Sharon finished her chemotherapy program in the middle of the summer, everyone felt like celebrating. "She wanted us to give her a party at work. She was so happy; everybody was happy!" Sharon celebrated so hard the first night that she was too hung over to come into work the next day. "It was so funny I just laughed. We had planned the party on that day, but she didn't come to work because of her damn hangover. When she did get back to work the following day, she realized, 'Oh there was no party for me.' So they got her a cake and had a little party. It was so happy because she was like, 'I've made it now. I went through my fifteen months of treatment. I've made it.'"

Four weeks after Sharon's celebration of the end of her chemotherapy treatment, however, Jeanine returned from a week off and received two messages from work. "Sharon was in the hospital. They thought she had a tumor. She'd started walking, to build herself back up from the chemo and the radiation, and was complaining about weakness. She had called the doctor that morning because it was getting worse and her leg was dragging. The doctor's office sent her over to the hospital for some tests, and while she was there she had a seizure.

"Arthur came home and we went to the hospital. Now, the last time I had seen Sharon was the week before, when she was looking good, really happy. We walked around the nurse's station and ahead of me I saw somebody holding onto a wheelchair. There was a nurse supporting the person. The person was dragging her leg. I got up closer and she turned halfway and—it was Sharon. My heart just dropped. The change in her, I couldn't believe it! She wasn't able to walk by herself. I'd just seen the girl a few days ago. When she turned and saw me, she just broke into tears, sobbing, 'I have a brain tumor.' I just held her and she cried."

Jeanine had to go out of town the next day, and Sharon made her promise to call to find out the results of her tests. "So I called that night. She answered the phone and in typical Sharon fashion said, 'I can't talk about this. Here, I want my mother to tell you.' Her mother had come to town the day before. Sharon put her mother on the phone. There were two tumors in her brain that were pressing in. There was swelling and that's what had caused the temporary paralysis in her leg. And it wasn't only the leg but her arm as well, and it was just horrible. Here this girl had just been celebrating less than a month ago. I got back on the phone with her, just talked and told her I loved her and that we'd figure this out.

"Sharon had a great fear of death. It was something she'd had since early childhood, didn't quite know where it came from, but it was close to a phobia. You can imagine, for somebody with that phobia to have cancer! Her way of dealing with it was that she didn't want to know the details about anything. She never wanted to know and asked them not to tell her anything about chances." She would learn about the medications or the chemotherapy schedule, "but nothing about prognosis. Nothing. She knew about the brain tests, but that's all. She didn't want to know. She actually made people leave the room when they talked about her."

When Jeanine got back to the hospital to see Sharon a few days later, there were "tons of visitors. People brought her flowers and they brought her stuffed animals and they brought her food, because she used to love to eat. She had a lot of support. I went in the morning and she told me she wanted a happy face T-shirt, so I went searching all over and finally found one. I went back to the hospital later, with Arthur, and took the T-shirt.

"She had told me that she wanted a bunch of people there, and Lynne was there, and Maggie and her partner were there, and Arthur, and two other people." In fact, Sharon was throwing a party for Lynne. The same day that she had been diagnosed with the brain tumors had been Lynne's birthday. Lynne had stayed with her that night, but was annoyed by all the visitors and left the next day for the weekend. To make it all up to her, Sharon had arranged for someone "to get a birthday cake for Lynne and bring it to the hospital. Even in the midst of all this stuff, Sharon was trying to take care of people."

When Jeanine arrived at the celebration, Sharon asked to talk to her, "and we left everyone in the room and went down the hallway. I could tell by Lynne's face that she wasn't happy. Sharon and I walked around a corner, sat down at a table and started to talk. She just wanted to tell me everything that had happened, how she was feeling.

"All of a sudden here comes Lynne with her little boy, Mitchell. She came around a corner and she shouted, 'I'm leaving!' and Sharon said, 'Well, wait, where are you going?' Lynne shot back, 'Obviously I'm not invited to *this* party you're having and I'm leaving!'

"She was hollering in the hospital from one end of the corridor to the other. It was awful. I didn't know what to do. I'm saying, 'Stay calm, Sharon,' and 'Lynne, come on over here. You come sit down. I'll talk to Sharon later.'"

But "Lynne wouldn't sit down, and shouted, 'No! All these people and you're not telling me anything!' I could see Sharon just melt before me. A nurse came out and peeked her head around the corner. She left because Lynne was hollering, 'I'm sick of this!' and on and on. And poor little Mitchell. He loved Sharon; she helped raise him. It was horrible." Someone had summoned a security guard, who arrived on one elevator just as Lynne and her son got on another one. Jeanine just held Sharon, who was crushed. Jeanine was furious.

Sharon got angry, but her anger was not directed at Lynne. "Sharon was angry at the oncologist. She was angry at the surgeon. They didn't do something right. She got a lawyer, Dan, who was also like a brother to her. They were investigating whether to sue. A lump had popped up on her arm. They had done a biopsy and said that it wasn't anything, that it could have been the medicine. Sharon also found out the pharmacy she used had incorrectly filled one of her prescriptions. Ultimately, that pharmacist was charged with a crime and was actually closed down because he was doing all this fraudulent stuff with people's prescriptions."

Certain that other mistakes must have been made, Sharon had arranged for a second opinion at a nationally recognized cancer center. "I went to the hospital that morning because I had bought a care package for her—the juice, the fruit, everything that she would need to go for the day. Sharon left the hospital, went to the cancer clinic and came back that night. She had the exam but she didn't want to know anything, so her mother and Maggie had left Sharon in the room and went to hear from the doctor. In typical Sharon fashion, she called me when she got back to say, 'I can't talk about this. I told Maggie to call you and Maggie will tell you.' She couldn't tell me because she didn't know what she didn't want to know.

"It was kind of funny, because she didn't want to know but she wanted everybody else to know. So Maggie told me that the cancer had spread. The second opinion was the same as what the other doctor had said. It had spread. Sharon did not want to accept that. The prognosis at that time was, could be six months, could be nine months." When Sharon returned home after this hospitalization, she was weak and dispirited. "Maggie and I tried to figure out what we were doing. Sharon needed a medical ID bracelet, so we got the application from the doctors and filled it out. The agency paid for the bracelet. She wanted gold, so we got her gold. Then I went to the pharmacy and got her a walker.

"Sharon was having such a hard time dealing with all of this. She was just numb and so depressed: 'I don't want to see anybody. I don't want to talk to anybody.' The people at work really wanted to see her, they were so concerned about her. Finally I convinced her to come down just for a while. I told her, 'I'll come and get you because you need to see them.' She really wanted to come but she was scared. She didn't want people to see her like that 'cause she was still dragging her leg some, but it worked out all right. People were glad to see her and she stayed for a while and that was the first step in getting her to come back to work.

"In September, Sharon came back. The medicine actually did help. She got to the point where she didn't need a cane and was walking better. The local paper did this big article on breast cancer. They featured five women, and Sharon was one of the women, and one male. And there was this beautiful picture. Sharon was a very stylish person and after her hair came out, she wore a kerchief around her head. Then she worked herself up and came in one day without the kerchief. She was bald but she was beautiful. A perfect-shaped head, just beautiful. Then we were laughing because she told me, 'You know there's something about this bald head—all these women are coming up to me.'"

Sharon's suspicion of her medical care persisted. "She was sure they hadn't done something right. I felt bad for her oncologist, who was a really nice guy. She treated him like shit. It was a wonderful office and he was a wonderful man. The times I went with her, she'd talk to the office staff, but she wouldn't even speak to him. He was the bearer of bad news: It was all the doctor's fault. If they had done this, then that wouldn't have happened; it was all their fault." In mid-September, Sharon went with Dan, her lawyer friend, to a world-renowned and more distant cancer center for a third opinion. "What the doctors there said was that it had spread, and that it had probably already started to spread at the time that Sharon had that first biopsy, even before she started chemo."

This actually helped in some respects, Jeanine reflected. Sharon's "anger level went down then: 'Well, maybe this isn't the doctor's fault.' Sharon had been so sure that they'd made some big mistake. But again, she didn't want to hear anything about prognosis."

Sharon continued to live by herself into October. "There were lots of people who would check on her, but we tried to think of other options. She was telling us that Lynne was staying with her at night, which sometimes Lynne would, but sometimes she wouldn't. Meanwhile, Lynne was going out partying and telling Sharon, 'I can't deal with this. It's part of the Barbados culture that we don't deal with illness.' Everybody was ready to kill Lynne because Sharon was so loved in this community and then people would go out and see Lynne out there dancing up a storm having a great time. A couple of times Lynne even left Mitchell with Sharon while she went out.

"Lynne had Sharon's sports car during the time Sharon couldn't drive. Then Sharon got it back, and Maggie had possession of the key. Lynne was angry about this, so she wouldn't come around. Sharon was worrying about her, and we were trying to slap her up, you know, 'What in the hell are you doing here? You've got to take care of yourself. You've got to let go of all that stuff, and Lynne is too much stuff. Why are you putting up with this?'

"Sometimes I could understand it, sometimes I couldn't. Ultimately, even though Sharon couldn't face her illness, I think there was a piece of her that knew what was happening, so I guess it was not a time to be separating yourself from somebody you loved. Even though that person was treating you like shit, I guess it's better to have something than to not have anything.

"So Sharon was living by herself. Lynne was there sometimes, being really . . . cruel. It was hard for us to watch. Sharon was getting to the point where the pain was getting worse, but she wouldn't take pain medication, because she was gonna do this homeopathically. She was eating Tylenol and none of that stuff was working. The pain was beyond it. The doctor had tried to tell her, but no, she wouldn't listen. Finally I was able to convince her. I said, 'Get the prescription. At least it'll be there. Even if you don't want to take it, you'll have it.'

"I also was the first one to have to broach with Sharon the idea of a will. Maggie had tried to gently mention it to her, but she didn't want to hear it. Because that would mean she's dying and of course she's not dying. So I talked with her about it, and this was the approach that I used: 'Sharon, you have worked hard for all you have.' She was proud of her car, the things in her apartment. I said, 'Do you want the state to get that stuff? Because that's what happens to people who don't have wills.' She said, 'I don't want to hear this. Let me tell you how I feel.' I said, 'All right, you can talk first, but then I get to talk.' We were sitting on the couch and I had my arms around her. We did one of those back and forth things.

"She said she'd think about it. I was slowly moving her toward this. Some time after she got out of the hospital in August, she had started noticing these little lumps. First in her back, and she'd say, 'Oh, I'm sure it's a side effect of some medication. It's something that I ate.' Two days later, there were four or five lumps. I didn't know, but I believed it was spreading. She hadn't told the oncologist about it, so I went with her to the next appointment and I told him. Just by the look on his face, I knew. He wanted to do a biopsy which Sharon refused. She had talked with her mother and her mother was of the mind, like a lot of people I guess, that if you do a biopsy to see if something's cancer, and you open it up to the air, that's what makes it spread through your body."

Sharon's refusal to discuss her status persisted through September. The situation seemed to reach an extreme in early October, when Sharon panicked over "something about her medication. She called the doctor on call, but she was so upset that she couldn't talk with her, so she got me on the phone. She had call waiting, so she had the doctor on the other line, and she said, 'Jeanine, I told the doctor that you'll be able to explain it to her so I'm gonna hang up and she's gonna call you.' So this doctor called me and I told her what was going on. Finally, she was able to tell me what to tell Sharon. Then I had to call Sharon back. This was the way it was working because it was the only way that Sharon could manage it."

Finally, later that month, "we got Sharon to agree to have the biopsy because the lumps were just coming everywhere now. They were on her back, on her arms, just everywhere. Maggie and I went with her, right there in the room. Maggie was watching the procedure, but not me." Jeanine laughed at herself as she described this. "I was sitting down in the chair. I didn't want to see it. I was just holding Sharon's hand. She was awake because they did a local. The doctor was really nice and said we'd have the results in a few days."

Then, Jeanine recounted, "the Monday before Halloween I was at work and there was an emergency call. Maggie was frantic. She'd been on the phone with Sharon and something was wrong. Maggie had hung up, called 911, the ambulance came, and Sharon was at the hospital. When I got to the hospital, she was better. What had happened was that because Sharon's appetite had started to decrease, she had not been eating. But she had started to take the pain medication and the effects were strong stuff on an empty stomach. She'd panicked and started to hyperventilate. By the time I got there, they'd calmed her down."

Sharon's oncologist came to the emergency room to see her and told her he had the results of her biopsy. "Sharon asked everybody to leave except for me and closed the curtain. What he told her was that it was skin cancer. It had spread to her skin. She wanted to know how aggressive it was. He said, 'Well, on a scale from one to ten with one being the least aggressive and ten being the most aggressive, it's a nine.'" This was the first time, Jeanine noted, that Sharon had ever asked for direct information. "And she turned to me and said, 'Will you help me do my will tonight?'"

The doctor told them, "'She can't be by herself. She should not be alone.' So I said, 'Well, Sharon, come on home with me tonight. You'll be on the couch; we'll get this all figured out.' As I was saying this to her, I was thinking, 'I'm gonna get her home and settled down, then I'm going to call her mother.' Sharon hadn't seen Lynne since Friday and this was a Monday, but I just know somebody's going to come for her. So my thought was that she was just going to stay the night.

"I have an oversized couch, so we took off the back cushions and made it up like a bed and put her there. Arthur was cooking dinner and here comes Lynne knocking on my door. At this point I was so angry at Lynne I didn't even want to see her. I had to grit my teeth and open up the door and be a hostess and invite her to come in. Lynne said, 'Oh Sharon I just heard,' and this and that and this and that.

"The next day I stayed home with Sharon and called her mother, and her mother said, 'I want her to come home.' Now, they had this conversation before, and in fact, one weekend in October, Sharon did go stay the weekend with her mother because she was really sick after a chemo treatment. We helped get Sharon ready and they came and got her and her mother took care of her. Her mother had begun to say, 'I want you to come here and live and stay with me,' but Sharon was adamant. She was not going to go. She made me promise, and she made Maggie promise, that she would not go home with her mother. This was before she even came to live with me.

"Sharon came to my house on a Monday. Her mother did not show up at my house until the following Saturday, almost a week. Sharon had chemo on Friday and it was horrible. Luckily, Arthur was outside when we got her back from chemo, because he had to come and help me. We had to carry her from the car into the house, she was so sick. She woke up during the night moaning with the pain and we just sat up with her, holding her hand. I thought she was gonna die that morning. It was that bad. She had this far-off look. I'd say, 'Sharon, where are you? Come back. Come back.' I really think she was close to death at that point from the chemo.

"I was trying to figure out, what are we going to do here? That week Lynne was telling Sharon, 'I just can't stay with you. I just can't deal with this.' I'm really pissed off! I thought, 'This woman is your lover. What in the hell do you mean you don't know what to do? I don't know what to do either, but you do what you gotta do! Sharon should be home in her own apartment, where she wants to be.' But she couldn't be there by herself. I felt so bad for her. The people who should have been there for her during this time weren't there, and it was that first week that I really realized all the dynamics with her family. There is no way in hell that I would have gone through any of this and my family not been there for me. So her mother comes on Saturday, and when she sees Sharon, her mother just starts crying. Sharon was in bad shape. Her mother was begging her, pleading with her, 'Come home. Come, I'll take care of you.'

'No, Mom. No, Mom. I'm not gonna go. I'm not gonna go.' The brother came, he was crying. The sister came. They probably stayed three hours. It was the first time that they were at my house. Her mother gave me a $50 check to help with stuff.

"Thursday, the day before the chemo, Sharon had to go to the doctor's for a checkup. She was really angry at him because she wanted to hear positive stuff from him and there was nothing positive. It had spread, but she still didn't want to know any details, nothing." Then Jeanine laughingly recalled having to secretly signal Maggie that they should talk with the doctor alone, and pilot Sharon out to the waiting room, where the staff would prevent her from suspecting what was going on. "So Sharon went out to the waiting room and the nurses were talking to her and we scooted back in. The doctor left one of his patients—you should have seen him—and quickly came in the office. Maggie and I were looking around. We felt like we were thieves or something. He told us that his best guess was somewhere between one and three months.

"So again, it was like, 'Oh my God.' I have a very, very hectic job. I was a zombie already, getting up in the morning and she'd be sick and the medicine was hard for her to take and she was getting weaker. Arthur and my daughter rallied around, but it was hard because there were tons of people at our house. I'd get off work and come home, and then I went to work and then I'd come home. I was basically going back and forth because she really couldn't be by herself." Jeanine sighed at the memory. None of this had been planned, but the overnight guest Jeanine had invited over would spend the next four weeks dying on her couch.

"I had to start making a chart of the medication because Sharon had five different ones. I didn't know anything about this stuff! At first, I was having to get up every two and a half hours to get her up to take the medication. I was a zombie. Then things started to get a little ugly with Sharon's family. Sharon's sister from out of state was calling, and what I found out is that the mother believed that the reason I had Sharon at the house was because I wanted her money, Sharon's money. And that Sharon really wanted to be with her mother, but I was keeping her from that. Like I was fucking keeping her, excuse me, hostage in my house! But this mother is very passive aggressive, so of course when she was in my face or when she was on the phone, she was very friendly: 'Oh I thank you so much and I'm never gonna forget you for this.' Meanwhile I was hearing from Maggie that Sharon's mother was asking, 'Who's Jeanine and what is she doing?' So the mother called my house and said that Sharon's dad was coming up and he wanted to know all of this stuff.

"Sharon and I had begun working on her will. Neither one of us knew anything; I just got a piece of paper, we listed what her benefits were from the city and who she wanted to have her stuff. In typical Sharon fashion, we got a whole list: 'I want the leather jacket to go here, I want this picture to go to this person.' We were itemizing every little thing. It was tough on her, it was tough on me and we didn't do it all at once. We'd work on it a little bit and then put it down.

"We spent a lot of time talking about stuff, about her life, about my life, about the cancer, about the doctors, about her mother, about Lynne, about what she really wanted. We had to make a very tough decision about the chemo. It wasn't going to do any good and it was making her deathly ill. After that last treatment on that Friday, she finally made the decision not to have any more chemo. Because I'm telling you, I thought the girl was gonna die on my living room couch that morning.

"That next week, I got information about hospice care, and Sharon and I went up to the hospice facility to visit. We talked about it before we went. It would be a last resort. If it came down to that, she would go to the hospice rather than go to her mother's. Sharon got sick while we were there, but she did get a chance to see it. It's a beautiful place and it's right here in town. I first went there when baby Joshua died of SIDS and a person from the community recommended the grief counselor to come and do some work with us. When I called him up he immediately said, 'Yes'—the nicest man.

"But meanwhile I was still thinking, 'Okay, we're gonna work something out here. I'm going to talk to her mom. Or, Lynne's going to come home.' At one point, Lynne came and made noises." In fact, one night she offered to take Sharon to an appointment the next day. "I was really wondering about that because she hadn't taken her to anything else. She'd made it clear, 'I can't deal with that stuff, and I need the support of my friends.' You bitch! What about what Sharon needs!"

Jeanine continued: "Lynne took Sharon to the appointment and they don't come back, they don't come back, they don't come back. I was worried. Finally, I called and they were at Sharon's house, 'taking care of bills,' which I was also curious about because Sharon had got to the point where she couldn't do that. A member of the board of directors at the agency, a friend of Sharon's, had been handling all of her financial stuff. So I wondered, what do you mean 'taking care of bills'? They came back to the house. Lynne told me that they had talked and that Sharon was going to go back home to her apartment and Lynne was going to take care of her. 'But,' Lynne added, 'I can't take care of her until next week because I have to take little Mitchell trick-or-treating.'

"I found out that when Lynne took Sharon to the appointment, she conned Sharon into giving her $600. Here the board has been doing fundraising, and people have been donating because Sharon could not work. She still had her full salary because the agency has a sick bank, but her job was not enough to cover her bills and she couldn't work part-time so she didn't have any freakin' money, and she gave Lynne $600! I was so pissed at her and I let her have it when I found out. This whole thing Lynne promised about 'You're going to come back home and I'm going to take care of you' was a crock of shit. She did that so she could get the fuckin' $600.

"And then Sharon's mother was pleading with her. One day, the mother called me, maybe two weeks after Sharon had been at my house. Sharon's dad was coming to visit from out of state and she said, 'He's concerned and wants to know what's going on and he's not happy. He thinks Sharon should be with me.' Now Sharon's mother and father do not have a good relationship. In fact, they only were talking because of Sharon's situation.

"Sharon was freaking out about her dad coming. She thought he was going to pressure her to leave. He had called up Maggie, because he knew her, and was asking her questions about me because he did not know me and he had not met me. Maggie told him, 'She's just doing this out of the goodness of her heart.' So he was fine about that. Then when he came to the house, him and his wife, I was so glad because it meant so much to Sharon. They spent good quality time together. He and his wife stayed at Sharon's apartment and I really liked him. I really liked his wife too, but there was still a part of me that was wondering: He worked, but I still couldn't figure out—your daughter has a month or two to live, why not come here, move in her apartment and take care of her? Because that's where she wanted to be.

"They stayed for four days. And in those four days it was wonderful because they talked, they made peace. When he left she said to me, 'The kind of time I spent with my dad I wish I could spend with my mother.' Because the few times that her mother would come, it would be, 'Are you eating? You're not eating enough. Please come back home. I'll take care of you. Come,' and not hearing."

It bothered Jeanine that Sharon's mother would not honor her daughter's wishes. This added injury to the insult that Jeanine felt at being characterized as greedy and dishonorable. "She called me up one day and said, 'I need some help and I think only you can give me the help.' She wanted me to tell Sharon that her being at my house was causing a hardship for us and we couldn't keep her anymore. She felt that if Sharon had to leave my house, she would come to hers. I said, 'Mrs. Alvarez, first of all, I'm not going to lie to Sharon, and second of all, even if I did that, you think Sharon would come to your house? She won't, Mrs. Alvarez, she is clear about that. She will go home by herself and die in that apartment before she goes to your house.' Then her mother got mad, 'Oh, so you won't help me.' I see her as a very bitter, unhappy woman.

"I said, 'Mrs. Alvarez, it's not that I don't want to help you, I understand. Please! Come here!' She said, 'But I can't.' She had a job. She worked. I said, 'Well, let's think about it. What about if you came on the weekends? Sharon could stay here during the week and you could come on the weekends. She doesn't have much time. Please, come here. That's what she wants. Then she can go.'

"Do you know what that woman said to me? She said, 'I can't do that," *because she was remarried.* Sharon liked her stepfather, a Mexican man, very friendly, just the kind of person she was. But her mother said to me, 'I have a husband. I can't leave my husband here. After all, Sharon is not his daughter. Even though he loves her, that's not his real daughter.' I was just flabbergasted! Your daughter has got a month or two to live and you won't come here and you won't compromise! She lived only thirty-five miles away! She and her husband worked at the same factory. They could have commuted! She wouldn't even entertain it. This was the way Sharon would say it was, and the way it was when she was growing up: It was her mother's way or no way, no compromise. Her way or no way."

Another family member was also problematic. Sharon's out-of-state sister was trying to help, not by coming to town and spending time caring for Sharon but by prescribing treatments from a distance. "There's this tea that has supposedly been known to cure cancer. She sent all this information about this tea and Sharon's got to drink it. If it won't cure the cancer—because Sharon's cancer may have progressed too far—it'll make the skin cancer lumps go away and it'll help ease the pain. So she was FedExing this stuff up here and she was calling and she wanted me to do this, asking me, what are you feeding her? But she couldn't come because she was trying to find a job."

"This is what I was having to deal with. I was watching Sharon's body deteriorate before my eyes. She really liked this homeopathic gel because she said it helped with the pain. So we'd have to put this gel all over her because by now the nodules, as we called them, were everywhere. She had two on her face, which was starting to change. She had nodules everywhere and I was having to rub these things everywhere.

She was losing weight, her ribs were starting to show. I was having to put this gel on her breasts, and they were just full of these nodules. You felt them as you're putting the gel over her. Nodules on her back, on her stomach, nodules between her buttocks, nodules in between her legs, nodules on her legs—her whole body was being covered. I'm not a nurse. This is not something that I wanted to do. If anybody had told me a month before that I would be doing something like that, I'd have said, 'You're absolutely crazy.' I don't know how I did that stuff, but I did it.

"And then the boys came. Three little boys who were missing their mother." The children had been removed from their mother's care because of her mental instability, and their father, Arthur's son, had died the year before. So Jeanine and Arthur took on this load as well. "The boys had spent a lot of time at our house in the past, but still, they were little boys, they missed their mother. It was just crazy. I don't know how I did it. I felt like a robot. I would just get up and turn the switch. We were able to get Sharon's medicine on a better schedule so it wasn't every two hours. But still I would get to bed at midnight and be up at five because she'd need the next medication, and this was going on and on. I finally was able to get Sharon's cousin, Brenda, to come stay at the house with her.

"We paid Brenda because the board was doing these fund-raisers for Sharon. They had a number of big community events. That was really hard for Sharon because it meant having to confront, 'Why are they doing this?' They held a candlelight vigil for her. It was just beautiful. They had this big raffle that netted a little over $5,000. People who had been her clients were coming. The support from the community was pouring in.

"We're watching her go down. She's getting weaker and weaker. As the tumors in her brain grew she had difficulties with smell. Things had to be exactly right, exactly. She was drinking hot water with lemon, and I don't know how many times I'd take her the water and it would be either too hot or too cold. So I would have to go back and put it in the microwave or add cold water, go back, it's still not right, go back, do it again. Now it's got too much lemon in it, so I would have to pour that out. I'm trying to get her to eat. She'd say she'd want something but when she'd get it, she couldn't eat it.

"Watching her go down, forcing her to drink Boost and take the pills and then finally it got to the point when she couldn't take the pills anymore because she got nodules in her throat. So then we had to get some liquid morphine but we couldn't call it morphine because she was afraid of getting addicted. By now we had the in-home services from hospice care. Even though the nurses explained to her that people who have this kind of severe pain don't get addicted, she was afraid. So then we get something called Roxanol, which is a form of morphine, but we called it Roxanol so she wouldn't know.

"It was in liquid form and you would have to show her the dropper because the tumors in the brain were starting to affect her. In the beginning she would ask me, 'How much is it?' I would tell her the dose that she wanted to hear but I'd give her more because of the agony that she'd be in. She didn't like the way it made her feel so groggy. I got to the point where I'd have to lie to her. She'd ask, 'Did I have a dose already?' 'No, you didn't have a dose. It's time for your dose now.'

"Then we had all the other medications. She was on medication for the swelling in the brain, medication to keep the seizures down, the medicine that she had to take when she was still on chemo—there was a whole bunch of stuff. We bought a little notebook and whoever was watching her had to keep track."

When Brenda wasn't available and Jeanine couldn't leave work, "staff people at the agency would come and sit at the house with Sharon." And there was other support. "People in the community got a meals list going, so after the first week people were bringing meals and that was great because then we didn't have to worry about it. Except then we had all this food!"

It was the third week of Sharon's stay that the little boys came, and "then it started getting worse because the boys were really active and as the illness progressed, Sharon couldn't stand the noise. The tensions were starting to really clash, and then my older daughter came home. It was a mess." Because Sharon had been close to Jeanine's daughters, the situation was especially difficult for them too. Its effects have persisted, "especially with the younger one. I'm seeing the impact in lots of ways now. She's failing in school this year. A piece of it is just typical teenage laziness, but a lot has to do with watching Sharon die.

"Watching her die—because that's what we did: watched her change, watched her body with the stuff on it—all of the things that we had to do, it was exhausting. And then Sharon would feel beholden to us and she'd feel really bad. She would ask me, 'How are you?' She'd say, 'You've got to take care of yourself.' But no sooner did I sit down than she'd say, 'Can I have some more water, please?' I don't know how we did it."

Jeanine was able to enlist the outpatient services of the local hospice, which sent a home health care aide, but Sharon didn't like the aide. "She smelled of cigarette smoke," so she only came one day. Sharon did permit the hospice nurses to make their visits. "She was constipated so they had to give her enemas. The nurses came at least once a day, more often if we called, and that was helpful. That's how Sharon ultimately ended up going to hospice.

"The week of Thanksgiving, she was mainly sleeping, so weak. The oncologist had tried to tell us about the dramatic changes that could happen, but I hadn't realized, from one day to the next, from one week to the next, how dramatic the changes would be. In some ways I was upset with Sharon because she wasn't handling this well, not wanting to know about things. But then I realized later that in many ways she *was* strong, and she had to handle this the way that she could handle it. Her will—I don't know where she got it from, but it was just incredible. But she started sleeping more and she was still changing; it was hard for me to look at her, it was hard.

"Just the year before we had lost Tom, Arthur's son. Tom had been stabbed and suffered a massive infection. Surgery to clean out the infection turned into a disaster. They had put him in a drug-induced coma to put him on a ventilator. The surgery was on a Thursday. He was supposed to come out of the coma on Saturday, but nothing happened. Arthur and I were thinking it was okay because Tom was a big guy and they'd had to give him a lot of drugs." But after a long wait, "the doctor came and he said, 'I have bad news, the worst news.' Tom was brain dead. We watched him deteriorate until he died two months later."

Now Jeanine and her family were taking care of Sharon a year later and those memories were still fresh. "A twenty-five-year-old man who was just so vibrant. He was the oldest of Arthur's four kids and everybody looked up to him. And he had so many friends! There was a trial for the young man who stabbed him, seventeen years old. What had happened is that Tom had carried the sickle-cell trait. When they did the surgery to clean out the infection, there was a kink in the oxygen tube. He lost oxygen and when you have sickle cell, that makes the blood start to sickle. And then a blood clot went to his brain. We didn't find that out until the trial. We were sitting there and the medical examiner told about the kink in the tube. Now there is a lawsuit but nothing will alter the devastation of watching him die.

"And not only that. Tom died in October; then, the woman who had helped raise Arthur died in December. Then Arthur's real mother died in February, unexpectedly. What was so eerie were the similarities. Mama goes for angioplasty. She'll be out the next day, so we didn't even go to Alabama, where she lived." But she too ended up on a ventilator and died. Arthur had lost his son, his surrogate mother and his mother within five months of one another. And then, Jeanine added, "his brother died unexpectedly the Saturday after Sharon's funeral. It has been horrible."

On the Tuesday before Thanksgiving, Jeanine was at work when the visiting nurse called. "She wanted to talk to us," but Jeanine was reluctant to explain this to Sharon. Instead, "we lied to Sharon. We said that Brenda had another appointment somewhere and that I had to go do something. We got one of the secretaries from the agency to stay while Maggie and Brenda and I went to the hospice. They told us that it's only going to be a matter of time now." The three of them went to lunch to discuss the situation, and the question came up: "Now, who's gonna tell her? And right away both of them said, 'I can't do it. Jeanine, you're gonna have to do it.'

"One of the most difficult things for me through all this was having to take on that role, to be the person who said, 'You've got to take your medicine now. Come on. Sit up.' Or, 'Sharon, come on. You have to get up and you have to go do this.' Just like when Sharon was angry at the oncologist, some of that turned toward me. That frustration was coming out, and I felt so bad because this was somebody I loved and I cared about. I didn't want this as it got closer to the end. I didn't want it, but in some ways that's always the role that I've played in her life. I'm the one who's had to set her straight when she didn't want to hear shit.

"So we went home after we ate lunch. We turned off the TV. The person from the agency left. Sharon woke up and she knew that something was wrong. We were surrounding her, and when I told her, the look on her face was, 'You betrayed me. You don't want me here.' That hurt me."

Jeanine then shared a recollection of an incident that had occurred two weeks earlier. Sharon had gone to spend the weekend with an old friend in a nearby city. "What a job that was, getting Sharon all ready to go, but I was glad that she wanted to go and she went. But it was the weirdest thing—two weeks she'd been with me and she's getting ready to go and she said to me, 'You know what? I feel like a teenager going out on my first date.' I said, 'You know what? I feel like the mom who's losing her teenager on the first date.'" Jeanine laughed at the memory. "Then Sharon said, 'I don't want to get too attached, because I know I'm going to have to leave at some point.' But this was when she was still thinking that she might go home."

Sharon spent Thanksgiving at Maggie's. "What a move that was, trying to get her there, because by now she was so weak. On Friday after Thanksgiving, the hospice called an ambulance and that's how Sharon got to the facility. Arthur and I had gone to her apartment and got a bunch of her things, then decorated her room at the hospice. It was beautiful, a corner room with windows on one side and big sliding patio doors on the other. At the agency they had made this huge banner, bright pink, with a tree with all these little hands on it. The kids and staff had written all these messages, and we had that across the back of her bed. I'd brought her stuffed animals and her blanket and some candles. She didn't want to go to the hospice because it was another step toward the end, but when she saw her little rag dolls and her little bunny that lived on her bed at home, this smile came over her face.

JEANINE STRONG ⟶ 223

"She was hardly talking then. Her mother came that day and the next, and then proceeded to stay until Sharon died. And even though I was really angry at her for not honoring Sharon's last wishes, I felt sorry for her because by the time she got there, Sharon could hardly communicate. It was just waiting and watching her daughter die. Sharon was starting to look like a skeleton. The nodules in the face were growing and the shape of her head had changed. She had lost weight and was so gaunt, it was just awful.

"The people at the hospice were really nice. There's a Native American, John, who works there, a spiritual man, and he does honor songs. A lot of people call them chants, but they're really honor songs to the patients. John was very good to Sharon. When we first got there and Sharon saw him, she told us she didn't want him in the room because he was a man and she didn't want him seeing her undressed or anything. They told John that and he was fine about it. The next day, John was chanting, singing an honor song to somebody down the hall, and Sharon heard that and this smile came over her face. From that point on, it was all right for John to be there.

"She had tons of visitors. We just made her comfortable as much as we could. Maggie and I went on Monday or Tuesday down to a funeral home to get information and start making arrangements, because we knew it was going to be soon. Her mother was not being nice to people, including us. Never mind that Sharon lived with me for weeks and Maggie was there every day helping out. Now *she* was in charge.

"She didn't want people in the room. Sharon had said, 'Don't leave me by myself. I don't want quiet.' Sharon wanted as much stuff as possible, so there was a lot of laughter and people talking and a lot of noise. But her mother's like, 'She needs her rest now.' Her rest?! She's getting ready to have eternal rest. This is not what she wanted!

"Her mother couldn't hear that. People at the hospice didn't quite know what to do with the situation, because I was the one who was the contact. I had signed her in. I took care of the bill, from the fundraising. You have to pay two weeks up front, $1500 for two weeks. If the patient dies during that two weeks that's just it. If a patient dies within a day, they still get their $1500. Then you can work out something after the two weeks.

"Aside from the $50 check that Sharon's mom had given me the Saturday after Halloween, that was it: nothing. But now she was gonna come in and take over. People were trying to give her her space but she was getting on their nerves—the nurse, the aides that were there at night—because she knows everything." For example, Jeanine and the others had spent days trying to convince Sharon and her mother to permit self-administered morphine, "the thing where you can just punch the button. But her mother's saying, 'What if she overdoses?' Even though the people told her that Sharon needs this now. She was moaning and grunting. Finally, finally, her mother agreed." Sharon died two days later. She had been in the hospice facility for six days.

"I felt so bad because I was there the whole time, but I wasn't there when Sharon died. Arthur and my daughter had come up the night before because we'd gotten a call, 'You should come now.' So we did the vigil. I stayed and fell asleep in the chair. I left the hospice about four in the morning. I had to get the boys up. I went home and laid down. The phone rings a little bit after six: 'You should get here right away.' I'm getting up and then the phone rang fifteen minutes later and it was Maggie and she was crying and she said, 'She's gone.' I drove myself, because Arthur and my daughter were going to get the kids together. My daughter was a wreck.

"I don't know why, but I was still thinking, 'Okay, Sharon's family is gonna step up here, right?' But Sharon's mother didn't even stay with the body. *We* stayed! She *left!* Her husband came and the sisters and brothers came. They viewed the body, they all left. We waited for the funeral home people to get there and watched while they took her body out. We asked them to please not zip up the bag, because Sharon had a fear about that. She had told Maggie that she didn't want to be in a body bag. The woman was very nice, so they had her in the bag but not her head. We watched while they pushed Sharon into the hearse and closed the doors and then we went back in the room. I had to pack up all the stuff there. Then everybody came to my house and just ate and hung around.

"The next day we went back down to the funeral home and Maggie and I made the funeral arrangements. We wrote the obituary. We got the flowers. We did all the arrangements. The family did absolutely nothing. Now that Sharon's gone, it's more obvious how the mother's feeling. She calls up and she gives the funeral home shit" because the obituary was not in the paper right away. "And I heard from friends that she was telling people back home that her daughter really wanted to come live with her but I wouldn't let her. I wanted Sharon's money.

"The funeral was a big deal. Sharon was a city employee loved by many people. Everybody had offered help. The mayor arranged that we could have buses for people, because the parking is horrible at the chapel where we held the service. The schools participated, released the kids for the day. They had school buses to take the kids up to the chapel.

"Sharon and I had talked about the funeral arrangements. Because she wasn't a Jehovah's Witness, she couldn't have a service in a Kingdom Hall. She had wanted to do that originally, because she thought it would make her mother happy. But they don't allow that if you're not a Witness. So then it was, what about if her mother's Brother—they don't call them pastors, they call them Brothers in the Kingdom Hall—what if he did it at the chapel? Well, they can't do that either. Ultimately we just found somebody else and it was a gorgeous service.

"It was a moving tribute to her, more of a memorial service. The whole community rallied around and we all supported each other. But wouldn't you know—it was the funniest thing—it was almost the end and the freaking fire alarm went off in the chapel! And everybody looked and I saw the woman from the funeral home coming up to me. She said, 'There really is something wrong, so we're going to get the body out and everybody has to go.' We had to laugh later," said Jeanine, laughing now, "because it was like Sharon said, 'Enough already! Let's get out of here!' What had happened was that a new PA system had been installed the week before and something went wrong with the wiring." After the trip to the cemetery, "we had a big reception at the agency. I put one of the staff people in charge of it and we got tons of donations. It was just beautiful."

But the difficulties with Sharon's family persisted. When everyone gathered at Sharon's apartment to go over the will, "her mother was so ugly. Sharon and I had written up all this. Maggie had seen the notes, and Sharon's lawyer friend, Dan, everybody. Dan had taken those notes and put them into a will format" for Sharon to sign, but when he brought the will to her, "Lynne was there. Lynne had a fit. 'How could you do this without me being involved? You know there are things I want in the house!'" Jeanine found this behavior appalling, but when Sharon asked her to put away the will, she complied.

Sharon never signed her will, and her mother eyed it with suspicion. She insisted on seeing all the paperwork, which Dan showed her and explained. In the end, she honored some of Sharon's wishes, but not all. "Sharon had all this stuff listed out, but if there was something her mother wanted, she took it. She didn't pay a dime for the funeral, didn't even offer, didn't buy family flowers, didn't pay for the obituary, spent not one dime. Made not one arrangement, nothing. We did it all—the people who were supposedly holding her daughter hostage because we wanted her money.

"The only money Sharon had was from the state retirement system. When you die, if you are still employed by the city, you get three times your salary. For Sharon that was a little over $60,000. Sharon had designated Maggie as the beneficiary years ago. Now, when we did the will, Sharon had parceled out that money to the penny" for Maggie to distribute. "Sharon had a number of students, kids" on the list. And she had "set aside about $6,000 for her funeral."

But "her mother didn't believe any of it, saying, 'I know my daughter would have talked to me!' She had asked me at one point if Sharon had done a will," and Jeanine had recommended that she speak with Sharon. Her "father knew because he came out and asked her. He got to see the drawn up will, even though Sharon never signed it. So he was fine with everything, but her mother believed we made the whole thing up and she wouldn't honor Sharon's wishes. Even though she heard her ex-husband say he saw it. He'd had a chance to talk with Sharon. He knew these were her wishes.

"I have not talked to them at all since we left there. They started giving Dan a whole lot of grief. The mother got an attorney because she wanted the retirement money, but there was nothing that she could do about that because Sharon had signed that beneficiary. Her mother even accused people of having altered that. It's horrible and it's really sad in many ways. I feel bad that Sharon's last days had to be in turmoil. Even in her final days, she couldn't get her family to be there for her, which was the epitome of their relationship."

Jeanine regretted the way that illness robbed Sharon of her pleasure in life. "Sharon lived her life to the fullest and with such zest. She was always doing something. And the thing that made it really hard was that this cancer just paralyzed her. She was so traumatized and so fearful that we had to encourage her to do things. The board was going to send her wherever she wanted to go—on a trip or just to go visit close friends, whatever—but she couldn't. She would sit in the house with the blinds closed. By the time she got to some place of acceptance," she was unable to do the things she might have. "That's the part that I feel bad about."

Looking back, Jeanine reflected, "This was all new and taken a day at a time. I've learned so much, but one thing I think I would have done differently is really have a clear conversation with Sharon about how the end would be. We'd talked about going to the hospice; what we didn't talk about is how and when the decision would get made. Did she trust me enough to know when it was time? I believe she did, but that piece wasn't so clear. I wonder if I might have been more up-front with her family about her really wanting them to come stay with her. Even though I talked with her mother and even though I talked with her father, I just wonder if there might have been some way to make some impact. I've thought about this, and I go back and forth. But to be honest, I don't think it would have made a difference." The family's dynamics had been in place long before Jeanine came on the scene.

As for the ordeal she had been through, Jeanine said, "One of the things that's been surprising to me is people being amazed that somebody would do something like this," that is, to take in a dying friend. "Whereas for me, it's how would you *not* do something like this. I would want somebody to do something like this for me. Fortunately, I have not had the experience of not having people there for me through bad times."

It has been gratifying to know that "I helped make Sharon's last days better. She said she felt safe at my house."

But Jeanine regretted the impact on the household. "I've really worried about Arthur because of all the deaths we've been through. I worry about my youngest daughter. My oldest daughter was home on some weekends while Sharon was with us, and she still can't sleep on the couch downstairs. When she comes home now, she's up in her sister's room. When I said, 'Why don't you just sleep on the couch?' she said, 'I can't.' I said, 'Is it because you're afraid?' She said, 'No, it's because I'm really sad.' She and Sharon were close.

"There were times during this, and even now, that I've wondered if I made the right decision having Sharon come. I talked with my family at the time, but not knowing it was going be as long term as it was. There's a part of me that feels bad about the impact on them and on myself. There's a bigger part of me that thinks that they've learned a valuable lesson and that they gave of themselves in a way that a lot of people do not. And that it will come back to all of us, what we did for Sharon. As hard as it was for us, it will come back to us in the end.

"It made us all closer in many ways. I don't know how we've lived through all of this. After what happened with Arthur's son, I couldn't imagine anything worse. So God works in mysterious ways, and we've had to deal with all of this. It's been rough to lose so many people you love in such a short span of time. So many and so close together. We got real good at this stuff."

The new year has been better, said Jeanine. "It has been hectic with the boys there, but little kids are just great. When the boys first came, I worried that they would be afraid of Sharon. She was on the couch, she was sick, there were trays with the medications, but how quickly they adapted! They'd come home in the afternoon and give us a hug, then they'd run over and give her one too.

"It's crazy, but I really do believe that it happened for a reason at the time that it happened. The boys are still with us. I guess I was meant to be a caretaker. It's what I do. People say I do a good job. I don't know about that; I just do what has to be done. You can't turn away family and family doesn't always mean immediate family. I believe that Sharon is up there looking out for all of us. She loved people. She gave of herself. The hardest part for her" was saying goodbye to the young people she had served and cared for in the teen program at the agency. "They wanted her to come to see them at the agency, but she couldn't face them. Ultimately, some of them just started coming to the house.

"It was so hard for her to see them" that Jeanine and a hospice counselor made special arrangements. "When we knew that the end was coming soon, we put this thing together to talk to the teens. Sharon couldn't come, but she wrote a letter that I read to them. She wrote that she would always be there for them, and that even when they couldn't see her, she would be up there looking out for them. And that's where I believe she is. That's where I believe she is."

Notes

When People Invite You to Be with Them as They Are Leaving the World, It's a Great Honor

Minister Jane Adams Spahr

Jane Adams Spahr describes herself as a lesbian evangelist. She was ordained as a Presbyterian minister in 1974, before she named herself as lesbian and four years before the church's 1978 ban on the ordination of lesbian, gay and bisexual people. She recalls knowing since the age of fourteen that God wanted her to be a minister, but that people did not take her seriously because she was a girl.

Although her work within the formal Presbyterian faith has been compromised since the late 1970s because of her sexual orientation, Jane has continued her ministry. At the urging of friends, she began working with gays, lesbians, bisexuals and transgendered people through Spectrum, a California-based interfaith spiritual ministry and social service agency that was established in 1982 with Presbyterian grant money. She has been with Spectrum ever since. When we talked with her, Jane was between speaking engagements about her work as an advocate, and she spoke with enthusiasm and conviction.

As a minister, Jane has been dealing with people dying ever since she was ordained in 1974. "In pastoring, I'm invited to be with people at very sacred times: when they are being born; when they are being married

232

or having a holy union, celebrating their relationship, however people choose to do that; and when they are dying. When people invite you to be with them as they are coming into the world or leaving the world, it's a great honor. I hadn't known how remarkable and how sacred it is. People teach you about living and dying. I've been with people as they have crossed over to the other side, and they have taught me about their dying process. I've learned to make it a workshop—to learn about their process of dying and how they want to do it.

"Everyone has their own way. I believe that people choose the people they want to be with when they die. And sometimes they don't want to be with anybody. They call me to be there at a time when their families might not be able to be there. I hadn't seen one man in years. I saw him three weeks before he died; I knew exactly why he had called me and what we were to do together. It's to be there and not get in the way. It's to be there and facilitate what they want to have happen.

"Spiritually, I know my place because the people who have asked me to be with them have made my place for me. There are social workers, hospice nurses—a lot of different people other than the family. But if people ask a spiritual person to be with them, it's very clear what they want. Sometimes it is to listen to the deepest, deepest things in their life; we talk about how they feel, sometimes about what they are afraid to talk about with other people, because they think somehow that as a spiritual person, I know about that. They'll ask me about other people dying. They'll ask me about what I've learned from others. And sometimes I offer that, and there is relief because nobody else is talking to them like this. Not even the hospice workers, though sometimes hospice workers are very spiritual people. They know how to help people cross over, so sometimes a hospice nurse will be able to talk to people in that way. But it seems to me that when I'm invited in, it is very clear to me that being there and talking is what they want from me. Maybe they want to find a way to heal from all of the pain that they have gone through in their lives, whatever their faith tradition, or maybe they want to talk about God, or a higher power, whatever the name, or about an afterlife. You know, that kind of thing, all of those kinds of questions. I don't care what a person's religion or spirituality might be or not be, because I believe a ministry of presence is what a person might want the most. It has taken me all this time to know what a person may need from me, just to be there and not get in the way. I *try* to do that."

Trying to be present without getting in the way is one of the most difficult parts of Jane's work, and it requires her full concentration. "I have to go through a whole thing inside. I really feel them, I really hear what they want me to say. And I want to do it how they want it, not how I think it should be. Like Doug, for instance. Doug was dying, and he wanted us to hold him and love him. Doug and I had had the most incredible conversations. When I did his memorial service, people said, 'God, Janey, you just captured who he was!' No, he shared with me who he was and I shared with others what he wanted me to say.

"Before I do these memorial services, I breathe three times, very deep breathing. It brings me into a different place. That's what I need to do for me. Everybody has their ways—people meditate, whatever. This is what I need to do for me. It's like, here we go . . . here *we* go. At a memorial service I feel a person's presence. The days preparing, if it's three days or two weeks, I feel their presence and I want so much to do what they ask. I feel that presence and try to respond to it until I get it right. I can't explain that to people, but I know when I get it. It's like, when you do your work, you know when you did it. When it's *done*, you see, then it's done. Helping with death has been the hardest thing for me, but I think it is the thing that I do the best.

"Sometimes people don't have to tell you what they want when they are dying because you become more and more intuitive, as you go through more and more of these sacred times." Jane believes that her intuitive skill derives in no small part from being an identical twin. "Because I'm a twin, I've had communion with another individual from birth. I know how to communicate in deep ways without talking. Being a twin has been a gift for me. It's a wonderful gift I can keep refining. Intuitively I can almost match what people want, and I build on that with what people tell me. They teach you. We are not the teachers here.

"In spiritual counseling, I am open to feeling all of these intense feelings, because when you match them, then you are affirming their feelings. I have wept with my friends. I've been angry with them that they are so sick. I've cried with them. My worst fear is, 'Don't, please God, don't let me not feel.' I want to be in touch with my feelings so I can be present as fully as possible to meet another. And that's a stress reliever right there, just to go with it and do it rather than build these barricades of professional ethics or policies. I mean, if you're not with them, don't bother."

Jane's experience as a twin and her experiences with the loss of her own friends and family members contribute to her perspective that as a spiritual caregiver, it is professional to be personal. "My grandfather's death was very, *very* torturing for me and my sister. As twins, we came into the world together. When I looked at my grandfather, that was the first time that I realized that you die alone. Family losses were very, very difficult for me. I could feel them, I could feel them everywhere. For me, when people are dying, they are close. All barriers that keep people from each other, those boundaries seem to be gone. So with family it's been the closeness that matters. And in a professional role, I feel the same.

"Our staff at Spectrum talks about this. We've buried so many of our friends. I mean, these are not casual relationships. Some of our friends don't have family, because lesbian and gay people many times don't have families who can deal with that kind of thing and we become like family."

Jane has been fortunate in her own family. She was a married woman with two children before she came to understand that she was a lesbian, and she describes how her husband, Jim, was instrumental. He was her best friend and she shared her feelings about women with him before either one of them understood the implications. But eventually, Jim would leave books about homosexuality around the house. Then one day in 1976, after ten years of marriage, Jane heard a lesbian Episcopal priest speak, and suddenly she understood. When she got home, she told her husband, "I want to say this out loud. I'm a lesbian, Jim."[35]

Now when she recalls this moment of truth, it brings tears to her eyes. Jim had then taken her in his arms and said, "I know Janey. I've known for a while. I've been waiting for you to tell me." Jane and Jim talked to their two sons and saw a family therapist together. Two years later, the Spahrs divorced, but Jane remains close to Jim and his second wife, a longtime friend of Jane.

The same year that Jane was divorced, the church banned gay ordination. For the next fourteen years Jane struggled for legitimate status in the formal organization of her faith. Then in 1992, she was surprised to be invited by a church in Rochester, New York, to become a co-pastor. She discovered that she had to get over her "church phobia," because "the church has so hurt lesbian, gay and bisexual people. I work with this. I see families going through this. It has been such an atrocity to me to see what people have said and done to lesbian, gay and bisexual people in the name of God."[36]

Jane's hiring at the Downtown United Presbyterian Church in Rochester was nullified by the top Presbyterian ecclesiastical court, which ruled that an openly lesbian, gay or bisexual person cannot serve as minister of any of its churches.[37] But Jane has not left the Presbyterian Church (USA). Despite "people who call her 'slime' and 'Satan,'" Jane insists that this is her church, the church in which she grew up and which she loves. And she believes that the church needs her: "It is time for this church to become the inclusive place that Jesus wanted it to be.[38]

"My job right now is to 'person' this issue throughout the country. The two churches, in Rochester and California, created a fund to pay me to go across the United States to speak about diversity within the church, to speak about sexuality and spirituality, and to challenge the myths and misinformation that many people believe. It's the first time they have created this position—lesbian evangelist! What we are really up to is transforming an institution that keeps people in secret. We are working to change *any* institutional policy that keeps people from being who they are, or keeps people from answering a call to leadership when all other qualifications are met."

Jane feels that her mission to make the church more inclusive is informed by her work with the dying and her efforts to be like family to them. She feels that her greatest contribution in ministering to dying people is simply to love them. She does this "through talking about things that people are afraid to talk about with them; loving through asking them, 'Have you seen everybody that you want to see?' Talking about or through their fears, their expectations, their hopes—it's so nice for people. There's something about God, you see, and not even God, but spiritual issues generally. Phil, an atheist friend of mine, said when he was dying, 'All right. You can come in and talk to me.' He said, 'Well, I'm an atheist and I don't believe in any of this stuff.' He was one of the first people with HIV who we worked with. He was a bisexual and we ministered to his wife as well. That was the most amazing experience. I'll never forget it in a million years. I think of him, getting ready. He just talked and talked and talked to me about his life: who he had slept with and what he had done and what he hadn't done; what he had done right and what he thought he had done wrong. We talked and laughed. I had only stopped in for a few minutes, but there was a different quality to his talking that day. Somehow, I knew he would be dying soon.

"It was the same with Trevor. I went in to the hospital, just to see Trevor for five minutes, and he told me about his trip to Greece and what he had been doing for all those months. As I was sitting there listening, I realized, 'He's dying.' It was like it was with the first woman who ever taught me about dying. Elizabeth was sixty-four and a member of the first church that I served in. She was one of the youngest people in my church. As I was talking to her, I could just tell by our conversation that there was more to it, although I remember thinking to myself, 'Oh, this is ridiculous that you're getting this intuitive thing.' But deep inside I knew. I have learned to listen to that deep place inside.

"The person is talking to you; it isn't someone really telling you they're going to die. But you know. It's like someone is going to leave you and, God, you know. That's what I felt from my conversations with Phil, with Trevor, and with Elizabeth. I knew they were dying. There's a different quality. There's an intensity and there's something inside of you that says, 'This is not just talking and listening to my friend about a trip to Greece, or to one of my older parishioners about her life, not anything like it.' It's how they are talking, the way they are talking about their lives, and I think, 'Whoa, they are talking about their life and I'm going to sit here because they are telling me they are going, they're giving me their life.' It's more of a summary, or closure, it's something they just *have* to tell me about. And the detail is very vivid. I could see Trevor walking along the path he was describing. We were there, in Greece. It was beautiful. He gave me that part of his life.

"It was the same with my friend Ralph. He was so sick. He'd said to me, 'I think I want to crawl away, Janey, in my tent and go away and die.' And I said, 'Ralph, I know you want to do that, honey, but could you let us love you until you go?' And so he did. He stayed so we could love him and hold him and be with him. He invited my partner and me and some other friends out to his house the week before he died. It was incredible. He had told his nurses that he wanted to look very nice for us. He loved the outdoors. He opened all the windows, and he played a CD of special music for us, and then he gave it to us. 'Here. Now, you take this.' People give us so much when they die. Ralph gave us a little bit more of himself and all of that beautiful music.

"I have just been with Martha and Eve, who have been together for forty-five years. These are two incredible women. Once, near the end, when they were talking to me about their relationship, Martha said, 'You know, Janey, I've got to go.' Of course Eve didn't want her to go; nobody wanted her to go. Everybody loved Martha. Martha was younger than Eve! She was seventy to Eve's seventy-five. But, you know, she was telling us that she wanted to go. We prayed and we talked. At a later visit, Eve looked at me and said, 'Martha is going to die in this month. My mother died in June.' This was how Eve gave Martha permission to go. Then we just touched Martha, held her and said, 'You can go.' We loved her, and we touched her and we told her we loved her. We loved that she was a lesbian, and I thought, what a wonderful gift that was, especially to the older lesbians who were there. It's so hard sometimes. We hugged her and prayed with her, and touched. We laid our hands on her and prayed. And we said, 'All right, now Martha, you just go when you want to go.' And so Eve went out for something to drink, and Martha left. She just left."

Jane's approach to ministering is to try to read and listen to her clients carefully, to jump into the place they make for her, to be there without getting in the way. Ministering to those who are gay, lesbian and bisexual has helped Jane to see that task and to enter that process with clarity. "Sometimes, when you're lesbian or gay, bisexual or transgendered, you do things kind of differently. For Martha they did the burial first and then we did the service. The service was so important. All of their friends did a ritual. They lit candles, and pictures of her were everywhere. Everyone just sat with Eve.

"So who makes the rules about this? We've learned to honor our own way about what death is, you see. Family or friends who take care of those who die with HIV or cancer are sometimes so exhausted from the caretaking that they don't have a memorial for two months. By then, people have revived a bit. That is a wonderful gift, I think, about being lesbian or gay, or bisexual or transgendered: We don't have to do it the way people say it has to be done."

Jane remembered working with Jeff and Terry, one of her earliest experiences ministering to a couple dealing with HIV. "Terry was so sick that it was hard to recognize his face. And he was quiet. Jeff was crying, but Terry was quiet. The quieter that he became, the more Jeff and I talked. We would talk for hours. We were taking care of each other. I was going through an incredible breakup with a woman who I had been with for some years. Terry listened and took care of me. I talked with Terry about his brother's fundamentalist Christian views and his brother's worry about whether or not Terry was 'saved.' We were able to work through that before he died. Terry's body got smaller and smaller, but his spirit took up the whole room. So you'd walk into this room of Terry. It was like, 'Terry's here!' Even though he was so little, it was like the littler he got, the bigger his presence became. And he was beautiful, even though you could not recognize his face.

"A good friend who is an intensive care nurse came to visit and told us that Terry's case was one of the worst she had ever seen. Now, some of the people we minister to don't want to go through this, so they think about killing themselves. Terry and Jeff had thought about it and had a plan about what they were going to do. People who are going to die do what they need to do, and we talked about that. Our friend had this wonderful thing she asked people to do when they were planning this. She would ask them, 'If you're going to do this, I would ask you to take a year to do it. And tell people what you are going to do so they can tell you how they feel about you.'

"You know, sometimes people can carry out their plans, and then sometimes they don't because they're so sick. But it helped me to hear all of this, to be able to talk with people who think like that. God love Terry—he never complained or anything; all he needed was more morphine. They thought they'd done it, but Terry woke up and said to Jeff, 'Is this heaven?'

"Jeff was such a good caretaker. They had a beautiful garden tended mostly by Terry. Every now and then, Jeff would say to Terry, 'Now, Terry, I have to go out in the garden. I'm going to lie down out there. I need to lie down on the earth and meditate and I'll be away for about half an hour. Because if I don't take care of me then I can't take care of you.' Imagine, to have that sense of oneself. They allowed me in there to see that and learn from them. They are forever with me."

Working with Jeff and Terry held additional significance for Jane. During one hospital visit, Jeff began a conversation. "He said, 'Janey, I saw my dad today.'

"And I said, 'Well, Jeff, I thought your dad died about twenty years ago.'

"'He did,' and he continued, 'I saw my dad today.'

"I said, 'Jeff, what did you see?'

"'My dad came to me and said, "Jeff, you could never handle me dying, it was so hard for you. It was so difficult." But he went on, "You will take very good care of Terry, and it will be healing for you and me, too."'

"Jeff won the first financial spousal support award. I didn't know how bad off Terry was until we went to testify at the spousal support case. There was a hospice nurse and myself. We were to testify about Jeff and Terry's relationship and what we saw. Hospice called to thank me and said, 'We've never heard love between two people like this.'

"Everybody deals with dying differently. They may be screaming maniacs, but when I walk in the room, because of who I am or because I've earned my stripes or whatever, they talk to me. I may be warned, 'Janey, God, he's a son-of-a . . . ' and then I go in and I might say, 'Hey! Acting like a little boy? Are you free? Is your little boy in charge right now? Is that what you're doing?' They're flabbergasted. But they want me to say, 'Stop. Honey, you're a two-year-old and you're so cranky, and I know it's terrible.' Sometimes I just hop up in bed with them and hold them, and they just lie there with me and cry. I suppose one becomes all different things, if you're not in the way, you see. You're not in the way; you are just there."

Jane continued: "I've had to earn my way though, especially with lesbian, gay, bisexual and transgendered people, because so many have been hurt spiritually by so many faith communities. Some people are just so angry. This one incredible guy said, 'I'm so fucking mad at the Catholic church, I hate you!' Just screaming and yelling, and then I said, 'Well, Mark, do you want to make some peace around that?' So I talked about this to my friend Father Lou Roberts, a monk, an incredible man, with white hair and twinkling blue eyes. He brought Mark and his partner to the Catholic center. He took them on retreats, and when Mark was getting sicker, he would have Lou come to his parents' home with him. The parents didn't want to meet Mark's partner. But on one visit Lou took Mark's parents aside and said, 'It is not me taking care of Mark; it is his partner. You need to hear about this.' It was so good that Mark's parents could hear it from a priest. This is some of what we're able to do as spiritual counselors. It's an amazing . . . entry."

Jane recalled Tom, a man who had gone from a robust two hundred pounds to a mere sixty. As he lay dying, and Jane and her partner were sitting with him, "he put his hands to our lips. And he said, 'I will pray for you.' You could hardly hear him. We went into the living room to see his family, who were Southern Baptists, and they didn't know exactly who we were. His mother whispered to me, 'Is he going to be saved?' They were afraid. Their son was gay and he had HIV. I looked at her and I said, 'Mrs. Wells, not only is he saved, but he is saving us.' And that struck home."

During her first experiences of ministering to people dying from AIDS, Jane remembered how purposeless it all seemed. "Nobody knew what the hell this disease was; all we knew was that our friends were dying.

That's all we knew. We didn't know what it was or what it was from. In the early days nobody would touch people with HIV. People would wear masks. We refused. We went in, we touched, we wanted to be with them. People were frightened when we came in the room!"

But within this context, miracles to reinforce her faith occurred. "When Phil was dying, we talked to him, told him his wife would be all right and his dogs; he loved his wife and his dogs; we told him they'd be all right. We just prayed him away into the light, 'Reach your friends, reach your family on the other side.' His breathing just went way down. Then we saw him see something. When he died, he opened his eyes. The lesions that were on his face came off his face. We stood there. It was like, oh my God! I mean, it's made a hell of a believer out of me."

Jane recalled another friend who had a near-death experience. Chuck "died of a heart attack and then came back. He said to my partner and me, 'I don't know why I've come back, but I want to tell you what happened.' He talked about the light, going down the tunnel, greeting people on the other side. He saw the light, and then he tumbled back down the tunnel into his body. He said, 'Well, I know why I came back—so I could tell you.'

"You can tell this to people if they want to know it. Some people ask, 'Janey, tell me about other people, what do they see, what do they do?' When they are dying, it is so remarkable to me that sometimes I don't know if am I with people here or there. Sometimes I feel like I've gone to the other side with them. Sometimes it's hard to come back. Because when people invite you, well, the course of a death will just take you in. When someone dies, it's like I'm not in the world anymore. After someone dies, often I go to water, or I have to go outside or go be with children. I have to go out and hear life or see it, to come back."

Having witnessed firsthand the spirituality of those she has ministered to, Jane is angered by the charge that gays and lesbians are not spiritual. She recalled another terminally ill gay friend, Bob, a Roman Catholic who was interested in all faiths and traditions. "At night he would sometimes have nightmares. He made these wonderful cards with mantras that he'd read, like, 'Oh God, how can I be in your presence?' His mother came about a month before he died and told him, 'I can't be with you when you die. Your daddy died. It would be too hard for me. I can't.' So that was real; we knew what she couldn't do, and thank God she was truthful. She was worried about his wish to be cremated and about the ashes. Half of them, he said, were going to his friends. She looked at me and said, 'What would God think about this?' I answered, 'Well, I think God would be fine with it, but how are you going to be with it?'

"With HIV one really has to decide who God is. You know, either God is the patriarchal, passion-wrenched thing or in fact a pretty vulnerable, open spirit that cries and weeps with us and isn't in control but is willing to go with us. Not a power-over God, but a co-creator. So you've got some choices here. For some parents, that means they have to change who God is to them. This is their kid and when it's your kid, you begin to hear it differently. In the end, people will do whatever they can for their own kid.

"We thanked Bob's mother for telling the truth about not being able to be with him, and afterward, I asked Bob, 'How is it? Mom isn't going to be here?' He said, 'Janey, Alan and I are partners and we have buried so many of our friends together. Don't worry, Alan will be my mother. I'll lay on his lap and he'll stroke my head and I'll die with him.' And he died with Alan. Alan was his best friend, was like a mother to him. So he had his 'mother,' because you create what you need. People choose what is to be and things can happen quite differently."

Jane has also seen that death can be reuniting and healing for many people who have been cut off from their family members. When Larry, who was bisexual, was dying, he was married to a Japanese woman with whom he had had two children. His wife knew he was bisexual and so did the children, and they somehow kept working this all out. It was very, very hard for them. About three weeks before his death, Larry called and asked Jane to come over. "He wanted me to somehow help his wife let him go, to help her heal the pain around him having relationships with men. For three weeks we loved her, we talked with him. We had expected him to die within two days, but he didn't. Toward the end, we would go over there at midnight, sometimes at three in the morning, and everyone would take turns and sit with him. We finally asked him, 'Who isn't here, Larry? Is there someone you want to see?' His wife answered, 'I know who he needs. It's the person that he loved, the male lover.' They were no longer lovers, but this was the person he needed, and Larry's wife had come to the point that we could invite that man in, even though he couldn't get there in person; we could still invite him to be there. That's how much healing had happened within the family. Eventually, after everybody said everything they needed to say, we all left and went to bed. It was six in the morning, and he slipped away; he was out of there.

"A dear Buddhist teacher of mine told me to just 'breathe with people. What can you do, what can you do? Breathe! Breathe with the people.' That's what you can do. Just breathe and be natural when people are dying."

Jane thinks that everyone has the intuitive capacity to minister to the dying but that we have learned to doubt our gut instincts, and we have relinquished our role in witnessing death to others—to institutions and to institutional or professional caregivers. At the same time, she acknowledged, hospice houses have been very important, and hospital deaths are very appropriate for some. "Some people are so exhausted that it's a relief when their partner goes to the hospital for two or three days. They're still so sad, and it's still a hell of a trek to go to the hospital, but you don't have to worry about feeding or changing or bandages. I mean, it is a huge, huge thing, caretaking. You just don't do anything else, because that's your work."

As a spiritual counselor, Jane too has bathed her clients, and diapered them and changed bed pans. For some people, "this goes on for years; it becomes the caregiver's purpose in life. You see it with partners, like my mother and dad, and it's sainting. On the other hand, we have to watch for abuse within all of that. There are many kinds of learning involved in this."

Having witnessed so many passings, Jane reflected on what she thinks really happens when we die. "I only know what people tell me. They tell me that they see lights. They tell me that they talk to people on the other side. I've been with dying friends who have had conversations with people on the other side. Dying people can see family and friends on the other side. I believe people love the dying to the other side. I believe we can help them over, just because of the number of stories that we've heard in our community. I believe, too, that the dying help the living after they've crossed over. Jeff told me that Terry and he made an agreement at the end that Terry would come to him in a dream so that Jeff would know he was all right. Terry did come in a wonderful dream; Terry was busy on the other side, and Jeff knew that Terry was all right.

"Friends of mine are concerned about me and the work that I do. They say, 'Janey, you're going to go out in the public and somebody may hurt you. I mean, somebody might want to harm you out there. There are people who don't like lesbians, gays, bisexuals and transgendered people out there.' But one day I came home and there was this message on my answering machine: 'Jane Spahr, I thought you should know that wherever you are, all the people that you've been with with HIV, all those people, they'll be protecting you. You don't have to worry about anything.'

"I want people to talk about this. I want people to talk about their fears. In the early years of HIV, one of my parishioner's mothers said to me, 'You know, Janey, nobody knows how terrible this HIV disease is until you're in it. How can you describe this to people?' But you know, she said, 'Night goes into day, day goes into night.' This is the other part of it. Some of the most wonderful conversations are at three in the morning. It's like there is no time. Cycles are backward, how people think, whether you are awake or dreaming, that kind of thing. Sometimes you can feel it when you walk in the house: Transitioning is happening here.

"I think we can make the same kind of preparations for death that we do for birth. I think we should celebrate. When Phil died at four in the morning, I left that hospital and I wanted to wake everybody up and say, 'Something incredible happened here. This was good, good work!' It's hard work to die! You know, it is hard work they are doing! It's like what it is for someone to 'come out.' I think dying is the same hard work as giving birth. I think it's the same kind of hard work. I think the dying are being birthed somewhere else. That's what I've thought about. The tunnel is like another umbilical cord. Why couldn't it be like that? I mean, this is how we come in."

Having witnessed many part company, Jane nevertheless views all leave-takings as important and striking. One of her most moving experiences "involved a couple who didn't go to my church. The mother was Native-American, the father was European-American. I met their family after their one-year-old daughter died of crib death. Their older daughter was five and freaked that her sister was gone. We went to the funeral home. They had her laid out in her little blue dress, little white anklets and little Mary Jane shoes. She was such a little girl. I talked about her little life and her family, but I could feel, could *feel* this child everywhere. We went out to the cemetery for a Native-American ceremony; only the Native-American people could talk. They had corn and they had roses. Everyone stood in a huge circle. The Cherokee people came forward and spoke in their native Cherokee, then in English, to honor this baby girl. Standing there in the circle I can remember to this day, I saw, I *saw* in my mind's eye, a huge man wearing a blue shirt. He had long, gray hair. I knew he was Native-American, I don't know whether he was Cherokee, but this man came and picked up this little girl and carried her away. I thought I'd lost my mind, but I decided to talk to the mother. 'I want to tell you something that I saw today,' I said. 'I want to tell you.' I remembered the face perfectly; I wanted to describe everything the person was wearing and that the baby had been taken somewhere. The mother said to me, 'Janey, you have described my great-grandfather.'

"That was first time that ever happened to me. No one else saw the vision. I just had to tell her. I thought, 'Hey, this happened to me and I'm telling you what I saw.' All I can do is what I'm told from inside. Maybe I'm a lunatic. It's okay if I say that! But that never had happened to me before. Although I have 'felt' people who have died. I've felt them around. Usually when people die, I feel them. Especially when I'm getting ready to do the memorial. Sometimes I feel their presence, as though they are helping me."

On the other hand, Jane sometimes feels no presence of the person who passed away. She recalled getting ready for the memorial service of a young man who had committed suicide. "He had been really troubled, because of a lot of things. When I walked in the church to do the memorial service, that young man was gone; there was not a trace of him. I knew how much he had wanted to be out of here. I mean he was gone, so then I said, 'Go, my friend. I pray for peace for you.' Usually, people are around a little bit. But this was very different for me, different from all the others.

"We haven't begun to know all that is involved, but whatever the case, I become a part of the family in a way. I was called on several years ago to help a family I'd known for a very long time to say goodbye to their dad who had died some sixteen years before. They wanted to say goodbye again. So we went to where the father was buried. The son, now eighteen, was two when his father had died. He hadn't cried or talked about it in all those years. He just couldn't do it. But at this time, we were sitting out in the cemetery at his father's graveside, and we began to talk about the father. From the moment that I began talking, the son cried, and sobbed and sobbed. The family had been afraid that he wouldn't even participate. He had not cried in sixteen years. And they just held him and they held each other and they cried and cried and cried, and each member of the family said goodbye. This was long after the death, and sometimes it can't happen any earlier, for lots of reasons—their fear, or maybe they're exhausted from caretaking, but then finally they're lighter. They're different, you see, and that's the thing for me. It's just to be there, with lots of intuition. Because in no way do I want to put words in people's mouths. For this memorial I went over the notes of the service I had given sixteen years earlier. I asked them, 'Do you remember this?' They didn't, but we talked about what they thought now. I'm forever connected to that family."

As a spiritual counselor, Jane's work with families involves many important events within a family's life cycle. Reworking the grief associated with this father's death was only one of these. Jane also buried the grandmother of this family and performed the marriage ceremony for one of the daughters. For Jane it is remarkable to be a part of the family. It is the kind of work that she thinks bears a strong resemblance to the work centuries ago of village wise women, who were present to help families with the important transitions in their lives.

Notes

When Did I Get to Be So Grown-up?

Barbara Frazier

Bright and ambitious by nature, Barbara Frazier, a twenty-two-year-old college senior, wanted her mother, Mary, to live long enough to see her graduate. Barbara, who was one of the first people we talked with, was the only one we interviewed twice—once before her spring graduation, as her mother's cancer was progressing rapidly, and three months later, after her mother's death.

Barbara's goal meant that she had to take extra courses, even as she made frequent four-hour trips home to be with her mother, father and older sister. Her story is one of being at the threshold of adulthood and trying to accomplish important life tasks while at the same time having to cope with the decline and loss of her mother. Her interviews reveal the cruel paradox of those who attend to the dying: the absolute certainty that death is closing in and the absolute uncertainty about when or how it will come.

At the first interview, Barbara explained that during the previous fall, her mother, Mary, had suffered a persistent bout of sinusitis with attendant headaches, including an especially difficult headache during an airplane flight. Mary had consulted several doctors, but nothing extraordinary had been detected. Then, shortly before Christmas, she started getting nosebleeds. During another exam, a growth was discovered.

At first, doctors were not especially worried about it, but a biopsy indicated malignancy. Surgeons then removed all of Mary's left sinus, cutting so far up that the layer between the sinuses and the brain was punctured. Following the surgery, Mary resisted having an MRI (magnetic resonance imaging) because she was claustrophobic. Three weeks later, she was scheduled for radiation treatment but felt too sick to go. Barbara's father insisted, however, and when he got Mary to the treatment facility, she was numb from her toes to her chest. Specialists were called who insisted on an MRI, and the results showed that another tumor had wrapped itself around the spinal cord. Additional tests revealed that more cancer had spread throughout Mary's body.

Although she received chemotherapy, Mary was soon unable to tolerate the toxic effects. By March, the middle of Barbara's last semester at college, the doctors had discontinued it. Although radiation treatments continued, Barbara was very aware that the disease was running its course quickly. She wondered how rapidly her mother would deteriorate. How would the family manage her care? Would her mother stay at home or need to be hospitalized?

Trying to anticipate what might happen, Barbara speculated that her mother would get weaker and weaker and eventually lapse into a coma. Mary had made a living will and did not want life support. "I think she just wants to die at home," Barbara reflected. "She loves her house. She's redone most of it, all herself, by hand; she has stripped all of the floors. She has put so much love into the house. My sister and I have sat down and spoken to my father and said, 'This family needs hospice and this family needs hospice *now.*'" Barbara was confident that hospice would help. She also felt that she was knowledgeable about death. As a child she had experienced a number of close family members' deaths. In each case, her parents left it up to her to choose whether or not to go to the funeral. She recalled that "funerals, for me, were a very good source of closure."

Barbara's earliest memory of death was when she was about five years old. Their family owned an apple orchard, and an elderly worker died there one day. His body was discovered by some children, who came to the house to tell Barbara's mother. Barbara remembered being confused: The children were telling her mother that the man was dead, but to Barbara it just seemed that he was lying there, asleep. She remembered not understanding the concept of "dead" at all: "He was there, but dead? He was there. It didn't make any sense to me."

In college, Barbara enrolled in a course on death and dying. "I had never done any reading and I was very taken with Elisabeth Kübler-Ross, how . . . she made it sound almost beautiful and it took a little bit of the fear out of dying." The course helped Barbara realize that she had always felt somewhat distant from her grandmothers because to her, they represented being old and near death. The course alleviated some of that fear, and she has since been able to communicate with her grandmothers as individuals, rather than as people closer to death.

Barbara's understanding of death was broadened even more as a result of her mother's illness. "It's not what Kübler-Ross describes. It's not what I imagined. It's long and it's hard and it's tiring. I watch my mother for all the things I learned in books. There is so much more than what the books say." Barbara acknowledged that she could match some of what she studied with what she was experiencing: "When my mother refused to talk to me, when she refused to sleep with my father, I could say, 'It hurts her too much; she's pushing us away.' And that was straight out of Kübler-Ross. That was right on. But," she continued, "there are no mushy talks at the bedside, and we're not getting along in perfect harmony. Everybody's stressed, and everybody fights and we get on each other's nerves. It's just so hard. And Kübler-Ross doesn't talk about what it's like to be four hours away and to have to do this by telephone."

Recently, there had been a major crisis for her mother, which Barbara only learned about by accident. "My father didn't even call me and tell me it happened. I just happened to call my sister to ask her a question. Nobody called me. When my mother is in the hospital, I call in the evening to see how things are." But if something happens when Mary is living at home, like a doctor's appointment, Barbara does not hear about it right away. Although this bothers her, she understands what the situation is like at home. "You're so busy, your mind is so full. The first thing that pops into my dad's head isn't, 'I have to call Barbara now.'" Barbara's mother has been both bitter and needy, "my father's always got to be there. Sometimes she doesn't want to be alone, and he can't say, 'Excuse me, I have to go call Barbara.' You are in so much guilt. Oh my gosh, the guilt . . . because I'm not there and I should be there, you know?"

Even when Barbara does manage to be at home, there is an emotional toll for her. "I feel so responsible that I do anything that anybody wants me to do. And I do it the best. I do things that nobody else would ever do. I cook and I clean and I run around for my mother. 'Dad, you sit down.' I take over because they deserve it, but I do so much to try and make up for the weeks I've been gone that I'm mentally and physically exhausted. When I come back to school from having been there I usually spend a day in bed."

Despite the fact that the immediate future was so uncertain, Barbara was making plans. In fact, she had prepared various options for finishing her course work in a way that would assure her early graduation, depending on the actual timing of her mother's death. She explained, "I have a three-credit leeway in the May term, which means I could drop one course if I had to. She won't die this semester because there's only a week left. If she dies first summer session, I still have the three credits and I can drop one class. And it's five weeks. So that's a lot of time to deal with. Or second semester summer session, if she dies then . . . "

Barbara paused and then confessed that having to make these plans "makes me angry. It makes me angry that I'm . . . " and then she began to discuss her relationship with her boyfriend, Jack. In fact, she was announcing for the first time that "Jack asked me to marry him, and we had to sit and talk about the date. There was when *we* wanted to do it. Then, maybe we should wait till *after* my mother died, about six months, because then it would be a reason to be excited. This is a twofold thing. When I go home today and announce it, it could give my mother something to live for, 'to see my daughter get married.' She could maybe make it to October. But what if she dies very quickly? Then, that's going to put a damper on . . . my whole life, graduation . . . graduation is for my mother. This is all for my mother. Everything. And I don't know why I resent it, because my parents did it for me. They changed their lives for me. But they chose to have me. I didn't choose this. Like my whole life now, I've planned around my mother. I have to tell my instructors, 'I might disappear. I'll be real conscientious about letting you know, but if this happens in the middle of the night, I'm out of here.' There's nothing, there's nothing I can do about it."

Barbara vacillated, sinking into resignation about her situation and then rising to the occasion, determined to make the best of it, but resenting having to face the challenge at the same time. "I just feel that at almost twenty-three years old you should be excited about graduation and getting married. You've got your whole life ahead of you, and I don't think you should have to think about living each day for the day because there might not be a tomorrow. There's just a lot more pain. I've had to question so many things. *Is* there a God? If there is a God, why is he doing this to my mother? Why is she suffering? And . . . me. Usually, people don't have to confront things about themselves till they're older. A lot of times it happens in a midlife crisis or whatever. But I've had to really sit down and look at myself. I'm questioning my values, and I see now that life is short and I want to live life the best that I can now."

At the same time that Barbara valued knowing life was short, she was angry about having to confront that reality so unremittingly. In fact, Barbara said, she was usually angry these days, and this anger has been hard to handle. "We had a kitten and the kitten was always doing everything wrong and it would just set me off. I would yell, 'Bad cat!' And I would be mean to my boyfriend, Jack, and start fights. I've just recently started working on that. I bought a journal, and I'm learning to put my anger into the book. I've gotten to the point now that if something's really wrong, I look for my book. I don't look for Jack. I find my journal and I just go."

She added that although she likes to exercise, nothing seemed to help until she and Jack got mountain bikes. "The mountain bike has really done a lot for me. I didn't buy it for that, but it takes my mind off things." And her closest friends have helped too. "Jack, my sister and two good friends have all just really been there. They listen. They don't try and correct it, but they're there and they're strong and they let me cry."

Barbara's sister, Lisa, had a degree in psychology, was married, and lived within five minutes of their mother and father. Barbara knew their mother's illness was stressful for Lisa too, but in different ways. She speculated that Lisa felt that she needed to be strong for Barbara, and that, because Lisa was older and a psychologist, she thought she ought to be able to handle the situation. Barbara sensed that Lisa was angry too, but could not admit it. "Lisa has always been older than her years. I've been mature, but I have always been a kid too. I liked to play in the mud and things like that. Lisa was always very old—too mature to say, 'This isn't fair.'"

Yet Barbara felt that her sister was one of the only people who understood what she was going through. For example, concerning Barbara's push to graduate early, "Nobody said, 'God Barbara, what a good kid you are for busting your butt so your mother could see you graduate.' But my sister understood. When I talk about having to arrange my life around this illness, people say, 'That's the least that you can do.' When I talk about how bitter my mother is, people say, 'You'd be bitter too.' But I'm not saying she shouldn't be bitter. My sister understands that."

Barbara was becoming frustrated with people who have not had any comparable experiences. "I don't like people who have no clue telling me how I should feel. There are catch phrases that I hate: 'Everything will be okay.' The one that will make me violent is, 'I understand.' Now, my friend whose mother died of cancer said, 'Barbara, I understand,' and she did. At first, Jack used to say, 'I understand.' And he didn't. He couldn't. He didn't have the slightest idea. You can't. I hate that!"

Other people have distanced themselves. "Some people who I grew up with haven't even called and asked me how I am, or even how my mother is. I think many people have such a hard time with death that they can't. It's not that they don't want to—it's just that they can't. I wish I didn't have to deal with it either, but it's not a choice.

"My friend Amy has a really hard time with death. But we've known each other since we were five, and she's there. She does the best that she can, and she talks to me about it. 'I don't know what to say to you. I don't know what to do for you. I don't know how to handle this.' She doesn't run away. She cries with me and for some reason that really helps."

Barbara then described the tensions in her parents' marriage. Her father owns his own business and throughout the years has been married to his work. Mary used to ask him to take vacations, but they never did because her father could not take the time. Now, her father was feeling a lot of guilt, re-evaluating the whole relationship and realizing how much he really did love and rely on his wife. This made it worse for her father. "If they had not really loved each other, this would have been easier, but can you imagine realizing how much you love your wife and knowing that in a few minutes she's going to be gone? It's possible that he could have come to this understanding before this, but probably not without a lot of work," Barbara sighed.

Now Barbara's father was trying to meet his wife's every need. But he could not, of course, and Barbara thought her mother was mean to him. Her father just kept apologizing over and over again, saying, "I'm sorry, I'm sorry, what can I do?" He did not get angry around his wife, although he was taking his anger out on Barbara and Lisa and sometimes the dog.

"I get mad at my mother for treating my father so badly. I said, 'Dad, the reason Mom doesn't want you around and the reason she pushes you away is that it hurts her too much.' I explained, 'I love you and admire you and you're doing the best that you can do and I think you should be proud of yourself.' I think it was the first time anybody gave him some credit, and he just fell apart. I guess he hadn't ever thought about it that way." That was "the hardest day of all, over April break when I held my father, who is six feet tall and weighs three hundred pounds, in my arms. He cried and said, 'Why? This isn't fair. How can she leave me? What am I going to do?' It was awful. What was I gonna say? I don't know what my father's going to do with himself when this is all said and done."

Neither had Barbara thought much about what life would be like after her mother died. The most she could do was address the immediate issues, such as the funeral and how her mother would look in the casket. Her mother's looks had changed markedly. She was much thinner, and the operation had changed her facial features. She wore an eye patch, her color was not good, and she was so angry that she looked angry. And that is how Barbara pictured her mother would look in the casket: really angry. "I see her as she is now, angry in person and character. I think about who will come. I think about standing there. I hope that I'm not, that I can . . . " Barbara struggled to define her expectations for herself. "I've had to cope with so many people. I'm the one whose mother is dying, but her friend will come over and fall apart, because *we're* so strong. I have to comfort people in their forties. But wait a minute, I'm the kid! When did I get to be so grown-up?"

On the subject of her personal future, Barbara's focused on her relationship with Jack, and their wedding. At first, "I told him we couldn't have a wedding because how could I have a wedding without a mother? Who was I going to plan a wedding with? She's just not going to get excited about planning a wedding. I think she'll be excited that I am getting married and that it's Jack I'm marrying. But thinking about what it would be like to have a wedding without my mother in the picture would be too painful."

Later, it would occur to Barbara that, "maybe I could have even more fun, because it wouldn't be my mother that I'm butting heads against. My sister is my best friend, and I have Jack and my friends Amy and Rebecca. But it would be different and it would be sad.

"I think about my children. My mom was such a fun mom. I've always thought about how she was going to spoil my kids, but she's not going to know them, and my kids aren't going to have the opportunity to know her. That really bothers me, because she's not going to see her grandkids and she wanted grandkids."

Barbara was ambivalent about broaching specific topics with her mother before she died. She wanted to confront her about how she could be so mean to the people who are taking care of her, for example. But Barbara also felt that being terminally ill gives you rights that other people do not have. Her mother did not have much time left, so why rock the boat? "We don't have any unfinished business. So it's not like there's anything we have to settle. It's just that I would like to talk. My mom and I always used to talk about me and about life. We just used to talk so much. I miss my mom—so much. She's still alive, but she's dead. I miss her and I think about that. And when my kids come, I'm not going to be able to call her and cry on the phone, 'They're just like you said; what am I gonna do?' I'm not going to have that."

Thinking about her mother's meanness, Barbara reflected that it was not only illness-related. In some respects, her mother had always been an unhappy person. Nothing was good enough or pleased her. "Everything was keeping up with the Joneses, how it looked to the neighbors. She was very superficial. So, the way she's dying is how she would have chosen to go, with people coming and calling and flowers all around, putting on this act, 'Oh, I'm tired today, but can I get you anything?' My mother is on her deathbed and she's still the hostess. This lady is going to go out a martyr. Her friends think she is just handling this so well and she's so strong."

Barbara was curious to know what her mother was thinking and feeling during this time. She wished her mother could explain what it feels like to die, but she has not been able to get her mother to talk. "My God, can you imagine what it feels like to die? Who knows? Who knows? The knowledge that I could get from my mother for what I want to do in my own life—I mean, that's kind of a sick twist but—'Tell me, tell me what it's like. Tell me what you feel. Tell me what you think.'"

These questions led Barbara to speculate on the idea of an afterlife. "What makes me feel good is to think that there's a heaven and there's this little cloud and my mom is going to get on it and she'll look down and know that I accomplished things. It's nice to think that some day I'm going to see my mom again, and I can talk to her and she'll be there. That's what I hold on to. That part of you that thinks has to go someplace. Sometimes I look around and I say this is hell; there is no heaven, because this is hell sometimes. Truly, nobody is free. And then, some people believe in reincarnation. I think, God, I *feel* brutally old; maybe I am. Maybe my soul is very old. I can't imagine *nothing*. So I hope she'll be up there, and I hope she'll be a happier person. Anything's better than this—even if there's no person."

Barbara felt that people going through something like this, especially people her age, should be sure to be around people they can rely on, "people who aren't going to go anywhere. Along with that, I think it's really important to say 'I'm sorry.' It's important to say, 'I love you.'

I've come to that from a lot of hard work. At twenty-two, I can say I'm thrilled to spend the rest of my life with Jack because I know myself now. I think that you need to remember that nothing is 'wrong,' that however you deal is how you are going to deal. It's really okay. I can be mad at my mom for dying and that's okay.

"This is the worst time of my life, but I am making some of the best connections that I've ever made. What a paradox, truly. I'm so excited about my internship, and my directed study, and Jack and I wouldn't be at the point we are now if we hadn't been forced to do this. How odd that the worst time of my life is the best time of my life. If my mother hadn't been sick, I'd have been slack. I wouldn't be done this semester. I never would have gotten as many A's. And it's because it was something to do instead of feeling sorry for myself. I never would have been in my advisor's office to get hold of that internship. I would just take things for granted."

In early May, Barbara reached her goal. Upon the condition that she complete her credit load by the end of the summer, she was able to march with her graduating class as her mother looked on. Six weeks later, Mary died. We spoke with Barbara again in September, and she recalled the day of her mother's death.

"She'd had a hard night. Around two, my dad and I had to put her back in bed. Somehow she got out. She was sort of crumpled onto the floor, and then she was up at seven in the morning and decided she wanted all of her clothes off. My dad and I knew that she was going to die that morning. I called my sister, but she took my head off for getting her up so early for nothing. For some reason, Lisa couldn't sense it.

"We made a pot of coffee, and some friends of the family were there. My mother always had coffee going, and one particular scene sticks in my mind. She was in a big brass bed, and I had my cup of coffee, and my father was on the edge of the chair drinking coffee. My sister was sort of leaning, drinking her coffee. I was hanging over the bed. We were all waiting for my mother to die, drinking coffee. It was all so very civilized, because we were expecting her to just stop breathing—no big deal—just all of a sudden she wouldn't be breathing anymore. And that's what we were waiting for. That bothered me, that we could sit around and drink coffee and watch my mother die.

"My mom was having very labored breathing. She'd get up and say things. She died at 1:45 P.M. My sister got there around eight, so between eight and one we never left the room. My mother said a lot of things. Her lungs kept filling up with fluid, so she kept trying to get up, and she'd stand up and say things. One time she asked my dad what was happening to her, and my father said she was going to heaven. Throughout the whole thing she kept saying, 'Okay, okay. Okay.' I interpreted it as when there's something that you don't want to do, you get yourself together, like, Okay, okay, I just need one more minute. And she'd say, 'Okay, I need fifteen more minutes. I need another half an hour,' asking us for more time.

"At one point she got up because she needed her ticket. And my father told her that she didn't need a ticket, and she was sure that she did and he told her that it was for free. It was strange for me. I have a good friend whose father died in December, and I knew that he died very soon after having delusions. When my mom started having delusions and hallucinations, I knew. She started having little ones. Her favorite meal was boiled ham with potatoes and beans. She loved that meal, and she dreamed about it a lot. She'd be eating ham. She'd ask for more beans. It was a recurring theme right up until she died. She was still eating green beans and ham.

"She waved a lot. Once she was waving at us like we were little children and I lost it. I have talked about this type of behavior to people who said it's not that unpleasant, that they're going back in their mind to favorite situations, and it's a wonderful thing, they thought, not painful for her. But it was really sad because she'd come up out of it and she'd know she'd been hallucinating and she was embarrassed."

But "she really had her wits about her up until the end. About forty-five minutes before she died, she said she wanted to talk to each of us alone. She talked to my sister for probably fifteen minutes, then asked for me. She said, 'I love you. I'll miss you.' And gave me this really strong hug. Then she talked to my dad for a while. She died about half an hour later."

Barbara did not know what made her so certain that her mother was dying. "I just knew. Jack and I got there on a Monday and she just got worse and worse every day. And we were all there. She was waiting for something. On Tuesday, I talked to my father, 'I have this feeling that she's waiting for something because we're all here and she's waiting and I don't know what she's waiting for.' Now I know what she waited for." It was the date, June 20th.

"Vicki was my mother's cousin and best friend and is now my father's lady friend, and Vicki's little girl had drowned. She died on June 20th. Vicki and my mom had a conversation about how Vicki can't remember things like birthdays. June 20th is a friend's birthday, and Vicki made the statement that she could never forget this person's birthday because that's the day that her daughter died. I think my mother died on June 20th so Vicki wouldn't forget. She did it on purpose."

When Barbara's mother stopped breathing that day, "it was horrible. There wasn't any sign of God there. It wasn't peaceful. There were no angels, no heaven. She fought to the end. Her eyes were wide open with fear. My dad was really wonderful. He just kept talking to her. 'It's going to be okay. It's going to be okay. We really love you. You've got to let go and just forget to breathe,' real soothing things. She started to die and you could tell because of the gasping, the choking, the clutching of my father's hand, the face, the noises. Her face and the noises are what I'll never ever, ever forget. My dad was sitting on the bed with her. I was leaning over the bed and my sister was behind me. As my mother was about to die, my father just lost it. He just sort of pushed her down and he started crying. Lisa came behind me and grabbed me and we grabbed my mother. She was in our arms when she died.

"We kept staring at her. We kept expecting, like in the movies, we just kept expecting her to sit up and talk or for her eyes to move or for her to take another breath. None of us could believe that she was dead. It could have been the biggest surprise to me in the world. Because she was lying there, a dead person. I'm touching a dead person. And she went all goosebumps, her whole body, and that was, uck. She had lost so much weight that her face was just teeth. The position that she was in, it was just so . . . awful. There's no word. It was so unpleasant. Everything was so negative for me. Ugh. And I left. I left her with my sister. We had to call the hospice people."

A hospice nurse had come earlier in the day to check on her mother "But," Barbara said indignantly, "it wasn't our regular nurse. It was just another nurse. It was the weekend. I said to the nurse, 'Where are you going to be today?' She said, 'Why?'

"'Well, in case we need to get in touch with you. Are you going to be far away or are you going to be able to come quickly?'

"'I'll be able to get here within half an hour, but I don't see any reason why you'd need me.'

"This nurse didn't think my mother was going to die that day. But it was so obvious—all you had to do was look at her and you knew."

After she left the room, Barbara went to her grandparents' house down the street. She wanted to break the news in person. When she told her grandmother, "she already knew. She had a sense, like I did. When I got there, there were newspapers and books all over the place and my grandmother was down on her hands and knees picking them up. I said, 'Grandma, what happened?'

"She said, 'I knew that your mother was going to die today and I got very angry. All the good people in this world die, like your mother and all the bad people live' and aiy-aiy-aiy. She freaked out.

"And then I came back home and there were more people there. By now the funeral people were there, and they cleared the room because they were going to take her out. I refused to leave. That's another very vivid picture in my head. The hallway was very narrow and it had turns in it and they couldn't get her out. They had to sit her up. And when they did, she shifted in the bag and made this really gross, body-shifting-in-the-bag noise, and they wheeled her out. I held the door and I watched them put her in the hearse. I figured a body bag would look different. It looked like luggage. It was navy blue. It was just like a carry-on garment bag. I guess I was expecting clear plastic, like the movies. She was just so tiny. It was like she just wasn't in the bag at all.

"People started to come, and it really bothered me that they were in my space. I didn't like that. And everybody wanted to hug me and touch me and I didn't want anybody getting near me. I didn't want to be 'comforted.' I just wanted people out of my face. Lisa and I went upstairs and we picked out the dress that we wanted our mother to wear and we went through some of her stuff. It was really kind of odd that, right after she died, we went upstairs and went through her jewelry. We each put on a bracelet of my mom's, I guess because we wanted something of hers to be near us." Ultimately, Barbara explained, the disposition of her mother's things would be done quickly and agreeably in the next couple of weeks. "Nobody got their feelings hurt."

Reflecting on the funeral, Barbara noted, "I definitely got closure from her death and from her funeral because my major question throughout had been, I wished somebody could just tell me, 'When?' I wished somebody could give me the date. The not knowing really bothered me.

"The casket part of the funeral wasn't bad because in the death and dying class, I had been inside one. The professor said it would come in handy if anyone ever did die, which I thought was a crock. But it wasn't. It turned out to be true! The dress we picked clashed with the casket we chose. It was odd, putting the dress in the casket to see if everything was color-coordinated. We chose something else for her to wear. She had lost so much weight in the face, so they tried to rebuild it. It didn't look like her, which bothered me."

During the visitation at the funeral home, Barbara recalled that "the morning was easy. There were all old people I didn't know. But at the night-visiting were all people I knew, friends I hadn't seen. After everyone left, I realized I hadn't been to the casket. We'd had it closed. And all of a sudden it struck me that even though my mother was dead, she'd been with us. There she was, lying right next to us. She was still there. She wasn't really dead because she was still right there. Then it hit me that I was never going to see my mother again. Jack was with me and I just fell apart. And my sister and my dad came up and my family just sat there and cried.

"Lisa and I both read at the funeral. Everybody else thinks this was the most miraculous achievement. 'How could you ever read at your own mother's funeral? You must be so strong.' But when it's you it's different. I chose to read a poem and something I wrote about her. I wrote the things people kept saying to us: 'Your mother was so good,' 'Your mother helped me here.' One person said they didn't know how they would have made it throughout their life without my mom. And I said that through that, I got a new awareness of my mom and that if there really is a God and a grand design, that maybe my mom was so good at what she did, that she did what she was sent here to do too quickly.

"Watching her being taken off in the hearse to be cremated wasn't goodbye. It was at the wake when I guess I said my goodbye."

Barbara noted that "lots of weird things have happened," things that have struck her as mysterious. "The Monday before my mother died, she went to radiation for her last treatment. This man came out and was saying goodbye to everybody, and he came up to my mother. She'd never seen him before, but he grabbed her hand, leaned forward, kissed her cheek and said, 'I'll see you real soon, Sweetie,' and walked out. My mother looked at my father and said, 'Do you know who that man was?' He said, 'He was from our home town; he was a postman before he got sick.' It turned out that he died on Saturday too. 'I'll see you real soon, Sweetie,' and he died on the same day. So maybe they went up together."

And then there was Barbara's bird experience. "Just a little background: When my mother was sick last spring, I used to sit with her and have the windows open. We have lots of trees. I love listening to birds sing and I'd just sit there and listen and watch her, and we'd be quiet together. Later in the summer, after she died, I was feeling very sorry for myself, so I went by my mom's grave, and I stopped, and I looked at it. And then I got frustrated because I didn't know what I was supposed to do there, if I was supposed to talk to her or sit there. I was only there a minute. When I got home, I was lying in bed and I couldn't sleep, and all of a sudden I could smell Eternity perfume. My mom used to wear Eternity. That freaked me out, and then I thought, 'Am I really smelling this perfume or is my mind smelling this perfume?' I got all upset about it. It was about midnight and I was still lying there, trying to think. And all of a sudden, this bird starts singing outside. I've never heard a bird sing at night, ever, in my life. I finally fell asleep and had a terrible dream about my mom in the casket, being all bones and rotted. I woke myself up screaming. As I woke up, I realized that that bird was still singing. It was like two in the morning and I woke up almost every hour and every time, until it was light out, that bird was still singing.

"In the morning, I asked my father, 'Do birds sing at night?' He said, 'Well, you know I never thought so, but about a week ago, this damn bird showed up, and it sits outside in front of my office and sings.' We gave each other the eye—spooky. Later I called my sister and told her the story. A few days later, there was a message from Lisa on the machine, 'Call me *now*.' So I called her, and she said that the night before, she'd had trouble sleeping and there was a bird sitting outside her window singing!

"So now I think my mother is a bird. It's happened here at school. It was on a Sunday and I was really sad. I convinced Jack to stay until Monday morning. But I couldn't sleep and Jack was awake, and this bird started to sing! I almost asked Jack if he could hear the bird, and it stopped singing. So I don't think anybody else can hear the bird. I also feel now that I'm not supposed to ask, because it happened just the other night. And the first thing that came to my mind was, 'God, I really want to know if Jack can hear this bird,' and right then it stopped singing."

Although her father and sister had both heard the bird, Barbara explained, "My dad doesn't know that I think it's Mom. So he hasn't mentioned it. And even though I talked about it with my sister, she hasn't mentioned it again either. I think that this is my special thing, even though my mother might have presented herself to everybody else."

Barbara reflected on how her mother had died the way she lived. "My mother was very conscious of always having to look good. She could be having the worst day of her life and if somebody came over, *bing!* she was always the hostess, 'Can I get you anything?' We liked it when people came over because she'd get very up; when they left, she was very tired from putting up that front. On another level, she was never happy with her life. She always felt that she got the short end of the stick, and nobody appreciated her. And I saw that come through too. She was very, very bitter, very angry, very evil, a nasty lady. But about a week and a half before she died, my mother wasn't angry anymore. It was a subtle calm change; it wasn't all of a sudden. I think she just felt that she was going to die soon, that there was nothing that she could do. It wasn't the kind of peace that I've been told some people get that makes them just a joy to be around—they just love every little thing, and every little thing is beautiful. It wasn't that kind of peace. It was just sort of like she accepted it. But you could tell that she was still scared. Her struggle was so visible at the end. It didn't help that we were there and all very scared too."

Though not much time had passed since her mother died, Barbara felt that it was becoming "much easier. It'll be three months next week," she sighed. "The way I'm staying sane is by talking about it. There are certain scenes in my head, and going back to one will make me cry, because it was just so powerful. The first time I talked about it, I sputtered and cried the whole thing out. But it's a lot easier to talk about now. I've gotten my closure. It's come full circle. She's dead. And I miss her very, very much.

"My sister did it the other way. I mourned as my mother was dying. My sister didn't mourn until after my mother died, so afterward it was very difficult for her. On the night of my mother's funeral, my sister went home and cried herself to sleep. I was out bowling, having beers with my friends. That's what I needed.

"See, my mom didn't worry about me. She worried about my sister. Because I always land on my feet and I do things my way and everything always works out and she knows that and she doesn't worry about me because I take care of myself. . . . My dad was the same way I was. He mourned before. And also, he's got Vicki now and I think they're mourning together."

Barbara and her sister had initially been very uncomfortable with their father's developing an intimate relationship with their mother's best friend, and so soon after their mother died. But gradually Barbara felt that she understood, to some extent, what her father was doing. He had tried to explain it to her. He'd learned, and not easily, a great deal from the loss of his wife. He regretted the mistakes he had made, especially the fact that he had not seized the opportunities for intimacy that had presented themselves over the years. He saw as his wife was dying that he had been too interested in his business and not interested enough in her. And so, when another opportunity for intimacy presented itself in the midst of this loss, he chose to grasp it and make it a higher priority than propriety.

As Barbara talked about how the experience of her mother's death had changed her, she revealed why she has been able to accept her father's perspective. "It's changed me a lot. I think I appreciate more. I cherish Jack in a way I wouldn't have if this hadn't happened. I try to laugh more. I try to laugh things off. I'm totally off the wall when it comes to money. We are in serious debt. Jack gets all stressed out about it, but I'm not going to waste my energy. I'm not irresponsible about it. I keep in touch with people that I can't pay. I call and say, 'I can't pay my bill. What are we going to do about it?' But I don't get stressed out about it.

"Jack and I have a conflict now about time. Once time is gone, time is gone. My mom has only been dead three months and it feels like she's been dead for years. It almost feels like she never existed. That's our biggest conflict, because for me time is so precious.

"He says, 'Let's wait four years for kids.' And I say, 'Don't talk like that, because you don't ever know if you're going to be here in four years. If we're still around in four years, we'll have kids.' He talks about how it's okay if he's thirty-five when we have our first kid because he's healthy. And I can't help but think, 'Yeah, that's what my mother used to say.' Sometimes I'm really mean about it. But my mother was the picture of health until she died six months later.

"Jack is very future-oriented and I'm like, *now*; we're going to do it *now*. We might not have the money, but fine, we'll find it. We'll do it and think about the money later. Next month, we're going on another trip. We're not sure where we're getting that money but we're going. We're going to be with his family and it's going to be a good time. A window of opportunity comes so infrequently, I'm not going to walk through it; I'm going to dive through it. Because there's just not enough time."

Barbara reflected on her thoughts and wishes about an afterlife, which have changed since she lived through her mother's death. "I don't have the sense that she's in heaven. I talk like she is. I still have a hard time because her death was so terrible to me, but a clergyperson said to me, 'Nobody ever said dying was going to be easy. If dying were easy, then God wouldn't have sent His Son to help us, and that's why we believe in God and Jesus: to give us the strength to get through the death.' This helped a lot, because it is such a difficult thing. I really hope that she is up there, hanging out on a cloud, with my friend's mom, looking down and saying, 'What great kids we have,' or 'Gee, I wish they knew we were up here.' I really like to hold on to that. You know, I . . . I . . . I don't know. But I really hope so."

Notes

Making Room for Death

Paulina G. McCullough

A nationally recognized authority on Murray Bowen's family systems theory,[39] *Paulina G. McCullough's experiences during the decline and death of her frail, elderly husband provide an intimate glimpse at what it means to put theory into practice. William McCullough was the dean of social work at a large urban university and a fifty-nine-year-old widower with three grown children when he married his thirty-seven-year-old colleague, Paulina, a native of Chile. They had been married for twenty-four years and raised two children who were twenty-three and twenty-one when he died at eighty-two.*

This is the story of gradual losses that occur with advancing age, and of death's coming in a timely manner to a mature, professional couple. It had been nine months since her husband's death when we spoke with Paulina. As she spoke, she revealed her signature style: a heavily accented Spanish delivery, punctuated with husky laughter, disarming metaphors and surprising insights.

"Bill died in July. He had been in declining health: first congestive heart failure and then what they call a transient ischemic attack [TIA], in which blood to the brain is temporarily blocked. He had already had some loss

269

of memory before that, but it became more accentuated after the TIA. The last time he was in the hospital, in December, they realized that there was another condition related to his heart, and some pulmonary stuff. So from January to July he became increasingly more debilitated and lost a lot of weight. He had some concerns about what was going to happen. His concerns were more about not knowing what was happening to him than about death itself. I think that he was quite ready. I don't think that he was *longing* to die, but I think that he was ready. Derek, our youngest child, had turned twenty-one in June. That would have been one of Bill's biggest concerns. He was thinking that he had completed launching his second family. . . . His concern was not with death itself but more with how he would perhaps not know what was happening to him at the end. But he talked about it, we talked about it."

On the day that Bill died, Paulina called home before leaving work. "I think it was seven. He tried to get up to go downstairs to have dinner with me, and he fell next to the bed and died right there. By the time I came home at 7:25, he was still warm, but he was not breathing anymore. I called the paramedics and they told me what to do, but he was dead. So that's how he died. I did not know that he was dying though! That death was approaching, I knew, but that he was dying, I didn't, because he was dead by the time I got there.

"What happens after you have gone through life and death with a number of people is that, although I'm sure there are stages, I saw it much more as a process that was unfolding. I have thought about Bill's death from the time that he had his TIA. So that's like four years, you know . . . for all that time.

"Bill would, in a way, have liked me to let him die. He kept telling me that he was old and that he was not long for this earth, which to him meant, 'Let me be.' That was not what we had written in our marriage vows, that I would ever let be, because I wouldn't have married somebody that I would have to let him be, so I didn't let him be. And I think that he appreciated that, in a way. In another way, I think he wished he wouldn't have to be engaged, although he appreciated being engaged. So I learned more about the paradoxes of life in the last year of Bill's life, about him and me. That he was much more available than he looked, that people are always there, no matter how their memory fails, but the ones who are alive have to work. Sometimes he got tired of working, and sometimes I got tired—fortunately, not at the same time, which was also true of our marriage. . . . His last six months were no different for us than the rest of our marriage, in that the lines were drawn as to what he was going to do and what I was going to do. But we were able to talk about most of these things. We did talk about just about everything we needed to talk about.

"I *believe* that a relationship has all the elements in it of life and death. You see it all the time. Therefore, the difference is not so great." But this is not how people usually perceive living and dying. It is usually more problematic. "There is so much unfinished business in death always. 'I wish, I wish, I wish; if only I had; if only I hadn't.' The guilt over stuff. If you do the best you can and forgive yourself for being imperfect—which I was, but what the hell? I was never perfect about anything else, so why was I going to be perfect about his death, approaching, encroaching? I wasn't. I didn't have a lot to forgive him for, and I didn't have a lot to forgive myself for, and therefore all that unfinished business was just not there. Not many regrets. The way we lived kind of prepared us for the death."

The need for increasing Bill's care progressed gradually, over time. "For the last year, somebody came to the house two days a week to look after him and to do a few chores. For the last five months, there was somebody who came three days a week. I would try to go home for lunch, and if I couldn't, I would make sure that somebody would be there for that time. Our daughter had moved back in the year before. She was in school all day, but she was quite a bit of help in the evenings."

Paulina reflected on her initial expectations of her children. "You know, these are gringo children. They were born in this country and raised in this country, so I assumed that they were going to be gringo children in relation to their father: 'If I'm that young, I am not expected to do a whole lot with a parent in the home.' But Derek spent a whole term at home after his second year of college. You would never think of

Derek as the type to take care of his father, but he did it better than anybody. And Andrea came home with the expressed idea of being here, because she knew that he was getting more frail. She did not know how long he was going to be around, but it was not going to be for the longest time. So she spent the last year with him."

But it was not always easy when both children were living at home, Paulina recalled. "I was ready to move out at that point. And it wasn't because of Bill. It was because of the two young kids, I mean, having those many birds in one nest, with those big flappy wings. *Not* easy. Interesting to me because I would have thought, being the Latin mother that I always pictured myself to be, that I would just be delighted to have them all there. But actually, the only one who wanted to be out of the nest was me. . . . When you always think of yourself as being the *center* of the family, and all of a sudden, no—they are all there, you don't have to do anything. You then say, 'It would not be bad to be out!'"

In fact, leaving the nest did become necessary for Paulina. "I knew that Bill could die when I was not around. I went to Chile in January when my mother died, and he told me in no uncertain terms that he didn't think it was a good idea for me to go for any longer than a week. I said, 'You better be alive when I get back here, man, because I can't take two at the same time. So you just make bloody sure that you are here when I get back. I am going to be in Chile for three weeks.' Now he could have died, and I always knew that.

"Those were the conscious choices. They *were* conscious choices. People don't make them. They say, 'He may die so I can't move.' And that's what part of all that fatigue is. I was anxious always; I was not fatigued. I came to work every day." This was not always easy for Paulina. Colleagues would notice how she "walked into this office sometimes without my coat on, without my stockings on, without make-up on, without having combed my hair, dash in, spruce myself up and straighten up my shoulders and go into my interview.

"I'm making the distinctions between death and grief, and I'm also making the distinctions between caring and caretaking. And the other distinction that I want to make is that most people put the anxiety on the caretaking. Okay? But because Bill and I were able to manage the anxiety between us, there was less anxiety" concerning the stresses and demands of caregiving. "But I do know that I was on call. How do I know it? Because when he died, I was not on call anymore. I knew that. The thing that I knew clearly was that I was no longer on alert. I was always very conscious of Bill, no matter where I was. Very. Now, I didn't let it stop me, because I don't let things stop me. In other words, I know that anxiety is just part of life and that I have to live with the anxiety and with its consequences. If I am not willing to live with the consequences, then I don't do it."

Paulina also discussed the impulse to infantilize, which is "absolutely connected" to the anxiety. "If I can deal with my anxiety, then he is going to have a better day. And that's really hard because as soon as somebody gets sick, then we can put all our concerns over there, and we do. Complaining all the way, naturally, 'Oh, look what I have to do to-day and look what I have to do tomorrow and look what I had to do last night.' It just focuses on that person, and that person doesn't need that. They are sick. They don't need all this other stuff on top of them.

"With the amount of memory impairment Bill experienced, he changed quite a bit, but not dramatically. Over the period of a week, he would be more there, the way one used to know him, than not 'there.' And he was a ripe old age. His death was timely. Not timely in the sense that you wanted it, but in the sense that you could see the gradual turn-ing down of that life. People have said that so many times about candles and made that image, and I think it was true, definitely true in this case.

"If it is a natural kind of happening, then one takes it as such. The unnaturalness of a death has much to do with how difficult it gets to be for us. In many cases, it is just very untimely and tough and difficult. But we have some responsibility in that too. The living people do not want to let go of the people who are ready to die! And they keep them for themselves, and make it more difficult for the one who's ready to go. It takes a big toll on the person who's dying.

"We had discussed with Bill what he wanted, and he said, 'If I'm wanting to take off, by all means let it happen.' We had discussed all that, which helps, I think." This openness was possible in spite of his memory problems. "By objective criteria, he had lost much more than it looked like. He had volunteered for a project on memory and aging, and the impairment was considerable. But I believe that we are more than memory and we are more than old. We are people, and if we are treated like people, we respond like people. He responded like a person until the end because we treated him that way. We did not let him off the hook, which is really important when it comes to dying. If you infantilize the person, if you consider him to be incapable before he actually is incapable, then you do mischief to him. And we never talk about that, how the living people prey upon the ill person and the dying person. We have to keep our little grubby, helpful hands off them and we don't. Thus we make it very difficult for them. We do not help them to do their leave-taking in an honorable way. We just interfere a great deal. It takes a lot of restraint not to do that."

For Paulina, talking about this period now is different from how it was before Bill died. "Nine months later, I am much more open. It's like a kaleidoscope. All the elements are there all the time, but they change in terms of the new awareness. There's always a new awareness, and you go deeper and deeper and deeper into the nature of the connection, which is very, very rich. I wasn't trying to defend against anything, but letting the whole of Bill come back in was a little difficult at first. In the kitchen I have two pictures of Bill when he was not looking so hot. I knew that those were the tough ones to look at. The tough parts are hard.

"I know all the time how much I'm letting in and saying, 'Well, you let in what you can let in.' 'Making room for the dead' is another phrase. All three of us—Derek, Andrea and I—wanted to spend Christmas by ourselves, so that Bill could be there rather than crowding him out. So we had a Christmas where we could talk about him the way we do. We are a little crazy the way we talk. We talked crazy about him while he was alive, we are still talking crazy about him. Derek particularly has this wicked sense of humor when he recalls how Bill used to do strange things. We were just roaring at dinner. We also made room, to just be, to have him around in our thoughts, alone and apart, together and apart. Slowing down and making room has been very important.

"Our anxiety about death is just monumental. I thought that for Bill, the hardest part of the last part of his life was his isolation. We let older people just die in isolation to a great extent. And by association, the person who loses the one who dies also has to experience that. . . . If I didn't have as much awareness as I do, I would have been in bad shape, because people have not been around for me. They just haven't. And I suppose I play a big part in that, in that I look like I don't need too much. So people don't call and say, 'How are you doing?' All this work that I've done has put me in a different place, I assume, because I don't know how else to read it. I'm traveling in a strange land. I got cards galore. I got a box full of cards, which means, 'I'm thinking of you.' But then where does that thinking go? It's not coming to me. It's not a connection that I experience in any kind of way."

We asked how this experience has changed her life, and Paulina replied, "I don't have a husband . . . Other than that, Mrs. Lincoln, how did you enjoy the play?" After prolonged laughter, she said, "I'm always turning everything upside down, because that's my way of thinking about stuff. That quote to me is the best way to say it, because what *can* you say? It has changed my life in profound ways, but has it changed it? No. It's always yes and no to the same extent.

"The person I was in most danger to get done in by, whose death was much more close, was my mother. Other relationships just don't touch that one. It is just so primary, it is just so gutsy. When I left Chile in 1960, I knew that I was going to live apart from that, and that therefore that's where most of my regrets would be if I had any. And I did not have regrets when she died. I miss her terribly, but I always did. She was one hell of a lady and I wish I could talk to her, but regrets about her I don't have. Regret always has this sting. We didn't have as much time as I would have liked to have, but it's true about everything else, right? I was not that good, but I was as good as I could be, which is different.

"I have been in touch with how my thoughts of both Bill and my mother get evoked by things. I came back from Chile in January. My cactus is blooming, and the cactus is not supposed to bloom this time of year. And I say, 'Oh Mother, I think of you when I see that flower,' because she loved flowers so much. When she was alive, I would call and she would say, 'I was just hoping that you would call because of this or that' or, when I just had been thinking about her, she would call within hours or minutes.

"I don't know what happens when we die. I wish I had the quote about the two sisters who went to see their mother's grave and took some flowers there. And one sister said to the other, 'What do you think happened to my mother when she died?' And the other one says, 'What tells you that my mother is not here in the flowers and in the wind?'

"It's a powerful thing, not knowing. How do you understand it? I hope that it remains a mystery, for all times to come. But we know some things about it. Death is not all that is. There's more than death, but what is it and how does it express itself? I'll be continued in my children, which is the natural thing that we all talk about. I am content to some extent with the mystery, with not knowing. We have been gifted, as humans, to be the only species that knows what's going to happen to it, to them, to me, to you. We know it, we live with that knowledge. That, I think, is a gift. I don't worry my head too much with it. But it is an impressive knowledge, and an impressive mystery."

Notes

We Think About the Details so That Families Don't Have to

Funeral Director Rhonda Wiles-Rosell

Rhonda Wiles-Rosell is a tall, striking young woman who would appear to many to be a very unlikely mortician. However, she has become a full partner in the New England family business in which she grew up, and in which the word "home" has always had a double meaning.

"I would describe my job, first and foremost, as a caregiving job. Some people would interpret that as a natural thing for women to do. I never take that as a putdown or as ridicule; I take that as a God-given blessing. That certainly is not to say that men can't do the same thing, but some people have more of the qualities of a caregiver than do others. People in this line of work have to have whatever those qualities are that make them a caregiver, not only to the family but also to the individual who has died.

"We are treating the deceased human body with respect, regardless of what disposition the family has chosen. We're treating the family with the same level of care, wanting them to approach this the best way that they need to, as individuals and as a whole grieving family. You've got two different things going on here, as I see it: You have an individual's personal response to the death that has occurred and you also have that individual as they fit into the whole family unit and what that whole family unit is doing in the grieving process."

Rhonda tried to explain the terminology of her profession. "I personally don't like the word 'mortician.' It sounds cold and outdated. Years ago we were called undertakers because we undertook the job that no one else wanted to do, or that the family backed away from, or no longer could do. We are technically funeral directors and embalmers. Now, in some states, these are two separate roles in terms of how they are licensed. You can be licensed in some states as just one or the other. In Maine you have to be licensed as both in order to run the establishment. And I can't imagine being only one or the other, because I see both roles as important to being the funeral service practitioner. That's another term that's used. Or a funeral service counselor. A lot of people now are using the term funeral service facilitator so that we're not caught up in the legal requirements of what constitutes a counselor.

"I can't imagine doing exclusively one role without the other. In a large city firm you may find people who are what they call trade embalmers. They may have half a dozen funeral homes that they are on call for. And they are their own free agents. They go to whichever funeral home needs them. Myself, I would not want to be doing only that. That, to me, is for someone who likes the technical aspect but does not like the human interaction with the family. I personally have to see it all functioning together. I have to see that the work that we do from a technical perspective has a positive outcome for the grieving family members. For instance, I have to know that being a good embalmer and making somebody look 'more presentable,' more natural, has a direct benefit to the grieving family members. When you do see that difference, it makes it all worthwhile."

Rhonda explained that gender never seemed to be an issue in her choice of profession. "I can remember my teachers in grade school asking me, 'You're the daughter of a funeral director. Do you think you'll be a funeral director when you grow up?' They might have never thought that it was possible and only asked that of my younger brother. But that wasn't the case. It may be simply that their reference point was the fact that funeral homes in New England were family owned and operated businesses and stayed family owned and operated."

However, Rhonda was not eager to take up the family business. "Throughout high school, I wanted absolutely nothing to do with it. It was the most barbaric thing to think that I had the privilege of getting a new prom dress because someone's grandmother had died. I thought, 'This is horrible.' Then one day my parents sat me down and said, 'You know, we can't help the fact that deaths occur. We have no control over that. But what we have control over is making other families' lives better by going through the grieving process and experiencing things in a real way and getting on with better living.' And I started to put the pieces of that together.

"When I was a senior in high school, a dear friend of mine was struck and killed by a drunk driver. His friends, myself included, were supposed to be doing the music for his upcoming wedding, and we ended up singing at his funeral. I never realized at the time the impact that that had on me. I went away to college thinking, 'I absolutely want nothing to do with this business.' I began doing an internship in public relations at Children's Hospital in Boston, and loved it. It was doing human interest stories and I was relating to people's family lives and all those tear-jerking stories that have good endings. I even toyed with the idea of going into social work, because I found that all the people that I would gravitate to were in nursing or social services, and I would love to hear about their work.

"Then I got mononucleosis and had to take a medical leave of absence. I found myself living at home, getting my energy back and doing simple, mundane routines, like answering the phone. Or the florist would come and I would make sure that the door was unlocked. I started thinking to myself, 'This is crazy. This is truly what I like to do.' Maybe it's just being brought up in it and not really knowing anything different, but in my process of running away, I was really just running right back toward it."

Helping people to have a good ending seemed to be Rhonda's destiny, whether writing public relations stories or becoming a funeral director. In both instances, she saw herself "making a positive experience out of something that is chaotic. When a death occurs, everything is happening *to* you and you have very little control over what is going on. You go through the motions as best you can. I had somebody just this morning who said to us, 'Gee, people in the funeral business really are coordinators.' And we are. We think about the details that are important to having everything orchestrated correctly, so that families don't have to think about them. This ultimately gives control back to the family because they're able to take care of their own basic needs in those frantic days, from nutrition to being able to get a little more rest—just taking care of their needs and getting their feet back on the ground."

Although Rhonda knew the ropes of being a funeral director, she still had to go back to school at age twenty-five. Yet she does not regret getting her college degree. For her, it has been "imperative. I cannot imagine, in this day and age, going into this kind of work without having a liberal arts background, whether it is two years or four years. And, that whole experience of taking care of yourself without depending on mom and dad, and of knowing that you are an individual. We have a lot of students who come to the funeral home. We do the tour every semester. Once in a while someone will say, 'Gee, I would really like to do this.' And we always say, 'Get the rest of your education. If you decide to go into this line of work, you need to be well versed enough and educated enough to deal with a variety of people. The better educated you are, the better you are at communicating with anyone from any walk of life.'"

Rhonda's technical training resulted in "an associate's degree in funeral service management, which ordinarily would be a two-year program, but I had already had four years of undergraduate work, so a lot of my courses covered each other." She studied as close to home as she could get, in Newton Center, Massachusetts. She had already had the experience of living away from home. "What I needed was my technical training and to be prepared to take the national board examinations, which started at eight in the morning and ended at four in the afternoon. They are very intensive exams, the same kind of thing as when a nurse or doctor goes for their national board certification."

Rhonda reflected on the nature of her business in rural New England, both as a child growing up and now as a professional. "My mother has pointed out to me that some of the caregiving role came not only from the funeral director but from the spouses of funeral directors, the ones at home baking cookies and who, for example, happened to be at the funeral home to receive the clothing that a family was bringing for the deceased. They have to be articulate and able to show support."

As in any family business, everybody has a role. "In a lot of rural areas you see families living in the funeral homes. Your place of business and your home environment are one and the same, separated by a folding door or a hallway. In large city firms maybe there is an apartment that an apprentice lives in—because an apprenticeship is also part of your educational process—but usually the owner of the funeral home is not living with family and children under that roof. They're out in the suburbs."

Rhonda likes it the old-fashioned way. "A death experience is a family experience, and how much nicer for a family to be served by a family. That's just a rural Mainiac's perspective. But I would be willing to bet that if you went to a metropolitan area to open a family-owned business and brought family-centered care to it, your doors would stay open. I am a firm believer that if there were a more family-centered attitude in the world, there would be less destructiveness."

Although Rhonda had been a professional for more than eight years when we spoke with her, she felt as if she'd been at it much longer. In fact, she laughed, "I've been serving in the funeral service much longer than I know. In high school there were times when we might be running short-handed, or I might have known a family particularly well and jumped in and said, 'I'll take visiting hours.' Or if I could see that my father needed to be doing something more technical and I could relieve him at the desk or something like that—that's been ongoing. We're technically called FDKs, funeral directors' kids. We are an interesting lot!

"You get a whole group of FDKs together, number one, they tend to be very fun-loving. They tend to be very . . . I don't mean to say 'eager to party,' but they tend to really know how to have a good time. Maybe that comes from having seen so much tragedy. They seem to take advantage of whatever moments come by, to have a good time or to do something different. In this profession our time is not structured at all. We're on call twenty-four hours a day, seven days a week. We don't get extra for weekends and we don't get paid extra for holidays. I say that sort of sarcastically because I hear people quibbling over, 'Gee, I had to work on Mother's Day.' Well, you know, death doesn't take a holiday. Those of us who have grown up in this business know how disappointing it can be when it's time to go to your first prom and your father can't be there to see you out the door. Or how disappointing it can be when you have a Thanksgiving meal planned and the whole family is there for a celebration, but then family members are called away to go to somebody else's home because Great-grandmother has died."

But there are compensations. "We have a very strong family tie. We probably better utilize our time together, we don't waste as much time as we might. And we end up with wonderful friends outside of family that we might never have had the opportunity to meet. We are privileged because we are able to adopt new friends very quickly. I remember once we had a call on Christmas Eve. It was a very, very sad situation. Of course, it's holiday time, everybody wants to be joyous and that's just not real, that's not life.

"So, automatically our holiday plans completely stopped. We ended up having visiting hours at the home on Christmas night. Some people were saying to us, 'Isn't that terribly difficult for you?' Well, in some ways it was, but if you yourself were in that position, you would want to be with your memories of your loved one no matter what day it was. So we allowed the family to have visiting hours, and there were lovely poinsettias all over the place—a very different, quiet, serene sort of setting. And it's something now when we see that family: We automatically think of the holidays. Automatically they do the same thing, and now we always exchange Christmas cards with them. You become like an adopted family member, if you will.

"Sometimes you have to be careful of that also. You have to know when it's really the right time to pull back a bit, for their sake as well as your own. Somehow you just know when that time comes. But even when you're not so closely tied to that particular family, there's always that unspoken friendship that goes on. I am thankful that I am in this kind of work. You see people at the worst possible moment in their lives.

The worst. It doesn't get any worse than that. It just doesn't. So when you are watching them get better, that is such an added benefit." There are occasional exceptions, however, when after "watching them in a limbo state for a while, there are times that we have to then suggest that they seek additional counseling."

Rhonda's clients vary in their approach to making arrangements and in their need for them. There is "the immediate at-need group. They have made no prearrangements for a variety of reasons." In the event of a long illness, a family may "splinter off into the people who take control and begin to push forward and make the prearrangements, and the group that hangs back and cannot deal with anything except what is happening at the present. There seems to be a real split like that. In the group that makes the prearrangements, sometimes they have a bit of a guilt reaction. They feel very peculiar about being in the office here, talking about what are we going to do when Grandfather dies, with Grandfather still living, in a hospice center or at home watching *Jeopardy!* On the other hand, when something does happen to Grandfather, they're not under pressure to make decisions that they might not have made if they had had to do it right away. A burden has been lifted from their shoulders a bit."

A sudden death requires special care for clients. "We try to almost be their inner mind so that they aren't here making decisions that are not going to be appropriate for them. You always hear the stories about funeral directors taking advantage of the bereaved and making them feel like they should, for instance, purchase something above and beyond what they can afford." But for Rhonda, the truth is, "you want to be fair with everybody. We also are regulated by the Federal Trade Commission, so you have to present the cost of everything. And that's fine." But it is no guarantee that the customer is able to "think clearly. So if somebody is feeling, 'This is the last thing I can do for them and therefore I need to get the most expensive casket,' I will talk them out of that. It is an ethical responsibility of anyone who's working with people under stress to bring them to a closer level of reality." Rhonda makes those calls by "instinct. That's really what it is. It would not be realistic if I said that it never happens, that anyone in this profession takes advantage. You do pick up the paper and read that someone feels they were taken advantage of. I think that you have to have a strong moral base."

Making prearrangements can be gratifying or problematic, and with this comes larger issues. For example, when "the next of kin comes in and makes the prearrangements, if they're doing what the dying individual really wants done, there is a great sense of satisfaction when the death occurs that you have done what that individual requested. And I think that is a huge leap in the grieving process." On the other hand, "occasionally we will see a person who will say, 'I'm going to make my own prearrangements,' without thinking about what's going to be good for those who survive. Occasionally we will get somebody who will say, 'My family has been nasty, so it's my turn to be nasty.' That is rare but I have seen it. Sometimes people just think, 'The best thing for the family is to keep it as simple as possible,' when in fact that isn't what's best. The family needs some of the processes: They need, perhaps, the private family visitation time or a public visitation time. They need the sense of community."

It can be hard on survivors when they lack a sense of community, and Rhonda sees this more and more. It may be that the people don't belong to a church or just "because some of society seems to be falling apart" but "when a death occurs, I think all of a sudden the fear of the lack of community gets real scary. Probably as scary as having lost a person by death. And sometimes we'll hear them say, 'No funeral service, no visitation, no nothing, just take care of the body as soon as possible.' Whether it's immediate earth burial, whether it's cremation, no ceremony. No religious rite. No anything.

"We try to counsel with the family and literally ask them why they are making some of the decisions they are. To have them become a little introspective and sort of soul search a bit is a difficult thing to do when they're under stress. Because you are not here to say, 'This is what I think you should do and you better do it because I know everything!'" Rhonda laughed. "But I think that if you give them careful information and have them toy with the idea, that's better than just accepting their first reaction.

You know, I think an awful lot of people are afraid that no one will send flowers, or that no one will make memorial contributions, or that they're just not prepared to have anyone come to visitations to support them as grievers. I think there is fear: 'Where do I fit in my community and do I have any community? Am I an individual who is a member of any clubs or organizations? Who is going to have any part in the religious ceremony or a burial custom?' The sense of a lack of belonging to anything is a tremendous additional burden."

Rhonda's thoughts turned to a recent funeral for a ninety-seven-year-old and the perspective offered in the eulogy. "The clergyperson said, 'You know, we shouldn't really be here mourning this thing that we call death. Let us instead celebrate a life that has been lived.' Sometimes we have to look to religious leaders, or just our whole selves, and find out, what are our feelings? Do we just forget this person now? Do we run away from our feelings and hide them? Do we keep that Puritan, stoic New England attitude, or do we open up and really celebrate a life? The Irish are not wrong! Or any ethnic group where they have elaborate parties and celebrations. Part of that is very much on target and is very appropriate for the grieving process, for anyone. A person was born and has had a life—that's worthy of a celebration and to be held in memory and with reverence and respect."

When clients come to Rhonda, they often have particular concerns about the appearance of the deceased, whether he or she "will look natural, will look okay. And this is part of our work. You are really an artist in many forms, and you're caught in this interesting, perplexing problem of making someone look 'natural.' Some people translate that to mean looking alive. But you cannot change completely the face of death, nor should you.

"We get lots of young kids who come to the funeral home and a lot of times we'll stand around the casket in a circle and hold hands and I'll talk to them. They might say, 'Gee, Grandma looks plastic.' Or, 'She looks like she's asleep.' Or, 'Grandpa looks like he's taking a long nap except his mouth is closed!' They associate death with sleep, because the eyes are closed. What we try to do is to show them the differences between life and death. We talk about how when people are alive they can touch and be touched." Squeezing each other's hands as they stand in the circle, Rhonda has them notice the feeling of warmth and explains that the heart pumps the blood which creates our circulation. "We do very tangible kinds of things. Never forcing children, or anyone for that matter, to touch the deceased human, but nine times out of ten, kids are just going to go, 'Whomp!'" Rhonda laughed as she slapped the table, "and go right ahead for Grandpa's hand anyway. When that happens, that's when they say, 'Oooh, he's cold.' And they begin to see the difference between life and death."

It can be a fine line, Rhonda said, and members of her profession may "overworry" about how natural the deceased should look. "What we have to do is make them look as natural as possible without overmystifying this thing that we call death." Yet, the importance of viewing the deceased should not be minimized. "If we have somebody who was killed in a very tragic accident, it is imperative for families to see that person. It is just amazing, the difference. When we had the Vietnam conflict, if you had told a family that they could see their son they would have done anything in the world to have been able to see him. Compare that with somebody who has the option, say, a ninety-five-year-old grandfather who has died in a nursing home. There is no reason at all why he would not be presentable to be viewed, but you'll find the family throwing away that option. They'll say, 'We've seen him at the nursing home. That's all we need to see him.' I'm always struck by how some people will take their option and discard it and other people have no choice in the matter."

For Rhonda, "it's very difficult to have the family who has the choice see how important it might be, even if it's just for one family member," to view the deceased. "I think the importance of it is that number one, it gives us perspective. The old saying that seeing is believing is really, really true. We have had instances where somebody has said, 'No, we don't wish to view the body at all,' and the casket will be closed. At the very last minute at the grave site, someone in the family says, 'Oh, I've got to see him.'" This happens even when family members have been present at the deathbed.

In addition, if death "has happened at a hospital, there's been all kinds of equipment and machinery and tubing." It's important, Rhonda said, that people get to view the deceased some time after the death, "even if it's only a twenty-four-hour time period. Your perspective is different than at the very moment that you know that death has occurred. That small time frame is a very . . . there's no word to describe it unless anyone has felt that time frame. I really do think that it is important that people give themselves a little time, a little breathing space, and, even if they do nothing else, have private family visitation.

"A lot of the time people think that if they opt for visitation, that means it's going to be public visitation and they have no privacy." Families need to know that there is an array of options for them, and that it is "important that they at least take that private family time. Whether it is five minutes, whether it is an hour or two hours, it gives people a time to really begin to physically recollect."

Yet letting clients know what they can arrange for is not always easy. "There are standards and yet there are no standards, all at the same time. We try to ask every family what is going to be appropriate for them. For instance, we find out, 'Do you want to come into the chapel last or do you want to be already seated before the service starts so that you're not on public display?' People may be very shy about the idea of public awareness and being afraid to cry in public. That's another reason why I love having kids at the funeral home, because they are not afraid to do or say whatever it is that they happen to feel for that person who has died. And to express their love for grieving family members that are around them. If you can capture that sincerity in little ones, they unlock the doors for the adults. They're the permission givers. They are the most in touch and yet we try to protect them the most, which is really kind of crazy. I think what people are trying to do is to protect the child within themselves.

"We have wonderful stories and really interesting things that have happened. We had a little boy once who came in—and the family knows that I tell this story anonymously, I don't use names—and his father was killed in a very tragic accident. He was about five years old and he came to the funeral home. There was much discussion as to whether or not it would be appropriate for him to be here. I kept saying, 'Of course it's appropriate. This is his dad!' So he came to the funeral home; he had Oreo cookies and a couple of crumpled-up dollar bills and a handful of rocks. I asked him, 'What are we going to do with all of these things?'

"Well, first of all, we got a chair for him to stand on, because otherwise he was looking into the side of the casket; his perspective was so different than the adults'. He stood up and—he just referred to me as, 'Hey, lady'—he said, 'Would you give these to my father?' These were the dollar bills. I said, 'Yes. What shall we do with them?'

"'Let's fold them up,' he said. Then we decided that we would put them in his dad's shirt pocket. Well, I put them all the way down. When I did that, all of a sudden the boy's face went from almost gleeful-looking to very sad. He couldn't see the dollar bills anymore. I pulled them back up so that he could see them, and then he was fine. Because with this child, once the bills were out of sight they weren't real anymore. They had vanished.

"Then I said, 'Can I ask you what those are for?' Oh yes, yes I could ask. Then there was this long pause, so then I literally had to ask him. He said, 'Well, Grandma tells me that God has life in heaven for all of us. So, Dad was always buying candy at the grocery store, and he's going to need some money for God's grocery store in heaven.'

"The boy's next step was a real separation step. He took the rocks and he gave them to me. He said, 'Lady, can you please put these in with Dad's body?' His reference was turning a little bit. I suggested that we put them under the pillow. He thought that was a good idea. I asked him if he'd like to put his hand with mine and put them under the pillow so that he would know that the rocks were there." Knowing that they were there even though he couldn't see them was important. "And when he did that, that was just wonderful.

"I said to him, 'What are those rocks for?' He said, 'Well, it's like this, lady. These stones are from the driveway into the barnyard. Dad's not going back to the farm with us, so I want to make sure that part of the farm goes with Dad so he'll never forget us.' Then he took his bag of Oreo cookies and he marched right out into the fireplace room of the funeral home. He sat out there and ate his cookies and then he announced that he was ready to go home. All the adults, in the meantime, were watching this process. The boy was saying a lot of what was going on in their own minds that they just couldn't, couldn't articulate. And he was kind of doing it for them.

"I now have had the privilege of seeing this boy as a teenager, and I have asked him what he remembers about that whole experience. He remembers having done everything. He doesn't remember specific people, but he remembers that lady. It tickled me that he remembers 'a lady' being there helping him. He told me, 'I remember saying goodbye to him.' I will always believe that something good happened in that process for him. I would have hated to have seen it if they had never let him come in. It's obvious that he has always carried the fact that he said goodbye to his father and found his own way in there."

Rhonda then described dealing with younger adults, who occasionally come to the funeral home to make prearrangements. The youngest adults she has seen are those who have been very ill. "Either coming in themselves or with another family member who they have sort of appointed as a spokesperson for them. It might even be someone who has power of attorney for them or who is a guardian for them of some sort. We've had as young as twenty-five.

"Between the ages of thirty and forty-five are couples who have chosen to come in and make prearrangements. Heaven forbid that something would happen to both of them in a common accident, they don't want the burden of responsibility to fall upon the next of kin and having all kinds of turmoil for their minor children. That probably is the number one reason why we see that age group coming in. And, because of AIDS as well, even in rural communities. I have a friend in Boston who works for a large funeral home; she does prearrangements exclusively. That's all she does, four days a week. She is seeing a real increase in the cases in which she goes directly to hospice centers or nursing homes and even to private homes to make prearrangements. We do the same thing here, but she sees more there, in the metropolitan setting, and sees more young people with AIDS. They know exactly where they are medically and are finding out where they are spiritually."

People seem to approach death with a combination of fear and practicality, Rhonda said, and she hopes "that we're becoming more spiritually based, although I sometimes think that's just in my little Utopic mind. I think it's imperative that that happen in our culture. An awful lot rests in the hands of clergy, and I think that there is room for a lot of growth there; I see part of my work as being an extension, if you will. I've had somebody tell me, 'You people are a lot like ministers or priests.' Well, priestesses maybe," Rhonda laughed. "I guess if you feel that you are called to whatever you are doing, to that extent we are all ministers. But it is amazing to me, when I talk to ordained clergy on a professional level, how little training they have had in death and dying. And I mean *little!* At one of the seminaries I know of, the death and dying class is optional. Can you imagine that? Almost everything that we deal with in life has something centered around death or loss. Loss probably is the best word. It might be divorce, it might be separation, it might be illness.

"Also, organized churches offer only one perspective. They are like filters that some groups of us have found useful, and then there's everyone else." There are many different varieties of "the human response to death," Rhonda believes.

Rhonda then reflected on what she has learned about death from doing this work. Very slowly, she stated, "It is not the end. If I ever thought that it was the end, I could not ever do this work. Another thing that I've learned is valuing the things in life that really are important. Overlooking the trivial things that you get so irritated with and learning that there are other things that are much more important to focus on. And a sense of family. I always come back to that, watching other families going through the grieving process."

What is disturbing to Rhonda is the "lack of family structure in today's society. Families lately have seemed so dispensable. In the funeral home here, we've noticed so many kids coming from broken homes. So many other losses in their lives that when you see them coming because of the death of an individual in the family, you can't deny them access here. Because they have already been experiencing loss. I say this to families."

Rhonda's personal philosophy "goes back to my experience when my high school classmate died. His grandmother had sat us all down and told us, 'You have a match, and that is the individual. You strike the match and that's their life, the flame that was burning. When the match is blown out, you have smoke.' Her point was that everything is a growth process and a change. Some things we know more about than other things, but there is a constant transformation all the time. And I really do look at death as being that way. I don't regularly attend a specific church and yet I feel like I attend church all the time. I am able to pick and choose what feels right for me as I watch other people's religions. There are things about different faiths that I like very much that ultimately for me all fit together. I look at death as not being an end, but it is the beginning to another journey that we know nothing of and yet it has to be something.

"My father always says, 'Would we go through all of this if there was absolutely nothing?' Would we be striving to be better people? Would we be working? Would we be doing *anything* in life at all if there was not something additional? I really do believe that there is something more. And sometimes, just working in this profession, you get a sense. I don't know what it is."

When she is working, what Rhonda thinks about life and death matters. "I firmly believe—and have grown up with our set of family values—that when death occurs, immediately, the soul leaves the body. Immediately. If anyone didn't feel that way, I don't know how they could do the technical aspect of our work. And you put your technical hat on, if you will. Just like a surgeon has to when operating on someone they know in the community, the perspective must be that you are the clinician. You are the technical person and you have the ability to do your technical work. You go in with that in mind, and you don't think about the circumstances of the death or the family that you'll be meeting with. When they come in for the first few moments, that's when you put those pieces together and see the value of your technical work. Maybe they have a few moments when they break down. That's normal! People shouldn't be afraid of that. Why should we be so afraid of tears when we are so eager to make everybody laugh, you know?

"The other thing I always think of when they come for funeral services is an example I use from a psychology class on death and dying at the local university, where I've lectured." This involves a pendulum swinging over a circle. One half of the circle contains "all of the worst feelings and horrible situations that you can think of. On the other side of it are the happiest, most euphoric things we can experience. That pendulum swings back and forth throughout life, and if you try to stop it from getting into all of that bad stuff, it doesn't ever go back to its fullest extent on the other side. Its swing begins to dwindle and will only go so far.

"I try to use that example in talking with families. If they're willing to do their grief work, and willing to be vulnerable and to open up, then they're going to have times in their lives when they are going to be able to feel the most euphoric they've ever felt. But if they try to block it, if they try to run away from it, they're gypping themselves out of ever having the greatest highs again."

Rhonda encourages her clients to be open with their questions as well as their feelings. "*Everyone* in this profession should have the attitude that the only foolish question is the unasked one. If people want to know how we dress the body, if they want to know what kind of cosmetics we use, or want us to use a person's lipstick or eye shadow or nail polish—whatever it is that they want to know, or whatever their request is—we should be able to comply with that."

But such openness is not easy to convey when the subject is death. It is not as if Rhonda can take an ad out in the papers to say, "Death isn't as bad as you thought." Instead, she watches for "teachable moments" within each family or when speaking to an organization. "We've had Cub Scouts come on tours here before. We've had Girl Scouts, Brownie troops." There are also college class tours, often psychology students. They are not shown bodies "out of respect for the deceased and for that family. We have visiting hours going on and there is no way that we would ever mingle the two. That would just not be appropriate." But they see a lot on the tour. "We show them all the legal paperwork that we have to go through. We walk them through it as though they might be making arrangements for someone. And what to expect and how to understand some of the legal requirements. We hit them with a lot of information in a couple of hours."

One college tour member approached Rhonda months later and

thanked her for the experience. Not long after her tour, her grandfather had died and her grandmother needed help with the arrangements. So the student "made her grandfather's arrangements. She knew a little bit of what to expect. She was educated. She was informed. And she came to thank us because had she not attended that program, she would have had no other frame of reference whatsoever. She was able to do what she felt was her family role at that time, where she was kind of their caregiver. She was able to say, 'Hey you people, we've got to pick up the pieces. We've got some decisions to make. We've got to get an obituary pulled together." Her coursework helped her to do that.

In this teachable moment, Rhonda offered helpful advice to readers of this interview. "Number one, I would invite people to list, on paper or in their own minds, all of their greatest fears or anxieties related to death. Try to articulate whatever it is that is going on in their heads as best as possible. And to call and, either alone or in a group, set up a time to come on a tour and to really come face to face with all of the myths that they may have carried with them for years about what happens when a death occurs. Years ago, to some extent funeral homes were their own worst enemies. The homes were draped in dark velvet with ugly dark carpets, the shades were pulled and crepes were put on the door. People talked in hushed whispers and there was dreadful, dreary music. If you weren't scared already, you were going to be after you had that experience. It was that much more fearful and ominous. I would welcome them to take a tour of a funeral home. Look and see what really takes place. Ask the questions."

The old perception was that the dead person was taken away to a funeral home and the living were kept at a distance. Yet today's funeral homes offer quite a few services to the living, including counseling, not that this is new.

"I look at my dad. He's always saying, 'I don't have the education you and your brother have.' Well, he may not have the degree plastered on the wall, but he has a wealth of knowledge and experience that is more than my brother and I may ever get. He's been my greatest teacher. There are times, watching him, when I can recognize that he's counseling a family and they don't even know it. They might say, 'Okay, Jerry, we want this, this, this and this.' And he'll very quietly go right back to step one and work through every single possible related issue. Even when he knows their answers, he'll do that so that everyone has a sense of commitment to the decisions that have been made. And that it doesn't end up being one spokesperson with six other people just nodding their heads in agreement. He makes sure that they each verbally respond, that sort of thing. And they don't even know that that's what is going on. Good funeral service practitioners do that, and in such a way that people don't feel as though they are being invaded. We're just making sure that that dialogue is going on and that care and attention is being spent on details. The little things can make the difference in whether something goes smoothly or not."

Ideas about the soul and the afterlife are natural issues for anyone in Rhonda's business. Sometimes clients report visions or visitation of their departed loved ones, for example. "We've had people say, 'You're going to think I'm crazy if I tell you this.' But no, I don't think they're crazy at all. In fact, I know of one funeral director who experienced a sensation that there was just a very real presence of this . . . spirit, if you will, that had just not left the home. It was above and beyond what you might think of as being normal when you heard the whole set of circumstances. This man is a very sane and normal, straightforward kind of person. When telling about this experience, he kind of chuckled and said, 'I finally asked that presence to leave.'

"I've had people who have said that they've heard their husband's voice when they've walked back into the house, or that they have had a sense that that presence has been there and they just kind of go along with it comfortably. I've had people who, three to six months after they have had a very close death in the family, come back for another funeral, and when they very first walk into the chapel, they see their loved one. A flashback can be explained as part of the grieving process. This probably will sound strange, but some people have given us something that was of sentimental value, like an antique, and have asked us to keep it in the funeral home. One of these is a lamp, and there are times when I will have consistent problems with it. I will repeat the owner's name and say, 'Cut it out, cool it.'" Rhonda laughed and wondered, "Who knows to what extent that may be real? I like to believe that the soul goes to the other side and works for our benefit. All of our benefits.

"My grandfather died a year and a half ago and my grandmother died six months later, to the day. I know in my own process that we in this business are not immune to grief, by any stretch of the imagination, nor should we be. Nor should we be put on any kind of a pedestal, nor should a member of the clergy be expected not to have very real feelings, like feelings of anger at the deceased for dying, or guilt for having not sent a grandfather's card on Father's Day in nineteen-whatever.

"I have had dreams about my grandparents that were so real! I had been contemplating whether in my line of work it would ever be appropriate if I became pregnant. Well, lo and behold, I am pregnant, five months along, contemplation or not. And I had a dream. My grandmother was in the dream and I *swear* to you it was as though I could have touched her. I would like to think that somehow there is a force greater than anything that we can imagine that allows us to have some kind of comfort and security in knowing that they know what is going on. Knowing that when something happens to us we will still have knowledge that life will be continuing. And so I look at it as a great comfort, and I'm not at all scared of any of it.

"Of course, growing up as a funeral director's kid, I can tell you that, boy, didn't the Girl Scout troop love to have a party at my house. 'Can we have a seance?' It was adventurous. It was a thrill. It was something that we just didn't know enough about but were willing to explore."

Becoming a parent had been a concern for Rhonda because of the time commitments required in her business. But she has come to realize, "Gee, what better person to be a parent of a funeral director's kid than a funeral director's kid? I will know an awful lot of what he or she may experience and think in growing up that I'll be able to share. And one thing that I have found with being pregnant and being in this line of work—it might sound strange, but I believe there have been times when people have felt closer, because of seeing a life extension. I had an experience just last week where this family brought a five-month-old baby to the funeral service and somebody said, 'Oh look, that's the youngest person here.' Another woman who was standing beside me said, 'Oh no, the youngest one is right here.' And I, I had this very odd sense about me. This service was for an individual for whom I had a great deal of affection and who had watched me grow up. I had known her for over thirty years, and I was looking at her granddaughter and having her daughter-in-law say this; and I was thinking, 'Wow.'

"That night I came home and said to my husband, 'Have you ever wondered when the soul enters the body? We always talk about when the soul leaves the body, but when does the soul enter the body?' He looked at me and said, 'I've been thinking about this too. What prompted you to mention it?'"

Notes

Commentary

Over the years we have spent speaking with caregivers, transcribing their words and editing this manuscript, we have read and reread these interviews many times. We became thoroughly engrossed with each individual and each interview, and remember vividly the insights we first gleaned from them.

We were somewhat surprised to find that each time we revisited the material, we came away with additional insights, different than those insights that had struck us when we first collected the stories. For example, we made lists of what we noticed about Claire's story when we first heard it, detailing what seemed meaningful or helpful in terms of what we had experienced with our family members. We also noted the parts of Claire's experience that seemed most at odds with our own experiences.

When we reread Claire's story months later, we discovered that new aspects of the story were prominent, although items from our original list remained compelling. We would have this experience time and again as we reworked and reread completed chapters. It was as if the material, in combination with our learning, had a life of its own. These chapters continue to generate new things for us to think about in light of our personal experiences and about our ideas concerning death-in-life.

These observations have made us leery of attempting to summarize or draw generalizations from the material in a didactic way. We did not want to repeat the error we had found in our earlier reading—an instructive tone suggesting that there is one right way to die and one right way to manage the death of a loved one. We remain firm in our position that the accounts we have presented stand by themselves to reveal much about death and dying without any interpretive comment, and we trust that readers will take from each story those firsthand insights that prove most meaningful and useful to them.

Nevertheless, as we reflect on this collection as a whole—on what doing this project has meant for us personally; on what it promises to mean to others in their private attempts to deal with death-in-life; and on our collective public policy efforts—we wish to offer a general commentary about what we have been learning. We offer these comments from the perspective that we assumed throughout the project—lay caregivers of dying loved ones who have insights of interest to others like ourselves and to policymakers who would help us in our task.

The Caregiver's Reality

What impresses us most about the reality that caregivers describe is the intensity of their caring. This intensity is dramatically amplified by the shock they experience about their loved one's physical deterioration. When Claire Levine was confronted with the physical devastation caused by her husband's cancer, she was unprepared for "someone so physically ill, his body being out of control." In the midst of caring for Robert, she couldn't really stop to think about it. She did it all and confronted it all, allowing herself only briefly to realize that she thought she couldn't stand it anymore, that this had become a nightmare and she wanted to run away.

Claire's around-the-clock care, interrupted by only brief interludes of respite from hospice personnel or relatives, proved to be almost too intense for her. It is hard to take care of anyone for twenty-four hours a day; ask any new parent. Claire's experience shows how taking twenty-four-hour care of one whose deterioration is a personal catastrophe amounts to prolonged trauma. Under such duress, the fact that Claire was unable to marshal the support she needed or to assert herself when she needed more time with Robert's body is hardly surprising. This is evidence of how thoroughly overburdened she was. Nor should we be surprised to learn that during her ordeal, Claire presented some of the classic reactions to experiencing trauma, notably nausea and full-fledged panic attacks, which still worried her a year after the death.

Susan Briggs Russell was also preoccupied with the physicality of her mother's death. She had been unprepared even for incontinence, a relatively typical change that many people experience as they age, and certainly as they die. Her mother's changes in consciousness were also surprising to Susan, who was able to respond to these more or less in stride because of forewarning from a hospice nurse. For Susan, managing her mother's agitation during the last week was nearly her undoing. Sleep deprived herself, Susan needed to medicate her mother every two hours and, in addition, be able to function well enough to navigate the health care system on her mother's behalf.

As had been Claire's experience, what Susan witnessed as her mother died was frightening. Learning that the brown liquid oozing from her mother's mouth and nose was a sign that her mother was drowning in her own fluids, Susan wondered whether or not—and how to—intervene. She had never suctioned before, and she feared rousing her mother into another bout of agitation. But if Susan merely wiped the fluid away, was she not responsible for hastening her mother's death? "Easing" her mother into death was not easy at all, but fraught with moral as well as physical challenges.

Jim Viviano was also disturbed by what he saw during his partner's dying: "The hardest part was getting rid of the ugly images of the violent processes that go on in the final throes." Worried at first that he would remember only those "ugly" parts of Don's passing, Jim was relieved when the bad memories eventually diminished. This was long after he came close to falling apart, however, as he pushed himself to care for his other partner, Alex. Jim eventually sought professional help because "the most common things didn't make sense anymore. . . . I couldn't make order out of the things in life." As with Claire, Jim's caregiving was a traumatic experience with lasting emotional effects.

Both Nell Mihalich and Lee Adler were similarly shocked at the distortions in their loved ones that death brought. But in addition, they experienced these distortions in the context of the larger shock of a sudden, as opposed to anticipated, death. Nell's husband suffered a fatal heart attack away from home and although Lee's mother had been an alcoholic, her death was not expected when it occurred. For Nell, the struggle to come to terms with the suddenness of her husband's death sharpened the degree to which she was unnerved by the disfigurement of his body during attempts to resuscitate him. Perhaps it was the sharp contrast of her husband's well-being and his demise that prompted Nell to see the paramedic and emergency room procedures as violations of, rather than ministrations to, both her husband and herself.

Lee's reaction to the shock of finding her mother lying dead in her house is one of the best descriptions we've heard of how the survivor, full of dread, must admit the certainty of another's death. She gives us a vivid picture of how one's conscious mind is active in providing alternative explanations to a conclusion we want to avoid. Lee doesn't have the luxury to ponder her loved one's passing gradually. She has to do it on the spot, as she discovers her mother's body. As she drives to her mother's house to check on her, she has a sense that something may be wrong, but past experience has provided Lee with an explanation—her mother has simply passed out. But then there is the door ajar, the TV that is too loud, the lack of response to her calling out "Mother" as she proceeds down the hall, and then the vision of her mother lying on the couch, very still and naked, her arm unresponsive to Lee's touch. Piece by piece, the evidence collects to lead Lee to the logical conclusion that her mother has died, but the emotional acceptance for Lee, as for many others, takes longer.

Although all of our interviewees worked hard to accept the loss of their loved ones, to understand more about the dying process and the mystery of death, and to make the transformations in their lives that death requires, we think that Nell and Lee worked especially hard at trying of make sense of it all. Perhaps this is because, of all of our interviewees, they had the least preparation for death when it occurred. We value their accounts because their struggle to make sense out of the senseless event that death can be is so prominent within them. What Nell and Lee do to comfort themselves and to help themselves make the adjustment to life without their loved ones reveals how, in the midst of it all, we cope and react, even as conscious reflection on these processes may be in short supply.

Nell remarked that it was helpful to spend a few days living at her parents' house after her husband's funeral. Returning to her childhood neighborhood provided both comfort and a means of preparing for a new life. Exemplifying how one's past is prologue, Nell recalled and sought to retrieve the identity that she had forged growing up, long before she identified herself as "married." She found strength in returning to those roots of self before heading off in a new direction.

Nell also found it helpful to become involved in hospice after the fact of her husband's death. For Nell the hospice approach represented leaving well enough alone, something she would have preferred to the intrusive interventions her husband's body was subjected to. That hospice could comfort her after the fact reveals its potential for survivors during bereavement, even if they did not access it during a loved one's dying.

It interests us that both Nell and Lee found their interactions with the emergency medical systems problematic. For Nell this added to the magnitude of her shock. She couldn't believe that her husband had died, much less that emergency crews had "mutilated" him. Her personal disbelief was thus exacerbated by what she perceived as "systemic" insults. Had Nell known about the perspectives on managing death and dying that underlie emergency medical efforts, she may not have felt as violated by all that happened.

Adding to the intensity of caring for the dying is the vast complexity of caregivers' lives. From the vantage point of an experienced family therapist, Paulina G. McCullough advises us to make room for death in our lives, although even in her own case she admitted that this was hard to do. All caregivers are busy people, but it is easy to disregard how difficult it is to rearrange the details of one's life to make room for death until one hears firsthand about how others try to do it. Most of our interviewees worked outside of their homes, and they talked about how difficult it was to juggle full-time jobs and full-time home care. Even Susan, who was off for the summer, worried about what would happen if her mother lingered into the time when Susan was scheduled to start her new job. Caregiving was trying for Susan and her family, but it was even harder for Claire, Jim, Paulina and Jeanine.

Jeanine Strong, perhaps more than any other of our interviewees, seems a quintessential caregiver. As the head of a social service agency, she tends an entire community and as such reminds us of how women developed the field of social work in the nineteenth century, when women's roles outside the home were limited to extending their domestic duties and talents in the community. Not only does Jeanine care professionally, but when the family of an employee could not fulfill what both believed were the family's caring obligations, Jeanine provided that care personally, making room for death on her living room couch. Her story provokes questions about how we, especially women, internalize the obligation to care for others, what the impact of this is on our well-being and how this defines our roles in our families and communities.[40]

Full-time student Barbara Frazier made room for death by accelerating her college career and to some extent, foreshortening her youth. She describes pushing through her resentment about dealing with things that she saw as more appropriately the concerns of older people, while at the same time struggling not to denigrate the inexperience of her peers. Her story made us think about how the developmental course is affected by death: The effort we make to meet the usual challenges of development must often be redoubled when death interrupts. More attention needs to be paid in developmental psychology to how we interpret death whenever it occurs in the life cycle, and how our experience of death-in-life influences our trajectory through any stage of development.

A further example is Susan, who had to come to terms psychologically with being the sole survivor of her family in early middle age. Coping with the loss of both parents—becoming an adult orphan—requires a readjustment of self-perception, another event little mentioned in the developmental literature. This life event was further complicated in

Susan's case by the death of her only sibling. Though her brother, James, suffered from mental and physical illnesses, Susan had expected him to far survive the deaths of their parents.

The transition in self-perception that accompanies widowhood has often been discussed in the developmental literature concerning psychosocial issues for the elderly, but in this collection we hear from several women who confront this transition at varying ages. Paulina is the eldest of the widowed women we interviewed; Nell is in middleage; and Claire is the youngest. Their insights about how this particular transition occurred for them enlarges our perceptions of what it means to lose a spouse. In addition, Jim's loss—not of one but of two intimate companions—affords an even broader view of the need to rework one's sense of self in the face of a partner's death.

These caregivers concerned themselves with these kinds of psychological reworkings even as they dealt with the more concrete tasks associated with balancing work, home care and, eventually, funeral logistics. We mention here just a few of these instances to make the point that these more abstract tasks also demand caregivers' attention. Yet these tasks are often ignored and unrecognized as part of caregivers' workloads, by the professionals who interact with caregivers and by the caregivers themselves.

Of course, caregivers' lives are also complicated by the other people in them. The context of home care for a dying loved one often involves a number of other family members or friends. These people bring their own needs and perceptions of death and dying to the situation, which can both support and distract the primary caregiver. In Barbara's case, her mother's dying affected Barbara's accomplishments as a student and the status of her relationship with her boyfriend, leading to their rather urgent decision to become engaged and set a wedding date. At the same time, Barbara found herself having to respond to her father's newfound insights on relationships, brought on by realizing too late that he had not shown enough affection toward his wife. It was discomforting for Barbara when her father found a new partner in her mother's best friend so quickly after her mother's death, and yet Barbara worked very hard to understand her father's perspectives and what he learned from death-in-life. Changes in self-perception must be recognized and assimilated by others with whom we interact. Such change does not occur quickly; rather, it evolves with others as they too process what the passing of a loved one means.

Two of our caregivers, Susan and Jeanine, were also parents of children living at home as a loved one was dying there. Their comments about how their children were affected are instructive for those trying to imagine how their children might react to the particulars associated with home care. Susan's story included the account of her eight-year-old son, Brad, of what it was like when his grandmother died in their house. Brad did not have direct responsibilities for tending to his grandmother, but he was asked to help out when he could, to the extent that he could see that even at his age he was more competent than his grandmother, or his uncle James. His role at the bedside is unique; his presence, playing video games in the room adjacent to his grandmother, conveys a sense of normalcy to the household. Brad, of course, has questions and fears, but generally finds relief in taking them to his parents. And he can frame his experience into advice for other kids his age.

Although we learn about it secondhand, Jeanine's teenage daughters also expressed emotional reactions, and the younger daughter seems to have suffered negative effects, at least in the short term. Barbara's experience is also pertinent. Although she is a young adult, she tells her story primarily from the vantage point of being a nearly grown daughter. She talks about how she mourns the fact that her mother won't be with her as she crosses the thresholds of marriage and parenthood. As an older child, Barbara has much to tell us about what it means to lose a parent on the cusp of one's own adulthood. She also tells us what it is like to be involved in home care less centrally than the primary caregiver. Like the other children mentioned by our interviewees, Barbara is acutely aware of death's intrusion into her life and into her family's life. She explains what some of the struggles are for people who, because of location, age or other circumstance, must care from a distance. Judging from the children who are represented in these accounts, we have concluded that their reactions to death-in-life are as varied as those of adults.

Some of our caregivers' lives have been complicated by dysfunctional patterns of relating. Our accounts include individuals who have struggled with alcoholism, mental illness, a lack of societal or familial acceptance of their sexual orientation, and the clashing of just plain difficult personalities. Although some professionals think it ill-advised for families with severe dysfunction to take care of a dying family member at home, we were nevertheless enlightened by the accounts of people who did so, even as they struggled within the constraints of their problems. Sometimes the dying loved one is the most difficult person to deal with. For example, Barbara's mother wanted to die as she had lived, a gracious hostess. But privately she was bitter and angry, and Barbara regretted that the intimate bedside chats she had hoped to have with her mother never happened.

Jeanine was challenged in a similar way. Although she was able to confront the facts and deal with them by talking about them or taking action of some sort, her friend Sharon was too scared to talk about dying and how she felt about it. Sharon's strategy was to deny that her situation was terminal for as long as she possibly could, leaving Jeanine in the odd position of being unable to talk to her directly about many things, because to do so would force Sharon to acknowledge that she was dying. Out of respect for the dying person, or sometimes because the dying person maintains the upper hand, the caregiver can only respond. When this happens, he or she must still deal with the discomfort of not doing what might really be best. This is especially taxing when one is invested in providing the best care that one can, and for the last time.

Finally, some caregivers are overwhelmed because they must confront multiple deaths within a short period of time. Jim was still caring for Don when he began assuming care for Alex. Susan, although not her brother's keeper in the same way that she was her mother's, must begin the process of managing his dying only three weeks after her mother's burial. Both interviewees describe beginning to wind down from the intensity of caregiving, only to have the frantic turmoil start again as the next tragedy loomed closer. Jeanine tended Sharon soon after dealing with a series of family tragedies—three deaths over the previous year—which Sharon's dying called back into focus. Death is unpredictable. At times it may appear to take a holiday, but it may also seem to go on a roll.

The fact is that death continues to happen in our lives. Sometimes multiple losses occur at once, but even in the case of a single loss, we try to understand the meaning of it by connecting it, consciously or not, with previously experienced deaths, tragedies or other losses.

Given all that caregivers must do, we were keenly interested in what they had to tell us about what comforted them in their travails. For some caregivers, psychic experiences—including dreams and visions in which they encountered their lost loved one—provided great comfort. Although Claire talked readily and enthusiastically about her psychic experiences—the appearance of the butterfly, her encounters with Robert in bed, and her vision—it was important to her that we did not perceive these experiences as "crazy." When she had told others about these experiences, their apprehensions about them, and her mental state, only added to her worries. Her relief was palpable when Claire described the therapist who not only validated her experience but assisted her in finding ways to manage these encounters with Robert.

Anthropologists have noted that in societies all over the world, the funeral begins a liminal period characterized by that which is "ambiguous, paradoxical, and anomalous."[41] But throughout our work on this book, we learned that caregivers experienced such occurrences not only after, but before and during the deaths they had witnessed. We conclude that the liminality of death-in-life includes anomalous events such as visions, visitations and dreams of the departed, which may last for some time.

Usually, the outcome of such encounters is a sense of peace and joy. For example, Claire's forest vision is a wonderful illustration of transcendent consolation, as were the appearance and meaning of the canary for Lee, the dream for Susan and the nocturnal singing bird that Barbara heard. Investigators have recently noted that there are many varieties of these of occurrences, especially (but not exclusively) among the bereaved.[42] As more is done to reveal and research the nature of these experiences, let us hope that they become known for the sacred healing they can bring. No survivors need to suffer, on top of their grief and pain, the fear that they are losing their marbles.

For some caregivers, a religious or other belief system made a difference. Nell and Claire, for example, discovered that their childhood religious affiliations provided much needed support after their loved ones had died. Most caregivers we interviewed were willing to speculate about what happens when we die and ventured an explanation that served to satisfy, at least in part, their quest for understanding. Barbara explained, "A clergyperson said to me, 'Nobody ever said dying was going to be easy. If dying were easy, then God wouldn't have sent His Son to help us and to give us the strength to get through death.' Which helped a lot, because it is such a difficult thing. I really hope that she is up there, hanging out on a cloud, with my friend's mom [who died], looking down and saying, 'What great kids we have,' or, 'Gee, I wish they knew we were up here.' I really like to hold on to that."

Jim was more hardheaded: "When man dies, that's it. The brain stops firing, there's no more experience, there's just blackness. There's not even a sense of emptiness because there's nothing more. Consciousness ends." Yet Jim's realism includes a vision of imperishability. He noted that "immortality is really what happens when you are dearly loved and you are incorporated into those people you have left behind. Then that part of you that is incorporated into them is then incorporated into others. Immortality is really that incorporation of your self into the living."

Jim relied on his training in psychology for guidance. He explained, "Because I've been trained in psychology, I turn to it. The thought of turning to the family didn't seem reasonable. Religion was out from the beginning. I turned to what my religion was, psychology. I look for answers there." As helpful as systems of belief were to individual caregivers, it was helpful to us to learn about the variety of beliefs that served others in understanding and coping with the mystery of death.

Caregivers Need to Know About Dying

It is an unfortunate truism that caregivers of the dying should expect to be confronted with some very serious challenges. First and foremost we believe that it is important, especially for first-time caregivers, to be prepared for the ugly poses that death can strike. Caregivers may or may not realize their need to know what death can look like, and even those who seek out information end up feeling shocked and aghast by what they see. Susan, for example, asked for concrete details about what her mother's dying might be like, and this approach helped her to stay organized and focused during the death-in-life she experienced. But when death came, Susan was nonetheless unnerved and panicky. Barbara was horrified in spite of the preparation she had undergone in her death and dying course. She remembered, "Her eyes were wide open with fear . . . she started to die and you could tell because of the gasping, the choking, the clutching of my father's hand, the face, the noises."

We viewed these caregivers' experiences through a personal lens, noticing with interest and empathy the details they offered about their loved ones' declines and actual deaths. As shocking and ugly as death was for some of the caregivers we interviewed, we appreciated this level of detail for its educational potential. In the death literature we consulted on our own, no account was as detailed as those in this collection. As people who sought concrete information to help us rise to the occasion we dreaded, we were frustrated. It seemed we could get only the palatable part of the story when what we wanted was to know the worst. Much like Claire, we too felt worried and ambivalent about "the worst" and understood how Claire both wanted and did not want to know, how she both asked for and then resented information about the outcome of her husband's illness. Many of us approach and avoid death and dying almost simultaneously; it is not one or the other.

This is why we say that for caregivers of the dying, God is in the details. As hard as the details were for each of us to learn about, not knowing about their possibility was worse, because we still had to deal with them—and from the disadvantaged position of having to act while scared and shocked. Thanks to the caregivers who have told their stories here, we have seen a number of death's discomforting poses. In this way the pasts of our interviewees have become our prologues. We will thus be better prepared in the future, not only to deal with our own losses, but also to assess what we cannot bear and will need help with.

We conclude that the intensity of caring could be alleviated to some extent if one were more prepared for how messy and ugly death can be, even though it is important to acknowledge that not everyone will welcome this information, and that our resistance to it is natural. We hope that health care workers will be even more sensitive to caregivers who offer clues about needing to know these details. We hope that they will work to recognize those clues readily, and when they do, that health care workers are brave enough to tell the truth about what can happen. We also hope that professionals will be proactive in providing this information, even for clients who seem to avoid the subject. Withholding these details in an attempt to shield a person from the ugliness that death can bring may prove to be a caretaker's undoing, especially when the shock of that reality must be borne by someone whose strength has been sapped by extended caring. Though the truth may hurt, what we *don't* know can hurt us more, especially in the context of caring for the dying in our homes.

As grim as the truth about death's ugliness may be, caregivers have shared other details that are as beneficial but more heartening. Hearing firsthand about all aspects of caregiving provides access to other caregivers' helpful hints, good advice and inspiration. We admire our interviewees and how resourceful they were able to be, even in times of extreme duress. We admire them even more for their dedication. Indeed, as this work progressed from initial conversations to transcriptions to editing, we became engrossed and in a heartfelt way devoted to each of our interviewees. And we have asked ourselves what would have made death-in-life more bearable for each of them.

Caregivers Need to Know About Professionals' Perspectives

We believe that lay caregivers will benefit from understanding what the professionals we must deal with are thinking about their jobs, their clients and death itself. The more we talked to people about their experiences with the dying, the more we noted a gulf that lies between the lay caregiver and the professional. For us, this gulf is largely characterized by issues of attachment and detachment.

Each of our lay caregivers was acting out of affection and loyalty. All of them felt an important attachment to the dying person for whom they took responsibility, and all of them were riding out a storm of loss and grief. The emotional attachment that drove their desire to care for a loved one is much stronger than any other aspect of that care. It is what makes the caregiver's task so exquisitely painful and so different from that of the professionals, for whom some degree of detachment is necessarily embedded in their work.

Contributing to their detachment is the fact that the professionals had far more experience of the realities of dying than any lay caregiver. They recognized the signs of impending death and were more matter-of-fact about it. Although they too noted the ugliness and messiness of dying, they never reported feeling shocked, as all of the home caregivers did. It is the professional's job to become familiar with the reality that when the human body "doesn't work, it can be really pretty disgusting," as oncologist Ted Parker puts it. Professionals assume different degrees of detachment that permit them to deal with this reality.

Dr. Parker is perhaps the most detached of all the professionals we interviewed. He described death as "cold" and expressed admiration for the hospice nurses who provide the hands-on bedside care. His remoteness seems to be reinforced by his status in the system. As the ultimate authority and responsible party on a case, he must always look to his legal liability. When he is called upon to prescribe for a distant patient, for example, he feels he must know and trust the nurse who makes the recommendation. To do otherwise may be to place himself in legal jeopardy. Yet the cost of this conservatism may be excruciating pain for patients and their loving caregivers, as we saw in the case of Don and Jim.

We noticed that as one who sees cancer patients exclusively and knows how capricious the disease can be, the doctor is not completely protected by his detachment. He must grapple constantly with his anxiety over his own well-being and that of his family. For those professionals whose work brings them in constant contact not only with mortality, but also with the grief and suffering that accompany it, there can be a lingering psychic toll. At the same time, however, Dr. Parker, the paramedic Michael Andrews and the funeral director Rhonda Wiles-Rosell expressed a sentiment that many professional caregivers have shared: Working with the dying leads them to "seize the day," that is, to enjoy and appreciate the present in ways that most people do not.

It is also important for lay caregivers to understand that not all professionals work from the same paradigm. For example, the legacy of "heroic medicine" and its notion of maximum intervention is evident in the interview with paramedic Andrews. For him death is an opponent he must defeat in order to "win the game." (And everyone who cares for a dying loved one at home needs to understand that if we call for an emergency medical team, we are summoning warriors trained to fight off death, unless a proper DNR is present and enforced.)

Contrast the paramedic warrior and his antagonistic approach with nurse Elena Martinez, who compared the last stages of life to the final stages of labor. She described "a certain state" that she recognized as

> different than when I'm just functioning in my head . . . with women in labor, I was able to tell a lot intuitively about what was going on with them, what would help them . . . [to] relax to the point where she can have the baby. . . . Around someone who's dying, when you feel the death thing, which comes way before the death occurs, most of us want to negate it. Then we say, 'I'm being pessimistic! Of course he's not going to die!' But it's not being pessimistic—it's sensing the upcoming death. . . . Death is coming and it's time to start getting ready . . . and go about the process of helping someone you care about go through this passage that we all have to go through."

Health care aide Richard T. Murray offers a more subtle alternative: a Zen-like neutrality. "I'm present in a way that doesn't need anything [from the dying person], that's very approving, very gentle, very accepting, and with a lot of trust in what's going on. So I'm not trying to fix them or change them or hold them to this level, and I'm not trying to push them off. . . . I do everything I can to make their lives easy and pleasant. And they slip off in my presence." Lay caregivers can gain insight from being aware that professionals are operating from within different paradigms. This can help us better assess where we stand with a professional caregiver, and better discern how to get what we need.

In addition, we noted that all of our professional interviewees were often guided by feedback from the client in determining a course of action.

This may be as explicit as Dr. Parker's patient's announcement that she is ready to die, and his planning his care accordingly, or as implicit as health care aide Murray's observation of a dying client's breathing, and advising her to let go. It may be as deliberate as paramedic Andrews's hypnotic technique to help a grievously injured man report his pain, and learning of his broken arm, or as intuitive as nurse Martinez's impression that death had arrived to take Mr. Lovejoy, leading to her decision to prepare to help him die.

Feedback from the patient's loved ones can be a source of direction as well, but it can also be a source of conflict. The doctor noted that family members are often too numerous and far-flung to deal with effectively. The funeral director had been confronted with a conflict between what a client has "prearranged" and what survivors prefer. The nurse wished she could be more frank about her patient's treatments with his family, but feared stepping over the line of medical propriety.

For a time, we were tempted to understand the differences among professionals as gender based. For example, the women—the nurse, the minister and the funeral director—all noted similarities between birthing and dying, and were inclined to describe dying as a journey. The paramedic and the doctor—both men—were more likely to compare their work to combat. It seemed we had been brought back to our historical research, with the stereotype of the pragmatic and intuitive "wise woman" contrasted with that of the heroic doctor and his invasive practices. This generalization has proved to be too simplistic, however.

We came to realize that our observations were confounded by a deep and pervasive polarity concerning the acute (curative) versus the palliative (comfort) models of medical care. (This confound is complex because, as pointed out in the introduction, acute care in the biomedical paradigm has been largely defined by male professionals, who for centuries excluded women from the formal practice of medicine.) Acute care subsumes those qualities that we recognize from the traditions of heroic, male-dominated medical practice—a continuous battery of invasive and even toxic procedures, tests and treatments to conquer disease and defeat death by every possible means. Within this paradigm, palliative care has been resorted to only when the battle against death has been lost, and seeks only comfort for the vanquished. Today the picture is changing, slowly. Palliative care is increasingly accepted as a negotiated peace settlement with the inevitable, rather than a humiliating defeat of the medical arts, and we are seeing more palliative care being provided by hospitals, which were formerly providers solely of acute care. Furthermore, the nature of what is considered palliative care is changing, as, for example, a physician may prescribe radiation or chemotherapy as a comfort measure for someone whose illness cannot be cured.

Many caregivers and family members find understanding these definitions and distinctions difficult. Indeed, even professionals at the forefront of these changes grant that such terms as "palliative care," "hospice" and "end-of-life care" (EOLC) are used interchangeably and refer to a number of different contexts in which care is provided. The linguistic confusion reflects the liminality of the situation. We are all, professionals and nonprofessionals alike, "betwixt and between" as these and other boundaries merge and blur. Perhaps the most closely watched of these boundaries is around the notion of euthanasia, or as it is being called more often, "physician-assisted suicide" (PAS).

Most of our professionals cited a desire to help dying clients who wanted to hasten the end of their lives. The home health care aide demurred for fear of losing his license. The nurse quit her job in the intensive care unit because she longed to help the suffering souls who begged her to disconnect them. The doctor stated that he has "no problem" helping a patient who announced that she was ready to go, but denounced Dr. Kevorkian's methods. Minister Jane Adams Spahr stood ready to acknowledge a couple's plan for an overdose, but made sure she pointed out the "down side" to them.

This is one of the most heartbreaking dilemmas of caring for our dying. We seem to make the decision easily when it is on behalf of our beloved pets—we want their suffering to end, and believe we are doing them a kindness when we put them out of their misery. Our own human lives, however, are seldom ended with such sure mercy. As this issue gains more ground in public debate, we can only hope that feedback from the loving caregivers of the dying, as well as that of the dying themselves, will be prominent.

We also hope that understanding the nature of our liminality during these times will help us to reckon with the challenges we face. For lay caregivers, liminality is prominent not only because we are helping someone we love over the threshold between life and death, but also because as survivors, caregivers are crossing a threshold too—into a new life without the presence of our loved one.

Liminality can also characterize death and dying for professional caregivers. The home care aide reported dreams in which he learned of patients' deaths at the time they were occurring. The minister described times when she has accompanied a dying person over the threshold, only to find that the boundary has vanished: "Sometimes I feel like I've gone to the other side with them. Sometimes it's hard to come back . . . the course of death will just take you in. When someone dies, it's like I'm not in this world anymore." Even the funeral director, who is usually in attendance after the fact, expressed how everything is "different" at the moment death occurs: "There's no word to describe it unless someone has felt that time frame." Indeed, the only professional we interviewed who did not describe liminal experiences was the doctor, who acknowledged that he prefers to keep his distance. When a patient is "in the hospital sick and dying, I'm spending minutes with them; I'm not in there for three hours talking to them."

Caring for a dying loved one, then, should be understood first in terms of *intimacy*—with the patient, with the realities of physical care and with death itself. In spite of the old saying that we all die alone, in today's world we are more likely to find ourselves surrounded by others, in concentric circles of care. As policymakers at the outermost circle seek to set standards for those in the center, home caregivers may be the only ones who can remind them of the prerogatives of intimacy.

Health Care Management: Collaborative Caring

We wonder whether alternatives to home care could have been offered to those who cared to the point of collapse and regression. Are outpatient staff sufficiently trained to evaluate caregiver exhaustion? They should be and moreover, they should be able to assert their evaluations within managed care when a financially cost-effective home care arrangement is becoming too costly in human terms. We are concerned about the wholesale acceptance of home care as the most appropriate and reasonable choice for end-of-life care, particularly in the absence of much real appreciation for what this can be like for the caregiver. We believe that there is not sufficient deliberation about undertaking home care in the first place. Furthermore, once home care is under way, the caregiver and the hospice staff may not agree on the necessity of respite care or other support. Although respite care and volunteer support are generally promised by the hospice organization, it may not be available when the caregiver requests it. We realize that the quality of hospice or respite care programs varies widely in this and other respects, but the public perception is that it does not and that home care is uniformly well-supported throughout these programs.

In thinking about who cares for the caretaker, both policymakers and the public at large need to recognize the extent to which the success of home care depends on the expectation that someone, usually female, will perform this unpaid labor for twenty-four hours a day, seven days a week. We urge policymakers to recognize the reality of home care for the dying and the likelihood that unpaid labor will be exploited by health management systems. A proper response would be to provide caregivers with more of the assistance they need to be effective at home, well before they begin collapsing from the social, physical, emotional or financial strain of the twenty-four-hour care they are expected to provide. This does not mean, as some support initiatives have suggested, the development of programs that are designed to squeeze yet more time and energy from already depleted home caregivers.[43] Although well-intended, such initiatives betray a lack of understanding of the caregiver's reality. Interestingly, in the early days of hospice, staff burnout was considered a risk, one that was averted when it was discovered that staff could and should expect more of family members.[44] Staff burnout is thus transmuted into family burnout, which some of our caregiver interviews reveal most poignantly.

In investigating the origins of hospice in the United States, we learned that some of these gaps were built in. Hospice policy is largely defined by the 1983 legislation which made it a Medicare benefit that is currently used by 80 percent of all hospice patients. The legislation mandates several components significant to this discussion. First, one had to elect the hospice benefit in lieu of acute care. This removed hospital care as a recourse for hospice patients, and after hospice was undertaken, there was no turning back. Second, although short-term and respite inpatient care were supposed to be available, hospice was intended to be "a home care, not an inpatient benefit."[45] A third feature was the management of care by an interdisciplinary team including "a physician, a nurse, a social worker and a counselor."[46] These features reveal a system that for the most part requires the primary home caregiver to withstand whatever extremes the circumstances demand of her. It is a structure that impels professional and lay caregivers alike to maximize the home caregiver's contributions to the exclusion of other forms of care. Reforms are needed that offer alternatives to this narrow and unfortunate course.

In a paper on improving end-of-life health care, medical specialists Jane M. Ingham and Kathleen M. Foley note that, "despite WHO [World Health Organization] recommendations, which advocate for palliative care services to become an integral part of all public health services programs, no such policy exists in the United States."[47] Among their recommendations are these:

> In light of the financial, emotional, physical and social burdens carried by family members who are willing to care for terminally ill patients at home, government should consider establishing formal systems of recompense for the principal family caregivers. . . . Government should recognize the singular importance of home care for dying patients and ensure that hospitals are able to offer appropriate back-up and support for home care.[48]

We think that listening closely to caregivers will help to ensure that efforts to improve support during end-state care will do just that.

It is hard to say when and whether such policy changes might be made. When this book was in its infancy, public debate about a program of national health care was becoming a focus of political and social action.

A central plank in the platform of the 1992 presidential election was a national health care initiative, and it looked as if policy on end-state care would be hammered out in the public arena.

This initiative failed in Congress, however, and currently health care policies in the United States are being set and administered largely by insurance companies and health maintenance organizations (HMOs). Although the government runs both Medicare and Medicaid, health care policy for the rest of population is being set in the free market. Every week offers new headlines and anecdotes about the many effects and outcomes of this state of affairs, and end-of-life care is no exception to the rule that everything is in flux. "Many HMOs that serve employed, non-disabled persons . . . have not developed their infrastructure to meet the needs of dying patients . . . no quality measures for end of life care are well established and ready to use."[49] The situation promises to remain controversial and unsettled for years to come, as public and private policymakers lock horns and as consumers become more sophisticated about their options.

Given the current climate, it is as consumers that we hope more individuals will approach the issue of home care. For although we may be strongly motivated by duty and affection, we must also realize that each of us is limited in how much we can expect to do and endure. And we must make sure that systems of support adequately serve our dying, even when we cannot. We would urge our readers to think very carefully about the extent to which they can afford—financially, emotionally and physically—to provide home care, and to try to define the point at which their giving may be too costly for themselves and may be serving the system better than the loved one they had intended to serve.

Thinking of oneself as a consumer is a reach when one is caring for a dying loved one. However, it is a fact of caregiving that we are the ones who must access services. That we may barely feel able to perform our caregiving duties does not change this. We saw how Susan Russell had to find a new doctor for her mother as she lay dying, for example, and we heard many other consumer complaints as we gathered our interviews.

Some caregivers found that their hospice organization did not provide good service. Dr. Joanne Lynn, president of Americans for Better

Care of the Dying (ABCD), has recently noted, "It is becoming clear that some who provide care under the hospice name are simply inept, and that the public should be protected from them. Hospice needs some standards, measurement, and accountability that really have some teeth. Patients and families need ways to seek rapid appeal and advice, since most cannot wait for days to get better information or services."[50] Unfortunately, few caregivers have the will or the time to demand improvements of inept institutions. We hope that reform-minded professionals such as Dr. Lynn will prevail.

Other caregivers spoke of the ordeal of finding adequate support at home, especially that of finding responsible home health care aides. Indeed, the problem is widespread. Forty of the fifty states "do not license medically unskilled in-home aides, even though they make up a major part of the home-care field."[51] A 1995 television exposé revealed that of ten home health care aides hired and viewed with hidden cameras, "only seven showed up for work. Of those, more than half made mistakes with the medicine. More than half picked through . . . the belongings [of the client]. Nearly a third stole from her."[52]

Of course, there are consumer precautions that follow such a report, such as using agencies that are accredited by a national organization, which promises some accountability. One should ask if an agency screens, trains and supervises its personnel, and one should check each worker's references personally. This is sound advice, but for the family caregiver managing a terminal illness, these may seem Herculean tasks. Of particular import to minority women, a caregiver shortage is projected and expected to worsen for years into the future. "The majority of all paid caregivers are minority women," whose elders "are growing in numbers at a much faster rate than Caucasians."[53] Therefore, minority women will be increasingly in demand, both in the workplace and at home.

An additional consumer peril is that after weeks or months of exhaustion and distress, the caregiver is often the one who must make funeral arrangements—and is likely to be gouged. A 1998 report on CBS's *Sixty Minutes* revealed that "a few big corporations are snapping up thousands of mom-and-pop funeral homes around the country. . . . Just three companies already handle nearly a quarter of all the funerals in the United

States."[54] But these corporations maintain the original names of the funeral homes they buy, and few consumers know that the real owner is a conglomerate, which quickly raises the already high prices of the independents. For example, the least expensive casket, which wholesales for no more than $200, is sold to the consumer for $1,000; and the service of digging a grave, which costs $50-$100, carries a charge of $800 to the grieving family. "This is a fundamental fact that sets the death-care business apart from all others: Most consumers are clueless. People don't shop around; they don't comparison shop and the conglomerates know that. . . . [They] want to keep the consumer in the dark as much as possible."[55]

Judging from our own experiences, keeping us "in the dark" should not be difficult for them. The funeral is usually an afterthought for sad and weary caregivers, who have had trouble getting enough sleep, let alone "comparison shopping." Once again, we note how loved ones are exploited by institutional practices and will continue to be unless some changes are made by policymakers, in both business and government.

However, legislators may seem more likely to interfere with, rather than assist, caregivers and their dying loved ones. In 1998 a bill was introduced in both the House (H.R. 4006) by Congressman Henry Hyde (R-Ill.) and the Senate (S. 2151) by Senator Don Nickles (R-Okla.) designed to prevent assisted suicide. It sought to authorize the U.S. Drug Enforcement Agency (DEA) to revoke or suspend the federal prescription license of a physician who "intentionally dispensed or distributed a controlled substance with a purpose of causing or assisting in causing" suicide.[56] According to Americans for Better Care of the Dying, this bill's "practical effect would be to create a barrier to appropriate pain management, as well as a serious threat to patient and family privacy and confidentiality."[57]

In her testimony before the Senate Judiciary Committee on July 31, 1998, Dr. Lynn explained,

We have a society that has scorned "drugs" for decades . . . We penalize physicians who might overuse drugs, but almost never do we even notice if a physician undertreats pain. Certainly, no physician fears

losing his license over non-treatment of pain. . . . The rates of bad symptoms near death are stunning. Half of conscious patients in one large study had severe pain most or all of the time during their last few days. . . . Appallingly inadequate care at the end of life is a serious public health problem, affecting hundreds of thousands of persons every year. There seems to be no good reason to worsen this situation by asking the DEA to engage in additional police investigations. This is especially true since the bill before you will not even succeed at reducing the actual rate of physician-assisted suicide.[58]

According to Dr. Lynn, by intimidating doctors into prescribing less rather than more narcotic treatment, legislation of this type would have the effect of increasing demands for physician-assisted suicide: Patients whose pain is unabated seek more actively to end their suffering once and for all. Indeed, as Lynn sees it, the whole issue of PAS is a symptom of the inadequate pain management already rife in the system. She believes that patients who receive sufficient pain management typically wish to live out their days rather than hasten the end by artificial means.[59]

As the situation currently exists, "We already have the drugs and methods to ensure reasonable comfort; we just do not have a care system which uses its capabilities well. Improving that performance requires attention to education, regulation, financing, and research—none of which are improved in this bill."[60] Fortunately, the bill died on the floor of the Senate in October, 1998.[61]

We have read about how Jim repeatedly called upon Don's doctor to relieve his partner's suffering, but in vain. Even the recommendations of the visiting nurses fell on deaf ears. And this was a physician with whom both the caregiver and the patient—a doctor himself who knew what he needed—were on a first-name basis. It is stunning to realize that their nightmare of untreated pain and suffering is not rare or even unusual. But by the time a caregiver is confronted with this state of affairs, it is often too late to do anything about it.

What is needed is a grassroots death-care consumer movement. At a 1996 symposium featuring research professionals and clinical experts at the forefront of care for the dying, there were calls for more public education and consumer advocacy:

> *The public must learn to understand insurance benefits, recognize appropriate care, and demand that which constitutes good care at the end of life. As health care consumers, people should learn to choose care based on quality and value and to provide useful feedback to quality improvement processes so that they are best served.*[62]

One speaker, noting the "additional but less tangible costs . . . of caregiving and bereavement on family members," proposed that we expand our notion of the term "family planning" to include facing death, one's own and that of other family members.[63]

We concur with these conclusions, and the stories of our caregivers underscore the need. However, we cannot ask of caregivers that they marshal their forces in the midst of their travail. We can ask that others help us to bring these issues into public focus and demand reforms that really work. We urge readers to join the fray when they are able. The climate is changing, thanks to a number of such reform-minded organizations such as Americans for Better Care of the Dying and the Project on Death in America. In addition, individuals seeking improvements in death care can enlist those grassroots organizations that provide consumer information and support, such as American Association for Retired Persons (AARP),[64] Common Cause[65] and Consumers Union,[66] and bring these issues to their attention and request action.

On a more personal level, as lay caregivers we can provide assistance and advice to others who are too burdened to become savvy consumers of death care. We can tell them what has worked for us and warn them of what has not. We can encourage caregivers to perceive themselves as purchasers of services, with the power of the dollar to make change happen. Reform will take dogged attention and persistence that most caregivers cannot begin to muster in their hour of need. But those of us who have cared for and buried our loved ones and remember the difficulties are practical experts who can and should apply our know-how on behalf of those who come after us.

Afterword

In our commentary we have tried to express some of what we have learned from the stories in this book. We have built the case that knowing more about caregiving can inform health care policy at the broadest level toward the important goal of creating a more supportive context for families living with a dying loved one. We have also examined how traditional and changing gender role expectations have affected and will continue to influence the ways we care for our dying.

But we want to stress that each caregiver's story is a springboard for many other issues in addition to those of policy and gender. We hope that our focus on these issues will not diminish the power of these stories for readers at the personal level. What initially drew us to the work, and what we have tried to preserve throughout, is the clarity of the details of caregiving. It was the power of those details that stimulated our thinking, and the sharing of these details has enriched us.

Which issues rise to prominence and which questions beg for answers will depend on the filter that each reader provides. We encourage readers to note the aspects of each story that seem most meaningful, so that you will be able to explore what is important to you in more depth and share your impressions with others.

We wish you well.

Appendix

Interview Questions for *Parting Company*

For lay caregivers:

1. Tell me how it was when your [loved one] died.
2. How did you know she or he was dying?
3. When did you know she or he was dying? (Tell me about the last weeks/days/hours.)
4. Some people have reported impressions or experiences that they felt were psychic or spiritual. Sometimes these are coincidences, or communications of some kind, or dreams they had before, during or after the death. In looking back, have you heard, seen, felt or dreamed anything that seemed significant?
5. Have others reported any experiences like these?
6. It is sometimes said that people die the way they lived. Would you agree with that in this case?
7. How is talking about this now different from how it was then?
8. How have you come to terms with this death? (What has helped you?)
9. Is there anything you would have done differently (practically, emotionally or any other way)?
10. What do you think happens when we die?
11. What advice would you give to someone going through a situation like yours?

For professionals:

1. What is your age?
2. What training did you undergo to do this work?
3. How long have you done this work?
4. How old, in general, are those you have accompanied/treated through the dying process?
5. What do you find satisfying about your work?
6. What do you find stressful about your work?
7. How do you deal with stress and the experience of multiple losses?
8. Have you had a loss of your own?
9. How has your own loss been different from your professional losses?
10. What is the greatest contribution you feel you give to patients?
11. What is the greatest contribution you feel you give to patients' families?
12. Has doing this work changed you, and if so, how?
13. Can you tell me about one death experience in particular that struck you?
14. Why do you think people choose to go through the dying experience with another person?
15. Are there families who should not undertake this?
16. What are the recognizable markers that you use to determine where a person is in the dying process?
17. Have you noticed patterns in how dying people perceive their passage in the dying process?
18. When people fear death, why do you think this is so?
19. When people feel comfortable with death, why do you think this is so?
20. In relation to any death, have you ever experienced anything you would call intuitive or psychic in nature?
21. Has a patient or family member shared these types of experiences with you?
22. What do you think happens when you die?
23. If you were to put together a survival kit for families going through this, what would you include?

Endnotes

1. Arnold Van Gennep, *The Rites of Passage* (London: Routledge & Paul, 1960) originally published 1909.

2. Cheryl B. Mwaria, "The Concept of Self in the Context of Crisis: A Study of Families of the Severely Brain-Injured," *Social Science and Medicine* 30, #8 (1990): 889–93.

3. Jeanne Acterberg, *Woman as Healer* (Boston: Shambhala, 1991), 1.

4. Barbara Ehrenreich and Deirdre English, *Witches, Midwives and Nurses: A History of Women Healers* (New York: The Feminist Press, 1973), 5.

5. Ehrenreich and English, *Witches, Midwives and Nurses*, 3.

6. Ehrenreich and English, *Witches, Midwives and Nurses*, 14.

7. Ehrenreich and English, *Witches, Midwives and Nurses*, 15.

8. Ehrenreich and English, *Witches, Midwives and Nurses*, 24.

9. Ehrenreich and English, *Witches, Midwives and Nurses*, 33.

10. The American College of Obstetricians and Gynecologists now officially recognizes certified nurse-midwives. See the Boston Women's Health Collective, *The New Our Bodies, Ourselves* (New York: Simon and Schuster, 1998), 451–54 for a fuller discussion.

11. At the time this pamphlet was published, only 7 percent of the doctors in the United States were women, a lower percentage than in any other industrialized country. By the mid-1990s this figure had risen to 18 percent and is still climbing (see the Boston Women's Health Collective, *The New Our Bodies, Ourselves*, 700). Bear in mind that more than

80 percent of all health care workers are women (see Acterberg, *Woman as Healer*, p.1).

12. Ehrenreich and English, *Witches, Midwives and Nurses*, 39.

13. Ehrenreich and English, *Witches, Midwives and Nurses*, 40.

14. Timothy E. Quill, *A Midwife Through the Dying Process: Stories of Healing and Hard Choices at the End of Life* (Baltimore, Md.: Johns Hopkins University Press, 1996).

15. Maggie Callanan and Patricia Kelley, *Final Gifts: Understanding the Special Awareness, Needs, and Communications of the Dying* (New York: Bantam, 1997).

16. Emily K. Abel, "Family Care of the Frail Elderly," in *Circles of Care: Work and Identity in Women's Lives*, eds. Emily K. Abel and Margaret K. Nelson (Albany, N.Y.: State University of New York Press, 1990), 65–91.

17. Baila Miller, "Gender Differences in Spouse Management of the Caregiver Role," in *Circles of Care: Work and Identity in Women's Lives*, eds. Emily K. Abel and Margaret K. Nelson (Albany, N.Y.: State University of New York Press, 1990), 92–104.

18. Abel, "Family Care of the Frail Elderly," 65–91.

19. Lynne Ann DeSpelder and Albert Lee Strickland, *The Last Dance: Encountering Death and Dying*, 4th ed. (Mountain View, Calif.: Mayfield Publishing Co., 1996), 151.

20. DeSpelder and Strickland, *Last Dance*, 153.

21. DeSpelder and Strickland, *Last Dance*, 153.

22. Philippe Ariès, *The Hour of Our Death*, trans. Helen Weaver (New

York: Alfred A. Knopf, 1981), 570.

23. Jack D. Gordon, "How to be Sure Our Last Wishes are Honored," *New York Times*, 29 November 1995, sec. A, p. 22, col. 4.

24. See for example George Caspar Homans, *Social Behavior: Its Elementary Forms* (New York: Harcourt, Brace and World, 1961), and Peter Michael Blau, *Exchange and Power in Social Life* (New York: J. Wiley, 1964).

25. Richard T. Murray, personal interview with the authors, June 1993.

26. Abel, "Family Care."

27. Abel, "Family Care."

28. Abel, "Family Care."

29. Jim Viviano, personal interview with the authors June, 1992.

30. Susan Gilbert, "Doctors Often Fail to Heed Wishes of the Dying Patient," *New York Times*, 22 November 1995, sec. A, p. 1, col. 1; Sherly Gay Stolberg, "Study Finds Pain of Oldest is Ignored in Nursing Homes," *New York Times*, 17 June 1998, sec. A, p. 1, col. 1.

31. Ariès, *The Hour of Our Death*, 570.

32. Ariès, *The Hour of Our Death*, 570.

33. Wilda B. Tanner, *The Mystical, Magical, Marvelous World of Dreams* (Tahlequah, Okla.: Sparrow Hawk Press, 1988), 105.

34. Philip Kapleau, *The Wheel of Life and Death: A Practical and Spiritual Guide* (New York: Doubleday, 1989), 156.

35. For more on this, see Ann Rodgers-Melnick, "'We Are There and We Have Gifts to Offer,'" *Pittsburgh Post-Gazette*, 28 February 1993, sec. B, p. 1, col. 1.

36. See Rogers-Melnick, "'We Are There and We Have Gifts to Offer.'"

37. See Ari L. Goldman, "Top Presbyterian Tribunal Bars Homosexual Minister," *New York Times*, 5 November 1992, sec. B, p. 21, col. 1.

38. See Rogers-Melnick, "'We Are There and We Have Gifts to Offer.'"

39. Bowen's family systems theory provides a means to understanding present situations in terms of past relationships and family histories.

40. There are many dimensions to this topic. Readers who want more information about the role of caring as an aspect of women's identity and well-being should consult the work of self-in-relations theorists, such as Judith V. Jordan, Alexandra G. Kaplan, Jean Baker Miller, Irene P. Stiver, Janet L. Surrey, eds. *Women's Growth in Connection: Writings from the Stone Center* (New York: Guilford Press, 1991); and Jean Baker Miller and Irene Pierce Stiver *The Healing Connection: How Women Form Relationships in Therapy and in Life* (Boston: Beacon Press, 1997). These theorists, building on Jean Baker Miller's *Toward a New Psychology of Women* (Boston: Beacon Press, 1976) and Carol Gilligan's *In a Different Voice: Psychological Theory and Women's Development* (Cambridge: Harvard University Press, 1982), have articulated an alternative perspective to the standard principle of the autonomous self within personality development. They encourage a revaluing of women's roles in building and strengthening relationships and in nurturing others, but also articulate the potential costs to women of caring too much. As women reconsider the parameters of caring, one cannot help but wonder how this will affect home care for the family members of the dying. For example, in our interview with the oncologist, he talks about how often he is confronted with a patient "who's been a very abusive spouse, and now he's sick and dying and he's expecting his wife to do everything to help." But what if

she doesn't? If women turn away from their traditional role in providing this care, who takes up this burden, and how, and at what costs? We urge policymakers especially not to underestimate the importance of both traditional and newly evolving gender role expectations in reformulating end-state health care options.

41. Loring M. Danforth, *The Death Rituals of Rural Greece* (Princeton, N.J.: Princeton University Press, 1982), 37.

42. See, for example, Patricia L. Garfield, *The Dream Messenger: How Dreams of the Departed Bring Healing Gifts* (New York: Simon and Schuster, 1997); and Bill Guggenheim and Judy Guggenheim, *Hello from Heaven: A New Field of Research Confirms that Life and Love Are Eternal* (New York: Bantam Books, 1996).

43. See, for example, programs reviewed in Nancy Emerson Lombardo, "Skills Training for Caregivers: A Policy-Relevant Supportive Service" *Research Report*, Wellesley Centers for Women (Spring 1998) 2, No. 2: 1, 11.

44. Marian Gentile and Maryanne Fello, "Hospice Care for the 1990s: A Concept Coming of Age," *Journal of Home Health Care Practice* (November 1990): 1–15.

45. Thomas Hoyer, "A History of the Medicare Hospice Benefit," in Joan K. Harrold and Joanne Lynn, eds., *A Good Dying: Shaping Health Care for the Last Months of Life* (New York: Haworth Press,1998), 65.

46. Hoyer, "A History of the Medicare Hospice Benefit," 65.

47. Jane M. Ingham and Kathleen M. Foley, "Pain and the Barriers to Its Relief at the End of Life: A Lesson for Improving End of Life Health Care" in Joan K. Harrold and Joanne Lynn, eds., *A Good Dying: Shaping Health Care for the Last Months of Life* (New York: Haworth Press, 1998), 96.

48. Ingham and Foley, "Pain and the Barriers to Its Relief at the End of Life," 97.

49. Elise Ayers and Joan K. Harrold, "Managed, Capitated Care: Opportunities for Good and Evil," in Joan K. Harrold and Joanne Lynn eds., *A Good Dying: Shaping Health Care for the Last Months of Life* (New York: Haworth Press, 1998), 34.

50. "Complaints about Hospice: Growing Up or Going Wrong?" Letter from the President in "ABCD Exchange," *Americans for Better Care for the Dying*, July 1998. Retrieved September 10, 1998, from the World Wide Web: http://www.abcd-caring.com/jul98.htm#president.

51. "Consumer Alert: Take Care," reported by Lea Thompson on *Dateline NBC*, aired on NBC November 17, 1995, Burrelle's transcript "Consumer Alert," 10.

52. "Consumer Alert," 19.

53. Lombardo, "Skills Training for Caregivers."

54. "The High Cost of Dying," reported by Lesley Stahl, produced by Rome Hartman, on *Sixty Minutes*, aired on CBS, February 1, 1998, Burrelle's transcript "The High Cost of Dying," 16.

55. "The High Cost of Dying," 18.

56. Americans for Better Care for the Dying (ABCD), *Urgent Action Requested to Contact Congress: H.R. 4006/S. 2151 Will Have a Chilling Effect on Pain Management*, retrieved September 10, 1998, from the World Wide Web: http://www.abcd-caring.com/laws/sb2152p1.htm.

57. ABCD, *Legislation: On the Hill*, retrieved from the World Wide Web September 10, 1998: http://www.abcd-caring.com/laws.htm.

58. ABCD, "Concerning S. 2151, A Bill to Extend the Authority of the DEA to Prohibit Use of Controlled Substances with Intent to Cause Death," testimony of July 31, 1998, retrieved from the World Wide Web September 10, 1998: http://www.abcd-caring.com/laws/sb2151p3.htm.

59. ABCD, "Concerning S. 2151."

60. ABCD, "Concerning S. 2151."

61. ABCD, *Legislation: On the Hill*, retrieved from the World Wide Web February 14, 1999: http://www.abcd-caring.com/laws.htm.

62. Joan K. Harrold, Elise Ayers, and Joanne Lynn, "Visions and Strategies: What Participants and Others Might Do," in Joan K. Harrold and Joanne Lynn, eds., *A Good Dying: Shaping Health Care for the Last Months of Life* (New York: Haworth Press, 1998), 42.

63. Dwight B. Borck and Daniel J. Foley, "Demography and Epidemiology of Dying in the U.S. with Emphasis on Deaths of Older Persons," in Joan K. Harrold and Joanne Lynn, eds., *A Good Dying: Shaping Health Care for the Last Months of Life* (New York: Haworth Press, 1998), 59.

64. The American Association for Retired Persons describes itself as "a nonprofit, nonpartisan organization with 32 million members ages 50 and over . . . established . . . to better the lives of older Americans through service, advocacy, education and volunteer efforts." It can be accessed on-line at http://www.aarp.org or call 1-800-424-3410.

65. Common Cause is a "nonprofit, nonpartisan citizen's lobbying organization promoting open, honest and accountable government" and "represents the unified voice of the people against corruption in government and big money special interests." Find them on-line at http://www.commoncause.org or contact the membership department at Common Cause, 1250 Connecticut Avenue NW, Washington, DC 20036.

66. Consumers Union, publisher of *Consumer Reports*, "is an independent, nonprofit testing and information organization serving only consumers." It includes the Consumer Policy Institute, which "promotes the consumer interest through research and education projects—conferences, policy papers, and comment on legislative and regulatory initiatives." Call 914-378-2000 or visit their website: http://consunion.org.

Both **Cynthia Pearson** and **Margaret L. (Peggy) Stubbs** have cared for dying family members. Cynthia is a writer, lecturer and independent scholar. She is the co-author of *The Practical Psychic* and creator of the website *Dream Journalist*. Peggy, a developmental psychologist and former professor, recently became a project coordinator for a health care foundation. While a research associate at the Wellesley Center for Research on Women, she contributed to *How Schools Shortchange Girls* and wrote *Body Talk*, a pamphlet series to help parents talk to girls about menstruation. Friends since they met in fifth grade, both authors live in Pittsburgh.

Selected Titles from Seal Press

The Black Women's Health Book: Speaking for Ourselves, expanded second edition, edited by Evelyn C. White. $16.95, 1-878067-40-0. A pioneering anthology addressing the health issues facing today's Black women. Contributors include Faye Wattleton, Alice Walker, Angela Y. Davis, Zora Neale Hurston, Audre Lorde, Lucille Clifton, bell hooks and Toni Morrison.

Chinese Medicine for Women: A Common Sense Approach by Bronwyn Whitlocke. $12.95, 1-58005-018-2. This introduction to the basic concepts of Traditional Chinese Medicine is an informative, accessible guide for women exploring alternative health resources and covers over fifty specific conditions.

Dharma Girl: A Road Trip Across the American Generations by Chelsea Cain. $12.00, 1-878067-84-2. Written to the unmistakable beat of the road, this memoir chronicles the twenty-four-year-old author's homecoming to the commune in Iowa where she grew up with her counterculture parents.

Dutiful Daughters: Caring for Our Parents as They Grow Old edited by Jean Gould. $16.95, 1-58005-026-3. A compassionate collection of women's experiences, these timely essays offer insight and support to anyone who is touched by the needs and love of an aging family member.

The Lesbian Health Book: Caring for Ourselves edited by Jocelyn White, M.D., and Marissa C. Martínez. $18.95, 1-878067-31-1. This practical and readable book brings together a wide range of voices from the lesbian community, including doctors and other health care providers, women facing illness or life changes, health activists and many others.

No Mountain Too High: A Triumph Over Breast Cancer, The Story of the Women of Expedition Inspiration by Andrea Gabbard. $16.00, 1-58005-008-5. The extraordinary story of seventeen women who battled breast cancer and then took on the challenge of climbing the Western Hemisphere's highest peak to raise public awareness about the disease.

The Single Mother's Companion: Essays and Stories by Women edited by Marsha R. Leslie. $12.95, 1-878067-56-7. The single mothers in this landmark collection explore both the joys and the difficult realities of raising children alone. Contributors include Barbara Kingsolver, Anne Lamott, Linda Hogan, Julia A. Boyd and Senator Carol Moseley-Braun.

Seal Press publishes many books of fiction and nonfiction by women writers. If you are unable to obtain a Seal Press title from a bookstore or would like a free catalog of our books, please order from us directly by calling 800-754-0271. Visit our website at www.sealpress.com.